Texts for Writing

English 110: Composition and Literature

First Year Writing Program

University of New Haven

Bedford/St. Martin's   BOSTON ◆ NEW YORK

Contents

Nature, the Environment, and Ecocriticsm

Cultural Studies

Creating a First-Year Writing Program Portfolio

1. Log into Blackboard.
2. From the My Institutions tab, scroll down to the lower left corner to a box labeled "Content Collection: My Portfolios."

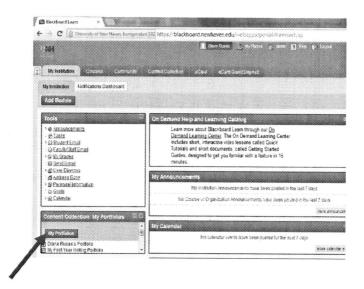

3. Click on My Portfolios.

4. From the portfolios homepage, click on My Portfolios.

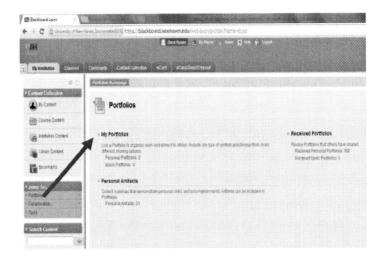

5. Click on Create Personal Portfolios.

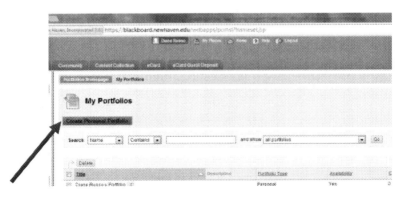

6. In the Properties tab, under Select Method, choose Select Existing and then in the pull-down menu, choose First Year Writing Portfolio and click on Submit.

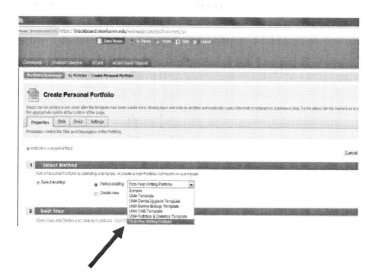

7. From the Edit Portfolio Page, click on Edit Properties, which will already be checked off.

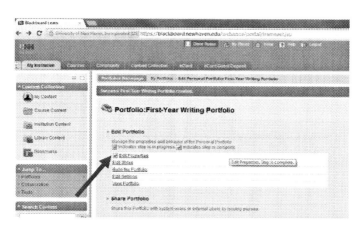

8. On the next screen, give your portfolio a title that includes your name, such as Jane Doe's Writing Portfolio, and click on Submit.

9. From the Edit Portfolio page, click on Edit Styles to customize the layout of your portfolio. Remember to hit Submit after you make your style choices.

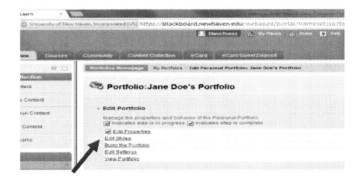

10. Once you have created the portfolio, you can insert material into it. This material is called artifacts. One of the most important artifacts is the homepage, which is the cover page welcoming the viewer to your portfolio. To begin adding artifacts, especially the homepage, click on Build the Portfolio from the Edit Portfolio screen.

11. To create the homepage, go the section titled Introduction to My Portfolio and click on Create New Artifact.

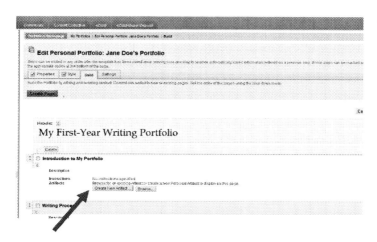

12. Once you click on Create New Artifact, a work area for creating the homepage appears. You should give the homepage a name, such as "my homepage" or "portfolio introduction." This title will not appear in the portfolio, but the title will help you to recognize the file you are creating as your homepage. Do not type in the box labeled "Description."

13. The next steps are to write the text and insert an image for your homepage in the composing space under Content. You will see there a typical toolbar menu for preparing a document and a space where you can write and insert video clips, images, and files. Once you are satisfied with the text and image, be sure to hit Submit.

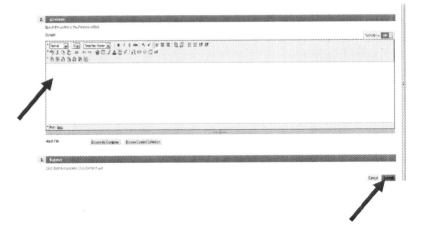

To insert a file, click on the attachment icon, and to attach an image, click on the image icon:

14. Once you hit Submit, you will be returned to the Build the Portfolio page. Be sure to hit Submit on that page as well.

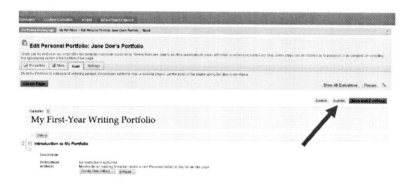

To add items to any page of the portfolio, you will follow the same steps for creating an artifact in the Build the Portfolio option. Please remember to hit Submit on both this screen and the Build Portfolio page, which comes up next, as is demonstrated in steps 13 and 14 above.

15. Once you have added materials, you should adjust the settings so that you can share the portfolio. From the Edit Portfolio screen, select Edit Settings.

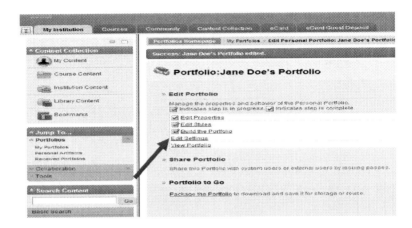

17. On the Edit Settings screen, check the box in the section labeled "Share Portfolio Settings" to make the portfolio available and click on Submit.

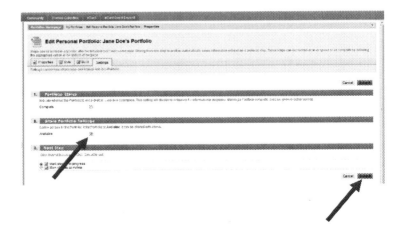

18. To look at your portfolio, from the Edit Portfolio screen, click on View Portfolio.

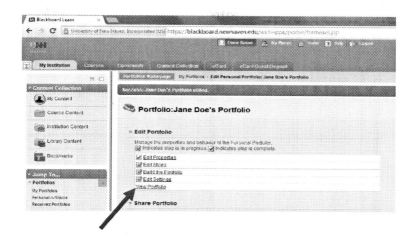

19. To send the portfolio, click on Share Portfolio.

20. On the screen that appears, use the pull-down menu to select the type of recipient with whom you would like to share your portfolio. The first option, User, is for any person with a Blackboard account. To share with your instructor, choose User.

21. On the next screen, insert the username of the person to whom you are planning to send your portfolio. You can choose to send a form email to notify the recipient that you have shared the portfolio. Then hit Submit.

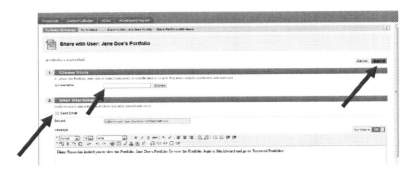

22. To edit your portfolio, go to the My Institution tab. On the left, click on My Portfolios. Once you get to the Portfolios page, in the center, you will find My Portfolios to click on.

22. The screen that appears lists all the portfolios you have created. To edit your portfolio, click on the arrow next to the portfolio you want to change, and click on Edit.

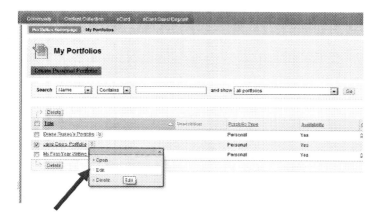

23. If you would like to edit or change an artifact that is already in your portfolio, including the homepage, you will need to come out of the portfolio and edit from the Personal Artifacts mechanism. To access that mechanism, return to the My Institutions tab and click on My Portfolios. Then click on Personal Artifacts.

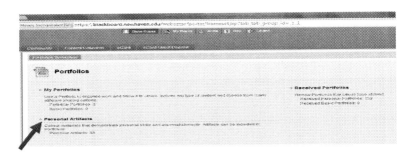

24. From the list of artifacts, click on the arrow next to the item you want to edit and then choose Edit. Once you make changes, be sure to hit Submit. Any changes you make to the artifact will be visible in the portfolio automatically.

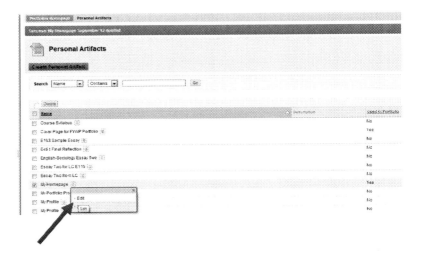

Why a Portfolio?

The process of writing is recursive. In many ways learning to write is a never ending series of iterations – each a product of its context. This constant going back to go forward can be dizzying, and discouraging. But, it can also be freeing, enlightening, and fundamentally rewarding, particularly when writers see for themselves evidence of their increasing sophistication.

Imagine attending a museum exhibit that depicts electronic technology as an evolution from the earliest light bulb to the electric adding machine to room-sized computers and finally, ending with your friend's iPad. Now consider the linearity of that exhibit – all the false starts and flawed contraptions that failed so spectacularly so as to never appear in the historical rendition of the iPad's antecedents. You know all about those false starts. You understand the blank screens, the late hours, and the multiple visits to office hours. Our companion textbook acknowledges this less-than-exhibit-worthy progression with the article, "Shitty First Drafts," by Anne Lamott. Your instructor also understands this part of the writing process. She or he will require you to participate in activities ranging from peer review to multiple drafts to drafting outlines to writing conferences.

When you collect, annotate, and reflect as you put together your writing portfolio for this class, you will be acting as the curator of the aforementioned iPad exhibit: you will be telling the story of your progression in writing. And, unlike the polished and perfectly linear museum display, your story should highlight the false starts, blind alleys, and ill-conceived lines of inquiry. Your portfolio will showcase your learning in ways that make visible all of those wonderful, frustrating, innovating, and sometimes exhausting, backward-and-forward steps that make up our attempts to engage with the texts of others through writing.

Dr. Michelle Trim
Director of First-Year Writing

WAYNE C. BOOTH   [1921–2005]

Boring from Within: The Art of the Freshman Essay

Wayne C. Booth was born in American Fork, Utah, and was educated at Brigham Young University and the University of Chicago, where he received his Ph.D. in 1950. After teaching for three years at the University of Chicago, he taught at Haverford and Earlham colleges, returning to Chicago as the George M. Pullman Professor of English in 1962. He served as the president of the Modern Language Association from 1981 to 1982. Booth's enormous influence on the way we talk about narrative began with the publication of *The Rhetoric of Fiction* (1961; second edition, 1983), which adapted Aristotelian theory to consider the reader and ways in which literary texts themselves shape the audience they require. Booth questioned the moral impact of certain narrative techniques and introduced such terms as "implied author" and "unreliable narrator," which have become common critical concepts. Booth wrote, cowrote, and edited more than a dozen books, many of which are taught as part of a core curriculum in colleges and universities, including *A Rhetoric of Irony* (1974); *Critical Understanding: The Powers and Limits of Pluralism* (1979); *The Vocation of a Teacher* (1988); *The Company We Keep: An Ethics of Fiction* (1988), which is widely thought to be one of his most significant works; and a memoir titled *My Many Selves: The Quest for a Plausible Harmony* (2006), which was published posthumously.

The following piece sets out Booth's ideas about what writing students need from their English teachers. The piece was adapted from a speech given to the Illinois Council of College Teachers of English in 1963.

Last week I had for about the hundredth time an experience that always disturbs me. Riding on a train, I found myself talking with my seat-mate, who asked me what I did for a living. "I teach English." Do you have any trouble predicting his response? His face fell, and he groaned, "Oh, dear, I'll have to watch my language." In my experience there are only two

Wayne C. Booth, "Boring from Within: The Art of the Freshman Essay" from an Address to the Illinois Council of College Teachers, 1963. Reprinted by permission of Phyllis Booth.

other possible reactions. The first is even less inspiriting: "I hated English in school; it was my worst subject." The second, so rare as to make an honest English teacher almost burst into tears of gratitude when it occurs, is an animated conversation about literature, or ideas, or the American language—the kind of conversation that shows a continuing respect for "English" as something more than being sure about *who* and *whom, lie* and *lay.*

Unless the people you meet are a good deal more tactful or better liars than the ones I meet, you've had the two less favorable experiences many times. And it takes no master analyst to figure out why so many of our fellow citizens think of us as unfriendly policemen: it is because too many of us have seen ourselves as unfriendly policemen. I know of a high school English class in Indiana in which the students are explicitly told that their paper grades will not be affected by anything they say; required to write a paper a week, they are graded simply on the number of spelling and grammatical errors. What is more, they are given a standard form for their papers: each paper is to have three paragraphs, a beginning, a middle, and an end—or is it an introduction, a body, and a conclusion? The theory seems to be that if the student is not troubled about having to say anything, or about discovering a good way of saying it, he can then concentrate on the truly important matter of avoiding mistakes.

What's wrong with such assignments? What's wrong with getting the problem of correctness focused sharply enough so that we can really work on it? After all, we do have the job of teaching correct English, don't we? We can't possibly teach our hordes of students to be colorful writers, but by golly, we can beat the bad grammar out of them. Leaving aside the obvious fact that we *can't* beat the bad grammar out of them, not by direct assault, let's think a bit about what that kind of assignment does to the poor teacher who gives it. Those papers must be read, by someone, and unless the teacher has more trained assistance than you and I have, *she's* the victim. She can't help being bored silly by her own paper-reading, and we all know what an evening of being bored by a class's papers does to our attitude toward that class the next day. The old formula of John Dewey was that any teaching that bores the student is likely to fail. The formula was subject to abuse, quite obviously, since interest in itself is only one of many tests of adequate teaching. A safer formula, though perhaps also subject to abuse, might be: Any teaching that bores the teacher is sure to fail. And I am haunted by the picture of that poor woman in Indiana, week after week reading batches of papers written by students who have been told that nothing they say can possibly affect her opinion of those papers. Could any hell imagined by Dante or Jean-Paul Sartre match this self-inflicted futility?

15

I call it self-inflicted, as if it were a simple matter to avoid receiving papers that bore us. But unfortunately it is not. It may be a simple matter to avoid the *total* meaninglessness that the students must give that Indiana teacher, but we all know that it is no easy matter to produce interesting papers; our pet cures for boredom never work as well as they ought to. Every beginning teacher learns quickly and painfully that nothing works with all students, and that on bad days even the most promising ideas work with nobody.

As I try to sort out the various possible cures for those batches of boredom—in ink, double-spaced, on one side of the sheet, only, please—I find them falling into three groups: efforts to give the students a sharper sense of writing to an audience, efforts to give them some substance to express, and efforts to improve their habits of observation and of approach to their task—what might be called improving their mental personalities.

This classification, both obvious and unoriginal, is a useful one not only because it covers—at least I hope it does—all of our efforts to improve what our students can do but also because it reminds us that no one of the three is likely to work unless it is related to each of the others. In fact each of the three types of cure—"develop an awareness of audience," "give them something to say," and "enliven their writing personalities"—threatens us with characteristic dangers and distortions; all three together are indispensable to any lasting cure.

Perhaps the most obvious omission in that Indiana teacher's assignments is all sense of an audience to be persuaded, of a serious rhetorical purpose to be achieved. One tempting cure for this omission is to teach them to put a controversial edge on what they say. So we ask them to write a three-page paper arguing that China should be allowed into the UN or that women are superior to men or that American colleges are failing in their historic task. Then we are surprised when the papers turn out to be as boring as ever. The papers on Red China are full of abstract pomposities that the students themselves obviously do not understand or care about, since they have gleaned them in a desperate dash through the most readily available courses listed in the *Readers' Guide*. Except for the rare student who has some political background and awareness, and who thus might have written on the subject anyway, they manage to convey little more than their resentment at the assignment and their boredom in carrying it out. One of the worst batches of papers I ever read came out of a good idea we had at Earlham College for getting the whole student body involved in controversial discussion about world affairs. We required them to read Barbara Ward's *Five Ideas that Changed the World*; we even had Lady Barbara come to the campus and talk to everyone about her concern for the backward nations. The papers, to our surprise, were a discouraging business. We found ourselves in desperation collecting the boners that are always a sure sign, when present in great numbers, that students are thoroughly disengaged. "I think altruism is all right, so long as we practice it in our own interest." "I would be willing to die for anything fatal." "It sure is a doggie dog world."

It is obvious what had gone wrong: though we had ostensibly given the student a writing purpose, it had not become *his* purpose, and he was really no better off, perhaps worse, than if we had him writing about, say, piccolos or pizza. We might be tempted in revulsion from such overly ambitious failures to search for controversy in the students' own mundane lives. This may be a good move, but we should not be surprised when the papers on "Let's clean up the campus" or "Why must we have traffic fatalities?" turn out to be just as empty as the papers on the UN or the Congo. They may have more exclamation points and underlined adjectives, but they will not interest any teacher who would like to read papers for his own pleasure or edification. "People often fail to realize that nearly forty thousand people are killed on our highways each year. Must this carnage continue?" Well, I suppose it must, until people who write about it learn to see it with their own eyes, and hearts, instead of through a haze of cliché. The truth is that to make students assume a controversial pose before they have any genuine substance to be controversial about is to encourage dishonesty and slovenliness, and to ensure our own boredom. It may very well lead them into the kind of commercial concern for the audience which makes almost every *Reader's Digest* article intelligible to everyone over the chronological age of ten and boring to everyone over the mental age of fifteen. *Newsweek* magazine recently had a readability survey conducted on itself. It was found to be readable by the average twelfth grader, unlike *Time*, which is readable by the average eleventh grader. The editors were advised, and I understand are taking the advice, that by improving their "readability" by one year they could improve their circulation by several hundred thousand. Whether they will thereby lop off a few thousand adult readers in the process was not reported.

The only protection from this destructive type of concern for the audience is the control of substance, of having something solid to say. Our students bore us, even when they take a seemingly lively controversial tone, because they have nothing to say, to us or to anybody else. If and when they discover something to say, they will no longer bore us, and our comments will no longer bore them. Having something to say, they will be interested in learning how to say it better. Having something to say, they can be taught how to give a properly controversial edge to what will by its nature be controversial—nothing, after all, is worth saying that everybody agrees on already.

17

When we think of providing substance, we are perhaps tempted first 10 to find some way of filling students' minds with a goodly store of general ideas, available on demand. This temptation is not necessarily a bad one. After all, if we think of the adult writers who interest us, most of them have such a store; they have read and thought about man's major problems, and they have opinions and arguments ready to hand about how men ought to live, how society ought to be run, how literature ought to be written. Edmund Wilson, for example, one of the most consistently interesting men alive, seems to have an inexhaustible flow of reasoned opinions on any subject that comes before him. Obviously our students are not going to interest us until they too have some ideas.

But it is not easy to impart ideas. It is not even easy to impart opinions, though a popular teacher can usually manage to get students to parrot his views. But ideas—that is, opinions backed with genuine reasoning— are extremely difficult to develop. If they were not, we wouldn't have a problem in the first place; we could simply send our students off with an assignment to prove their conviction that God does or does not exist or that the American high school system is the best on God's earth, and the interesting arguments would flow.

There is, in fact, no short cut to the development of reasoned ideas. Years and years of daily contact with the world of ideas are required before the child can be expected to begin formulating his own ideas and his own reasons. And for the most part the capacity to handle abstract ideas comes fairly late. I recently saw a paper of a bright high school sophomore, from a good private school, relating the economic growth of China and India to their political development and relative supply of natural resources. It was a terrible paper; the student's hatred of the subject, his sense of frustration in trying to invent generalizations about processes that were still too big for him, showed in every line. The child's parents told me that when the paper was returned by the geography teacher, he had penciled on the top of one page, "Why do you mix so many bad ideas with your good ones?" The son was almost in tears, his father told me, with anger and helplessness. "He talks as if I'd put bad ideas in on purpose. I don't know a bad idea from a good one on this subject."

Yet with all this said, I am still convinced that general ideas are not only a resource but also a duty that cannot be dodged just because it is a dangerous one. There is nothing we touch, as English teachers, that is immune to being tainted by our touch; all the difference lies in how we go about it.

Ideas are a resource because adolescents are surprisingly responsive to any real encouragement to think for themselves, *if* methods of forced feeding are avoided. The seventeen-year-old who has been given nothing

18

but commonplaces and clichés all his life and who finally discovers a teacher with ideas of his own may have his life changed, and, as I shall say in my final point, when his life is changed his writing is changed. Perhaps some of you can remember, as I can, a first experience with a teacher who could think for himself. I can remember going home from a conversation with my high school chemistry teacher and audibly vowing to myself: "Someday I'm going to be able to think for myself like that." There was nothing especially unconventional about Luther Gidding's ideas—at least I can remember few of them now. But what I cannot forget is the *way* he had with an idea, the genuine curiosity with which he approached it, the pause while he gave his little thoughtful cough, and then the bulldog tenacity with which he would argue it through. And I am convinced that though he never required me to write a line, he did more to improve my writing during the high school years than all of my English teachers put together. The diary I kept to record my sessions with him, never read by anyone, was the best possible writing practice.

If ideas, in this sense of speculation backed up with an attempt to think about things rigorously and constructively, are a great and often neglected resource, they are also our civic responsibility—a far more serious responsibility than our duty to teach spelling and grammar. It is a commonplace to say that democracy depends for its survival on an informed citizenry, but we all know that mere information is not what we are talking about when we say such things. What we mean is that democracy depends on a citizenry that can reason for themselves, on men who know whether a case has been proved, or at least made probable. Democracy depends, if you will forgive some truisms for a moment, on free choices, and choices cannot be in any sense free if they are made blind: free choice is, in fact, choice that is based on knowledge—not just opinions, but knowledge in the sense of reasoned opinion. And if that half of our population who do not go beyond high school do not learn from us how to put two and two together and how to test the efforts of others to do so, and if the colleges continue to fail with most of the other half, we are doomed to become even more sheeplike, as a nation, than we are already.

Papers about ideas written by sheep are boring; papers written by thinking boys and girls are interesting. The problem is always to find ideas at a level that will allow the student to *reason*, that is, to provide support for his ideas, rather than merely assert them in half-baked form. And this means something that is all too often forgotten by the most ambitious teachers—namely, that whatever ideas the student writes about must somehow be connected with his own experience. Teaching machines will never be able to teach the kind of writing we all want precisely, because no machine can ever know which general ideas relate, for

15

a given student, to some meaningful experience. In the same class we'll have one student for whom philosophical and religious ideas are meaningful, another who can talk with confidence about entropy and the second law of thermodynamics, a third who can write about social justice, and a fourth who can discuss the phony world of Holden Caulfield. Each of them can do a good job on his own subject, because he has as part of his equipment a growing awareness of how conclusions in that subject are related to the steps of argument that support conclusions. Ideally, each of these students ought to have the personal attention of a tutor for an hour or so each week, someone who can help him sharpen those connections, and not force him to write on topics not yet appropriate to his interests or experience. But when these four are in a class of thirty or forty others, taught by a teacher who has three or four other similar sections, we all know what happens: the teacher is forced by his circumstances to provide some sort of mold into which all of the students can be poured. Although he is still better able to adapt to individual differences than a machine, he is unfortunately subject to boredom and fatigue, as a machine would not be. Instead of being the philosopher, scientist, political analyst, and literary critic that these four students require him to be, teaching them and learning from them at the same time, the teacher is almost inevitably tempted to force them all to write about the ideas he himself knows best. The result is that at least three of the four must write out of ignorance.

Now clearly the best way out of this impasse would be for legislatures and school boards and college presidents to recognize the teaching of English for what it is: the most demanding of all teaching jobs, justifying the smallest sections and the lightest course loads. No composition teacher can possibly concentrate on finding special interests, making imaginative assignments, and testing the effectiveness and cogency of papers if he has more than seventy-five students at a time; the really desirable limit would be about forty-five—three sections of fifteen students each. Nobody would ever expect a piano teacher, who has no themes to read, to handle the great masses of pupils that we handle. Everyone recognizes that for all other technical skills individual attention is required. Yet for this, the most delicate of all skills, the one requiring the most subtle interrelationships of training, character, and experience, we fling students and teachers into hopelessly impersonal patterns.

But if I'm not careful I'll find myself saying that our pupils bore us because the superintendents and college presidents hire us to be bored. Administrative neglect and misallocation of educational funds are basic to our problem, and we should let the citizenry know of the scandal on every occasion. But meanwhile, back at the ranch, we are faced with the situation as it now is: we must find some way to train a people to write responsibly even though the people, as represented, don't want this service sufficiently to pay for it.

The tone of political exhortation into which I have now fallen leads me to one natural large source of ideas as we try to encourage writing that is not just lively and controversial but informed and genuinely persuasive. For many students there is obviously more potential interest in social problems and forces, political controversy, and the processes of everyday living around them than in more general ideas. The four students I described a moment ago, students who can say something about philosophy, science, general political theory, or literary criticism, are rare. But most students, including these four, can in theory at least be interested in meaningful argument about social problems in which they are personally involved.

As a profession we have tried, over the past several decades, a variety 20 of approaches attempting to capitalize on such interests. Papers on corruption in TV, arguments about race relations, analyses of distortions in advertising, descriptions of mass communication—these have been combined in various quantities with traditional subjects like grammar, rhetoric, and literature. The "communications" movement, which looked so powerful only a few years ago and which now seems almost dead, had at its heart a perfectly respectable notion, a notion not much different from the one I'm working with today: get them to write about something they know about, and make sure that they see their writing as an act of communication, not as a meaningless exercise. And what better material than other acts of communication.

The dangers of such an approach are by now sufficiently understood. As subject matter for the English course, current "communications media" can at best provide only a supplement to literature and analysis of ideas. But they can be a valuable supplement. Analysis in class of the appeals buried in a *New Yorker* or *Life* advertisement followed by a writing assignment requiring similar analyses can be a far more interesting introduction to the intricacies of style than assignments out of a language text on levels of usage or emotion-charged adjectives. Analysis of a *Time* magazine account, purporting to be objective news but in actual fact a highly emotional editorial, can be not only a valuable experience in itself, but it can lead to papers in which the students do say something to us. Stylistic analysis of the treatment of the same news events by two newspapers or weeklies of different editorial policy can lead to an intellectual awakening of great importance, and thus to papers that will not, cannot, bore the teacher. But this will happen only if the students' critical powers are genuinely developed. It will not do simply to teach the instructor's own prejudices.

21

There was a time in decades not long past when many of the most lively English teachers thought of their job as primarily to serve as handmaids to liberalism. I had one teacher in college who confessed to me that his overriding purpose was to get students to read and believe *The Nation* rather than the editorials of their daily papers. I suppose that his approach was not entirely valueless. It seems preferable to the effort to be noncontroversial that marks too many English teachers in the Sixties, and at least it stirred some of us out of our dogmatic slumbers. But unfortunately it did nothing whatever about teaching us to think critically. Though we graduated from his course at least aware—as many college graduates do not seem to be today—that you can't believe anything you read in the daily press until you have analyzed it and related it to your past experience and to other accounts, it failed to teach us that you can't believe what you read in *The Nation* either. It left the job undone of training our ability to think, because it concentrated too heavily on our opinions. The result was, as I remember, that my own papers in that course were generally regurgitated liberalism. I was excited by them, and that was something. But I can't believe that the instructor found reading them anything other than a chore. There was nothing in them that came from my own experience, my own notions of what would constitute evidence for my conclusions. There I was, in Utah in the depths of the depression, writing about the Okies when I could have been writing about the impoverished farmers all around me. I wrote about race relations in the south without ever having talked with a Negro in my life and without recognizing that the bootblack I occasionally saw in Salt Lake City in the Hotel Utah was in any way related to the problem of race relations.

The third element that accounts for our boring papers is the lack of character and personality in the writer. My life, my observations, my insights were not included in those papers on the Okies and race relations and the New Deal. Every opinion was derivative, every observation second-hand. I had no real opinions of my own, and my eyes were not open wide enough for me to make first-hand observations on the world around me. What I wrote was therefore characterless, without true personality, though often full of personal pronouns. My opinions had been changed, my *self* had not. The style was the boy, the opinionated, immature, uninformed boy; whether my teacher knew it or not—and apparently he did not—his real job was to make a man of me if he wanted me to write like a man.

Putting the difficulty in this way naturally leads me to what perhaps many of you have been impatient about from the beginning. Are not the narrative arts, both as encountered in great literature and as practiced by the students themselves, the best road to the infusion of individuality that no good writing can lack? Would not a real look at the life of that bootblack, and an attempt to deal with him in narrative, have led to a more interesting paper than all of my generalized attacks on the prejudiced southerners?

I think it would, but once again I am almost more conscious of the 25 dangers of the cure than of the advantages. As soon as we make our general rule something like, "Have the students write a personal narrative on what they know about, what they can see and feel at first hand," we have opened the floodgates for those dreadful assignments that we all find ourselves using, even though we know better: "My Summer Vacation," "Catching My First Fish," and "Our Trip to the Seattle World's Fair." Here are personal experiences that call for personal observation and narration. What's wrong with them?

Quite simply, they invite triviality, superficiality, puerility. Our students have been writing essays on such non-subjects all their lives, and until they have developed some sort of critical vision, some way of looking at the world they passed through on their vacations or fishing trips, they are going to feed us the same old bromides that have always won their passing grades. "My Summer Vacation" is an invitation to a grocery list of items, because it implies no audience, no point to be made, no point of view, no character in the speaker. A bright student will make something of such an invitation, by dramatizing the comic family quarrel that developed two days out, or by comparing his view of the American motel system with Nabokov's in *Lolita*, or by remembering the types of people seen in the campgrounds. If he had his own eyes and ears open he might have seen, in a men's room in Grand Canyon last summer, a camper with a very thick French accent trying to convert a Brooklyn Jew into believing the story of the Mormon gold plates. Or he could have heard, at Mesa Verde, a young park ranger, left behind toward the end of the season by all of the experienced rangers, struggling ungrammatically through a set speech on the geology of the area and finally breaking down in embarrassment over his lack of education. Such an episode, really *seen*, could be used narratively to say something to other high school students about what education really is.

But mere narration can be in itself as dull as the most abstract theorizing about the nature of the universe or the most derivative opinion mongering about politics. Even relatively skilful narration, used too obviously as a gimmick to catch interest, with no real relation to the subject, can be as dull as the most abstract pomposities. We all know the student papers that begin like *Reader's Digest* articles, with stereotyped narration that makes one doubt the event itself: "On a dark night last January, two teenagers, were seen etc., etc." One can open any issue of *Time* and find this so-called narrative interest plastered throughout.

23

From the March 29 issue I find, among many others, the following bits of fantasy: #1: "A Bolivian father sadly surveyed his nation's seven universities, then made up his mind. 'I don't want my son mixed up in politics.' . . . So saying, he sent his son off to West Germany to college." So writing, the author sends me into hysterical laugher: the quote is phony, made up for the occasion to disguise the generality of the news item. #2: "Around 12:30 P.M. every Monday and Friday, an aging Cubana Airlines turbo-prop Britannia whistles to a halt at Mexico City's International Airport. Squads of police stand by. All passengers . . . without diplomatic or Mexican passports are photographed and questioned. . . . They always dodge questions. 'Why are you here? Where are you going?' ask the Mexicans. 'None of your business,' answer the secretive travelers." "Why should I go on reading?" ask I. #3: "At 6:30 one morning early this month, a phone shrilled in the small office off the bedroom of Egypt's President . . . Nasser. [All early morning phones "shrill" for *Time*.] Already awake, he lifted the receiver to hear exciting news: a military coup had just been launched against the anti-Nasser government of Syria. The phone rang again. It was the Minister of Culture. . . . How should Radio Cairo handle the Syrian crisis? 'Support the rebels,' snapped Nasser." Oh lucky reporter, I sigh, to have such an efficient wiretapping service. #4: "In South Korea last week, a farmer named Song Kyu Il traveled all the way from the southern provinces to parade before Seoul's Duk Soo Palace with a placard scrawled in his own blood. . . . Farmer Song was thrown in jail, along with some 200 other demonstrators." That's the last we hear of Song, who is invented as an individual for this opening and then dropped. #5: "Defense Secretary Robert McNamara last spring stood beside President Kennedy on the tenth-deck bridge of the nuclear-powered carrier *Enterprise*. For as far as the eye could see, other U. S. ships deployed over the Atlantic seascape." Well, maybe. But for as far as the eye can see, the narrative clichés are piled, rank on rank. At 12:00 midnight last Thursday a gaunt, harried English professor could be seen hunched over his typewriter, a pile of *Times* magazines beside him on the floor. "What," he murmured to himself, sadly, "Whatever can we do about this trashy imitation of narration?"

Fortunately there is something we can do, and it is directly within our province. We can subject our students to models of genuine narration, with the sharp observation and penetrating critical judgment that underlies all good story telling, whether reportorial or fictional.

It is a truth universally acknowledged, that a single man in possession of a good fortune must be in want of a wife.

However little known the feelings or views of such a man may be on his first entering a neighborhood, this truth is so well fixed in the minds of the surrounding families, that he is considered as the rightful property of someone or other of their daughters.

"My dear Mr. Bennet," said his lady to him one day, "have you heard that Netherfield Park is let at last?"

And already we have a strong personal tone established, a tone of mocking irony which leaves Jane Austen's Mrs. Bennet revealed before us as the grasping, silly gossip she is. Or try this one:

I am an American, Chicago-born—Chicago, that somber city—and go at things as I have taught myself, free-style, and will make the record in my own way: first to knock, first admitted; sometimes an innocent knock, sometimes a not so innocent. But a man's character is his fate, says Heraclitus, and in the end there isn't any way to disguise the nature of the knocks by acoustical work on the door or gloving the knuckles.

Everybody knows there is no fineness or accuracy of suppression; if you hold down one thing you hold down the adjoining.

My own parents were not much to me, though I cared for my mother. She was simple-minded, and what I learned from her was not what she taught. . . .

Do you catch the accent of Saul Bellow here, beneath the accent of his Augie March? You do, of course, but the students, many of them, do not. How do you know, they will ask, that Jane Austen is being ironic? How do you know, they ask again, that Augie is being characterized by his author through what he says? In teaching them how we know, in exposing them to the great narrative voices, ancient and modern, and in teaching them to hear these voices accurately, we are, of course, trying to change their lives, to make them new, to raise their perceptions to a new level altogether. Nobody can really catch these accents who has not grown up sufficiently to see through cheap substitutes. Or, to put it another way, a steady exposure to such voices is the very thing that will produce the maturity that alone can make our students ashamed of beclouded, commercial, borrowed spectacles for viewing the world.

It is true that exposure to good fiction will not in itself transform our 30 students into good writers. Even the best-read student still needs endless hours and years of practice, with rigorous criticism. Fiction will not do the job of discipline in reasoned argument and of practice in developing habits of addressing a living audience. But in the great fiction they will learn what it means to look at something with full attention, what it means to see beneath the surface of society's platitudes. If we then give them practice in writing about things close to the home base of their own honest observations, constantly stretching their powers of generalization and argument but never allowing them to drift into pompous inanities or empty controversiality, we may have that rare but wonderful pleasure of witnessing the miracle: a man and a style where before there was only a bag of wind or a bundle of received opinions. Even when, as with most of our students, no miracles occur, we can hope for papers that we can enjoy reading. And as a final bonus, we might hope that when our students encounter someone on a train who says that he teaches English, their automatic response may be something other than looks of pity or cries of mock alarm.

A Note About Our Student-Authored Selections

Two essays, "Deep-Seated Daddy Issues," by Kaitlin Mahar and "Vita: a Journey from Childhood Innocence to Acceptance," by Jessica Damon, have been generously contributed to this collection by recent UNH students of English 110. These essays exemplify what scholars term a "close reading" of a literary text. In each essay, the author presents a specific interpretation of a literary text that is supported by well-chosen examples and properly cited in MLA format. The purpose of including these essays is to provide you with examples of working closely with a text before choosing a critical lens, not to provide you with models for your final products.

You should recognize that student authors often contribute interesting, insightful, and worthwhile ideas to conversations about literature. Like you, these students likely developed their own opinions of the texts they read; some inspired sleep while others evoked excitement in learning more about a time, place, or author. Learning that we share a like or dislike doesn't provoke much conversation beyond a knowing look or a shrug. But, discovering how someone else read a text differently, or more precisely, interpreted a significance in an author's work unseen by others, adds to our shared knowledge and gives us much to talk about. Read these essays as examples of effective approaches, and engage in the kind of discussion about their interpretations that goes beyond the interaction we experience when we click "like" online.

KAITLIN MAHAR

Deep-Seated Daddy Issues

Before coming into one's own, every individual looks to model his or her self after a peer who is believed to embody "perfection." The main character of Wendi Kaufman's "Helen on 86th Street," Vita, seeks to do just that. Initially, the reader may believe that Vita idolizes Helen and Vita's jealousy of Helen is the motivation of her character, but through character analysis, one may get to know Vita, and her motives, in greater depth. As is the case with any literary character of particular value, there is more of a complex entanglement of emotions than what appears on the surface, stemming from her relationship with her father. Vita idolizes Helen because she is "perfect," yes, but if one digs deeper, it is evident that she is motivated by her issues with her father and her need to have him back in her life.

Vita wants to play to role of "Helen of Troy" in her school's play, but even more so, she wants to be Helen, a fellow student who has been chosen to portray the mythical beauty because the director of the play, Mr. Dodd, says "she most embodies Helen of Troy" (97). As is the case with much of the pre-teenage population at some point during adolescence, Vita is jealous of her classmate. While Helen was chosen to play a role that Vita feels she can perform better, Vita also wishes she was more like Helen physically, noting how others say that the girl is "beautiful as a statue," and complaining to her mother about her peer's use of her beauty to her advantage and how she is constantly "flirting with the boys" (98, 97). This alludes to Vita's underlying jealousy that she cannot behave that way because it is not like her personality to do so, as well as her anger at how Helen seems to be "slacking off," further ascertaining that she, Vita, is more capable of handling the responsibility of playing "Helen of Troy."

Vita wishes that she was more like her classmate, or even the mythological beauty Helen of Troy, because she feels that if she was more like the girl for whom "men traveled great distances just to fight," then her father would find her worthy enough for him to return home (100). From Vita's point of view, if she had been as perfect as ancient mythical Helen or modern-day Helen, then her father would never have left. This is further proven when Vita asks her mother at the conclusion of the story whether or not her father would think she was beautiful: "'Would Daddy think I was beautiful?' 'Oh Vita, he always thought you were beautiful.' 'Would he think I was like Helen?' ... 'He would think you were more beautiful than Helen...'" (101).

Vita turns a blind eye to the fact that her father left her family (presumably for another woman, since her mother blames his departure on "wanderlust – emphasis on 'lust'"), and furthermore tends to romanticize her father (97). She imagines his adventures based on what her mother and she have heard from others: "...that he has travelled across the ocean, that he is living on an island... that he misses us" (98). She also reveals that since her father left, she has written him copious letters and keeps them in shoe boxes in her closet. In one letter, she wants to write, "'Do you ever sit on the shore at night and wonder what we're doing, what we're thinking? Do you miss us as much as we miss you?'" (99). This is a reference to Homer's tale of Odysseus, who fought in the Trojan War and faced a plethora of obstacles while trying to return home. While trapped on an island, the hero sat on the beach and imagined his wife and son, who were the sole reasons he was fighting so hard to return home. Vita thinks that her father is trying to do the same, but, like Odysseus, has some obstacles to face first.

While her father is off on "his own odyssey," Vita writes him letters (97). She discloses that in the current letter she is writing, she wants to ask him "[Mom and I] are both thinking of you... Are you thinking of us?" but instead writes about her play and says "Even though we [the Trojans] win the war, it will be many, many years before I return home. Until I see my family again. In this way, we are the same. I will have many adventures... Is that what you are doing? I wish you could come to the play" (99). These letters are more than just a way through which Vita tries to communicate with her father; they act as a catharsis to help her cope with her loss, which is why these letters mean so much to Vita.

Vita also compares her father to Helen's father, Zeus, who according to myth disguised himself as a swan and raped her mother, thus conceiving Helen. Throughout the story, there are allusions to swans, such as when Vita dreams about a swan - and subconsciously, her father: "That night I dreamed about a swan. A swan that flies in circles over the ocean. This is not the dark water that snakes along the West Side Highway and slaps against the banks of New Jersey but the real ocean. Open water. Salty, like tears" (99). Since Vita continuously compares herself to Helen of Troy, she of course also compares her father to Zeus. Her dream refers back to her idea that her father is out in a foreign area of the world, trying to find his way home. She says the ocean is "salty, like tears" because they symbolize the grief Vita endured when he left (99).

Because she views her father solely through rose-colored glasses and refuses to see any negative aspects of his character, Vita has a strong dislike for her mother's current boyfriend, whom Vita not-so-affectionately refers to as "Old Farfel." Vita obviously has some feelings of resentment stemming from her idea that he may be trying to replace her father, and that her mother may be allowing him to do so. Vita also worries that her father may return home and find her mother has moved on with Old Farfel, and will subsequently see he is not wanted or missed and leave again.

All of these factors come into play when Vita ultimately makes her own ritual in her apartment. She chooses to burn what matters most to her—her letters to her father—in exchange for his return home, and eventually, acquiring the role of "Helen of Troy" and Old Farfel's departure, since Vita asserts that "everything I have heard says that wishes are granted in threes" (100). Vita chants every Greek word she knows as a type of prayer for her wishes to come true. She truly believes that her prayers will be answered, and this is proven by her willingness to sacrifice her letters. This scene and its details remind the reader that while Vita may try to be strong and mature, she is still a young girl at heart. So, of course, as any little girl would, Vita's hopes continue to rise as she is given the role of "Helen of Troy," and her mother does not bring Old Farfel to the play, citing that "he wasn't what I wanted" (101).

This is why it comes as such a crushing blow to Vita when her mother bluntly tells her "'...Greek polytheism is an extinct belief'" (101). Vita refuses to believe her mother not only because two out of her three wishes came true, but also because the one wish she wanted most, her father's return, had not yet come to fruition. When she reaches the end of the play and realizes her father has not shown up, she comes to a painful realization that the gods are not real and that receiving the part of Helen of Troy and her mother breaking up with Old Farfel were mere coincidences. As the childhood innocence of her imagination significantly diminishes, if not dies completely, Vita is forced to come to terms with the fact that her father is most likely never going to return home to her family. As she pauses, all of this hits her, and Vita notes "in the stillness, there is a hole, an empty pocket, an absence" (102) This is not just her silence as the audience waits for her final lines, but also the inherent absence of her father at the play. This realization takes hold in her mind as she is giving her final monologue in her performance, and the raw emotion she is feeling is conveyed over to the audience. As the audience gives her a standing ovation, completely unaware of the pain she is experiencing, Vita says "I look into the darkened house and, for a second, can hear the beating of a swan's wings, and, then, nothing at all" (102). Her hope that her father will return, symbolized by a swan's wings beating as it flies away, disappearing into the darkness of the house and making Vita lose a little bit of her naïveté that is akin to one's childhood.

Through the use of character analysis, the reader comes to know that Vita does experience jealousy of Helen because she possesses everything Vita wishes she had, but even deeper are the insecurities derived from Vita's conviction that if she was more like either modern-day Helen, or even the fictional Helen of Troy, then her father would come back. Unfortunately, Vita comes to realizes that this frame of mind, which motivates her throughout the story, is incorrect – her father did not leave because she was in any way imperfect, and therefore he would not come back if she was more like either Helen.

Work Cited

Kaufman, Wendi. "Helen on 86th Street." Legacies: Fiction, Poetry, Drama, and Nonfiction. Ed. Jan Zlotnick Schmidt, Lynn Crockett, and Carley Rees Bogard. 5th ed. Boston: Wadsworth Cengage, 2013: 97-102. Print.

[2012]

JESSICA DAMON

Vita: a Journey from Childhood Innocence to Acceptance

The Greek Gods were once believed to be the most supreme beings of the world; the people of ancient Greece both prayed to them and feared them. Today, many know that believing in the Grecian Gods is a long-dead tradition, but for Vita in Wendi Kaufman's "Helen on Eighty-Sixth Street" the Olympians are still very much in existence. Vita's belief is so extreme that she performs her own burning ceremony to the Gods with the hope that they will give her what she wants—to be Helen of Troy in her sixth-grade play and for her father to come home. However, when Vita is told that people stopped believing in the Gods centuries ago, everything that she believes is shattered in that moment. She is forced to change the way that she views the world. Kaufman crafts a story that follows the coming of age of a young girl, Vita, and presents Vita as a dynamic character as she transitions from childhood hopes and desires to her final acceptance of her father's absence.

Vita, being an eleven-year-old girl, still possesses some of her childhood innocence at the beginning of the story in her desire that her father will come home. Vita initially implies that she no longer believes that her father will return. However, it is clear to the reader that she wants to appear as if she no longer believes this, but her actions tell otherwise. Every night Vita writes a letter to her father that she is not able to send. She believes that her father is merely on a trip. She informs him of her part in her school play and writes, "I will meet giants and witches and see strange lands. Is that what you are doing? I wish you could come to the play" (99). Vita thinks that her father is on a mysterious journey resembling that of Odysseus; this belief emphasizes just how desperate Vita is for her father to come home. She also thinks about writing "mom is talking about water again. I think this means she is thinking of you. We are both thinking of you, though we don't mention your name" (99). The previous quotation alludes to the shaky relationship between mother and daughter, and makes Vita that much more desperate for a relationship with her father. Vita's yearning for her father continues to appear when asking her mother if her father would think that she is a beautiful Helen of Troy. There is still some part of Vita that wants to be everything she thinks that her father will want. In reality, he most likely did not leave because of his daughter at all. It is important for Vita to understand and come to terms with her father's absence.

Vita's ignorance and childhood hopes are further expressed in her performance of the burning ceremony to the Greek Gods, whom she believes still exist. Vita puts all of her emotion into the ritual she "[thinks] about everything that [she] wants: to be Helen, to have [her] father come back" (100); she continues by chanting random Greek words that she happens to know to go along with her reoccurring thoughts. When Vita finds out that the girl to play Helen becomes sick, Vita truly believes that the ritual caused this to happen. She states, "It's all my fault. Helen McGuire got chicken pox. Bad...I know my burning ceremony did this" (101). In Vita's mind, she prayed to the Gods, and they answered her. Consequently, this leads her to believe that her father will definitely return to watch her play. Therefore, this event can also be connected back to her childhood desires. The belief that her father will return is an extremely dangerous thought for Vita to have and only reinforces her ignorance of the world around her. It can also be interpreted that because Vita will now play the part of Helen, she will finally be someone that her father can be proud of. Vita's mother tells her, "[Your father] would think you're more beautiful than Helen" (101). This gives Vita false hope. Vita is a child she does not understand why her father left, and she does not understand that it is not her fault. Her only belief is that she and her mother must not have been good enough, and if the Greek Gods helped her become Helen, then they must also bring her father back, right? An action as simple as a burning ceremony has revealed much about Vita's character and what she believes. However, Vita soon discovers the truth about polytheism, and her whole world changes.

The essential moment in the story serves as Vita's epiphany as she discovers the truth about the Olympians and her father's absence. Just before Vita is about to give her first performance, her mother drops the bomb and tells her that polytheism is a dead belief. She is confused; she reviews every moment over again in her head thinking, "Didn't I get the part of Helen? Didn't Old Farfel leave? I made all these things happen with my offering. I know I did. I don't believe the gods disappeared. At least not Athena" (101). Through the whole story, Vita has clung to the idea of the Greek Gods and their power. Now the gods do not exist which means her father is not on a journey resembling that of Odysseus, and he is not coming home. This is the realization the Vita faces at the end of the story. Her closing words as Helen of Troy embody all of the emotions that she feels with this newly discovered information. She says, "Troy, I have come to ask you to forgive me... And to say goodbye" (102). Vita herself is asking for forgiveness. She is asking her father to forgive her and her mother for not being what he wants. She is finally accepting that her father is gone forever. She is finally saying goodbye. Vita has completely changed her view of the world, and she has changed her attitudes toward her father.

Kaufman writes of the coming of age of young Vita as she comes to terms with her father's decision to leave. She was willing to do anything to make him come back, but in the end she realizes that he will never return. Vita's childhood hopes are embodied in her excessive letter writing to an absent father. It is also evident in her performance of the burning ceremony that she dedicates to the Olympians. She has changed her beliefs and will no longer try to be everything that she thinks he wants because nothing, not even the gods, will bring him home. Vita's experience is in one in which anyone who grew up without a parent can relate. There is the initial anger and confusion and longing evident in Vita's written letters, and there is the final acceptance that her father will never return.

Works Cited

Kaufman, Wendi. "Helen on Eighty-Sixth Street." Legacies: Fiction, Poetry, Drama, and Nonfiction. Ed Jan Zlotnick Schmidt, Lynne Crockett, and Carley Rees Bogarad. 5th ed. Boston: Wadsworth Cengage, 2013: 97-103. Print.

[2012]

ANNE FADIMAN   [b. 1953]

Never Do That to a Book

An award-winning author, essayist, orator, and editor, **Anne Fadiman**
(b. 1953) was raised in a literary household. After graduating from
Harvard University in 1975, she worked as an editor for *Life* and was a
founding editor of the Library of Congress's *Civilization* magazine. For
seven years she took the helm as editor of *The American Scholar,* a much-
esteemed literary quarterly, and in 2001 gleaned the National Magazine
Award for the best American magazine with a circulation under 100,000.
She taught nonfiction writing at Smith College and is currently a professor in the English department at Yale University. Her essays and articles
have been published in the *New York Times, The New Yorker,* and *Harper's,*
among others. Her first book, *The Spirit Catches You and You Fall Down:
A Hmong Child, Her American Doctors, and the Collision of Two Cultures*
(1997), which won the National Book Critics Circle Award for nonfiction,
narrates the story of the misunderstood spirituality of a refugee Hmong
family in Merced, California, their epileptic infant daughter, and their
ongoing conflicts with the American medical system. Fadiman's second
book, the best-selling *Ex Libris: Confessions of a Common Reader* (1998),
is a highly acclaimed collection of essays written entirely about books
and their readers.

Fadiman's enchanting and wholly inviting "Never Do That to a
Book," an essay from *Ex Libris: Confessions of a Common Reader,*
cleverly categorizes book lovers into two classes–those courtly lovers
who stand in awe of books, idolize books, and maintain their pristine
"just-bought" appearance, and those carnal lovers who write in
margins, break spines, and dog-ear pages in the passion of their
embrace.

When I was eleven and my brother was thirteen, our parents took us to
Europe. At the Hôtel d'Angleterre in Copenhagen, as he had done virtually every night of his literate life, Kim left a book facedown on the bedside table. The next afternoon, he returned to find the book closed, a

piece of paper inserted to mark the page, and the following note, signed by the chambermaid, resting on its cover:

SIR, YOU MUST NEVER DO THAT TO A BOOK.

My brother was stunned. How could it have come to pass that he—a reader so devoted that he'd sneaked a book and a flashlight under the covers at his boarding school every night after lights-out, a crime punishable by a swat with a wooden paddle—had been branded as *someone who didn't love books?* I shared his mortification. I could not imagine a more bibliolatrous family than the Fadimans. Yet, with the exception of my mother, in the eyes of the young Danish maid we would all have been found guilty of rampant book abuse.

During the next thirty years I came to realize that just as there is more than one way to love a person, so is there more than one way to love a book. The chambermaid believed in courtly love. A book's physical self was sacrosanct to her, its form inseparable from its content; her duty as a lover was Platonic adoration, a noble but doomed attempt to conserve forever the state of perfect chastity in which it had left the bookseller. The Fadiman family believed in carnal love. To us, a book's *words* were holy, but the paper, cloth, cardboard, glue, thread, and ink that contained them were a mere vessel, and it was no sacrilege to treat them as wantonly as desire and pragmatism dictated. Hard use was a sign not of disrespect but of intimacy.

Hilaire Belloc, a courtly lover, once wrote:

Child! do not throw this book about;
Refrain from the unholy pleasure
Of cutting all the pictures out!
Preserve it as your chiefest treasure.

What would Belloc have thought of my father, who, in order to reduce the weight of the paperbacks he read on airplanes, tore off the chapters he had completed and threw them in the trash? What would he have thought of my husband, who reads in the sauna, where heat-fissioned pages drop like petals in a storm? What would he have thought (here I am making a brazen attempt to upgrade my family by association) of Thomas Jefferson, who chopped up a priceless 1572 first edition of Plutarch's works in Greek in order to interleave its pages with an English translation? Or of my old editor Byron Dobell, who, when he was researching an article on the Grand Tour, once stayed up all night reading six volumes of Boswell's journals and, as he puts it, "sucked them like a giant mongoose"? Byron told me, "I didn't give a damn about the condition of those volumes. In order to get where I had to go, I underlined them, wrote in them, shredded them, dropped them, tore them to pieces, and did things to them that we can't discuss in public."

Byron loves books. Really, he does. So does my husband, an incorrigible book-splayer whose roommate once informed him, "George, if you ever break the spine of one of my books, I want you to know you might as well be breaking *my own spine*." So does Kim, who reports that despite his experience in Copenhagen, his bedside table currently supports three spreadeagled volumes. "They are ready in an instant to let me pick them up," he explains. "To use an electronics analogy, closing a book on a book-mark is like pressing the Stop button, whereas when you leave the book facedown, you've only pressed Pause." I confess to marking my place promiscuously, sometimes splaying, sometimes committing the even more grievous sin of dog-earing the page. (Here I manage to be simultaneously abusive and compulsive: I turn down the upper corner for page-marking and the lower corner to identify passages I want to xerox for my commonplace book.)

All courtly lovers press Stop. My Aunt Carol—who will probably 5 claim she's no relation once she finds out how I treat my books—places reproductions of Audubon paintings horizontally to mark the exact paragraph where she left off. If the colored side is up, she was reading the lefthand page; if it's down, the right-hand page. A college classmate of mine, a lawyer, uses his business cards, spurning his wife's silver Tiffany bookmarks because they are a few microns too thick and might leave vestigial stigmata. Another classmate, an art historian, favors Paris Métro tickets or "those inkjet-printed credit card receipts—but only in books of art criticism whose pretentiousness I wish to desecrate with something really crass and financial. I would never use those in fiction or poetry, which really *are* sacred."

Courtly lovers always remove their bookmarks when the assignation is over; carnal lovers are likely to leave romantic mementos, often three-dimensional and messy. *Birds of Yosemite and the East Slope,* a volume belonging to a science writer friend, harbors an owl feather and the tip of a squirrel's tail, evidence of a crime scene near Tioga Pass. A book critic I know took *The Collected Stories and Poems of Edgar Allan Poe* on a backpacking trip through the Yucatán, and whenever an interesting bug landed in it, she clapped the covers shut. She amassed such a bulging insectarium that she feared Poe might not make it through customs. (He did.)

The most permanent, and thus to the courtly lover the most terrible, thing one can leave in a book is one's own words. Even I would never write in an encyclopedia (except perhaps with a No. 3 pencil, which I'd later erase). But I've been annotating novels and poems—transforming mono-logues into dialogues—ever since I learned to read. Byron Dobell says that his most beloved books, such as *The Essays of Montaigne,* have been writ-ten on so many times, in so many different periods of his life, in so many colors of ink, that they have become palimpsests. I would far rather read Byron's copy of Montaigne than a virginal one from the bookstore, just as I would rather read John Adams's copy of Mary Wollstonecraft's *French Revolution,* in whose margins he argued so vehemently with the dead author ("Heavenly times!" "A barbarous theory." "Did this lady think three months time enough to form a free constitution for twenty-five millions of Frenchmen?") that, two hundred years later, his handwriting still looks angry.

Just think what courtly lovers miss by believing that the only thing they are permitted to do with books is *read* them! What do they use for shims, doorstops, glueing weights, and rug-flatteners? When my friend the art historian was a teenager, his cherished copy of *D'Aulaire's Book of Greek Myths* served as a drum pad on which he practiced percussion riffs from Led Zeppelin. A philosophy professor at my college, whose baby became enamored of the portrait of David Hume on a Penguin paper-back, had the cover laminated in plastic so her daughter could cut her teeth on the great thinker. Menelik II, the emperor of Ethiopia at the turn of the century, liked to chew pages from his Bible. Unfortunately, he died after consuming the complete Book of Kings. I do not consider Menelik's fate an argument for keeping our hands and teeth off our books; the lesson to be drawn, clearly, is that he, too, should have lami-nated his pages in plastic.

"How beautiful to a genuine lover of reading are the sullied leaves, and worn-out appearance . . . of an old 'Circulating Library' Tom Jones, or Vicar of Wakefield!" wrote Charles Lamb. "How they speak of the thou-sand thumbs that have turned over their pages with delight! . . . Who would have them a whit less soiled? What better condition could we desire to see them in?" Absolutely none. Thus, a landscape architect I know savors the very smell of the dirt embedded in his botany texts; it is the allu-vium of his life's work. Thus, my friend the science writer considers her *Mammals of the World* to have been enhanced by the excremental splotches left by Bertrand Russell, an orphaned band-tailed pigeon who perched on it when he was learning to fly. And thus, even though I own a clear plastic cookbook holder, I never use it. What a pleasure it will be, thirty years hence, to open *The Joy of Cooking* to page 581 and behold part of the *actual egg yolk* that my daughter glopped into her very first batch of blueberry muffins at age twenty-two months! The courtly mode simply doesn't work with small children. I hope I am not deluding myself when

I imagine that even the Danish chambermaid, if she is now a mother, might be able to appreciate a really grungy copy of *Pat the Bunny*—a book that *invites* the reader to act like a Dobellian giant mongoose—in which Mummy's ring has been fractured and Daddy's scratchy face has been rubbed as smooth as the Blarney Stone.

The trouble with the carnal approach is that we love our books to 10 pieces. My brother keeps his disintegrating *Golden Guide to Birds* in a Ziploc bag. "It consists of dozens of separate fascicles," says Kim, "and it's impossible to read. When I pick it up, the egrets fall out. But if I replaced it, the note I wrote when I saw my first trumpeter swan wouldn't be there. Also, I don't want to admit that so many species names have changed. If I bought a new edition, I'd feel I was being unfaithful to my old friend the yellow-bellied sapsucker, which has been split into three different species."

My friend Clark's eight thousand books, mostly works of philosophy, will never suffer the same fate as *The Golden Guide to Birds*. In fact, just *hearing* about Kim's book might trigger a nervous collapse. Clark, an investment analyst, won't let his wife raise the blinds until sundown, lest the bindings fade. He buys at least two copies of his favorite books, so that only one need be subjected to the stress of having its pages turned. When his visiting mother-in-law made the mistake of taking a book off the shelf, Clark shadowed her around the apartment to make sure she didn't do anything unspeakable to it—such as placing it facedown on a table.

I know these facts about Clark because when George was over there last week, he talked to Clark's wife and made some notes on the back flyleaf of Herman Wouk's *Don't Stop the Carnival*, which he happened to be carrying in his backpack. He ripped out the page and gave it to me.

Literary Criticism and Literary Theory

Anytime you sit down to write about literature, or even to discuss a story, play, or poem with classmates, you are acting as a literary critic. The word *criticism* is often interpreted as negative and faultfinding. But literary criticism is a discipline and includes everything from a glowing review to a scathing attack to a thoughtful and balanced interpretation. Criticism can be broken down into two broad categories: **evaluative** and **interpretive**. Evaluative criticism seeks to determine how accomplished a work is and what place it should hold in the evolving story of literary history. Book reviews are the most common form of evaluative criticism. Interpretive criticism comprises all writing that seeks to explain, analyze, clarify, or question the meaning and significance of literature. Although you may engage in a certain amount of evaluative criticism in your literature class, and while your attitude about the value of literature will likely be apparent in your writing, the criticism you write for class will consist largely of interpretation.

All literary critics, including you, begin with some form of literary theory. Just as you may not have thought of yourself as a literary critic, you probably haven't thought of yourself as using literary theory. But you are doing so every time you write about literature, and it is a good idea to become familiar with some of the most prevalent types of theory. This familiarity will help you understand why so many respected literary critics seem to disagree with one another and why they write such different analyses of the same work of literature. It may also help to explain why you might disagree with your classmates, or even your instructor, in your interpretation of a particular story, poem, or play. Perhaps you are simply starting from a different theoretical base. You will be able to explain your thinking more eloquently if you understand that base.

Literary theory has the reputation of being incredibly dense and difficult. Indeed, the theories—sometimes called *schools* of criticism—discussed in the following pages are all complex, but here they are presented in their most basic, stripped-down forms. As such, these

Janet E. Gardner, "Literary Criticism and Literary Theory," from *Writing about Literature: A Portable Guide*, Second Edition with 2009 MLA Update, pages 143–152. Copyright © 2009 by Bedford/St. Martin's.

explanations are necessarily incomplete and selective. You should not feel you need to master the complexities of literary theory right now. You need only be aware of the existence of these various schools and watch for them as you read and write. Doing so will give you a better sense of what you're reading and hearing about the literature you explore, and it will make your writing more informed and articulate. There are many other schools and subschools in addition to those described here, but these are the most significant—the ones you are most likely to encounter as you continue to explore literature.

FORMALISM AND NEW CRITICISM

For a large part of the twentieth century, literary criticism was dominated by various types of theory that can broadly be defined as **formalism** and **New Criticism**. (New Criticism is no longer new, having begun to fall out of prominence in the 1970s, but its name lives on.) Formalist critics focus their attention, unsurprisingly, on the formal elements of a literary text—things like **structure**, **tone**, **characters**, **setting**, **symbols**, and linguistic features. Explication and close reading are techniques of formalist criticism. While poetry, which is most self-consciously formal in its structure, lends itself most obviously to formalist types of criticism, prose fiction and drama are also frequently viewed through this lens.

Perhaps the most distinguishing feature of formalism and New Criticism is that they focus on the text itself and not on extratextual factors. Formalist critics are interested in how parts of a text relate to one another and to the whole, and they seek to create meaning by unfolding and examining these relationships. Excluded from consideration are questions about the author, the reader, history or culture, and the relationship of the literary text to other texts or artwork. Chances are you have written some formalist criticism yourself, either in high school or in college. If you have ever written a paper on **symbolism**, *character development*, or the relationship between sound patterns and sense in a poem, you have been a formalist critic.

FEMINIST AND GENDER CRITICISM

Have you ever had a classroom discussion of a piece of literature in which the focus was on the roles of women in the literature or the culture, or on the relationships between men and women? If so, you have engaged in feminist criticism. Some version of feminist criticism has been around for as long as readers have been interested in gender roles, but the school rose to prominence in the 1970s, at the same time as the modern feminist movement was gaining steam. Most **feminist criticism** from this time was clearly tied to raising consciousness about the patriarchy in which many women felt trapped. Some feminist critics sought to reveal how literary texts demonstrated the repression and powerlessness of women in different periods and cultures. Others had a nearly opposite agenda, showing how female literary characters could overcome the sexist power structures that surround them and exercise power in their worlds. Still others looked to literary history and sought to rediscover and promote writing by women whose works had been far less likely than men's to be regarded as "great" literature.

It was not long, however, before some critics began to point out that women were not alone in feeling social pressure to conform to gender roles. Over the years, men have usually been expected to be good providers, to be strong (both physically and emotionally), and to keep their problems and feelings more or less to themselves. Though the expectations are different, men are socialized no less than women to think and behave in certain ways, and these social expectations are also displayed in works of literature. Feminist criticism has expanded in recent years to become **gender criticism**. Any literary criticism that highlights gender roles or relationships between the sexes can be a type of gender criticism, whether or not it is driven by an overt feminist agenda.

MARXIST CRITICISM

Just as feminist criticism came into its own because of the political agenda of certain critics, so too did **Marxist criticism**, which originally sought to use literature and criticism to forward a socialist political program. Early Marxist critics began with Karl Marx's (1818–1883) insistence that human interactions are economically driven and that the basic model of human progress is based on a struggle for power between different social classes. For Marxist critics, then, literature was just another battleground, another venue for the ongoing quest for individual material gain. Literary characters could be divided into powerful oppressors and their powerless victims, and literary plots and themes could be examined to uncover the economic forces that drove them. According to this model, the very acts of writing and reading literature can be characterized as production and consumption, and some Marxist critics have studied the external forces that drive education, publication, and literary tastes.

The sort of Marxist criticism that ignores all forces but those that are socioeconomic is sometimes referred to as *vulgar* Marxism because, in its single-mindedness, it ignores certain complexities of individual thought and action. Its sole purpose is to expose the inequalities that underlie all societies and to thus raise the consciousness of readers and move society closer to a socialist state. Such Marxist criticism tends to be full of the language of Marxist political analysis—references to *class struggle*, to the economic *base* and *superstructure*, to the *means of production*, to worker *alienation* and *reification* (the process whereby oppressed workers lose their sense of individual humanity), and so forth.

But just as feminist criticism soon opened up into the broader and more complex school of gender criticism, so too did some Marxist criticism break free of a single-minded political agenda. You no longer have to be a committed Marxist to engage in Marxist criticism; all you need to do is acknowledge that socioeconomic forces do, in fact, affect people's lives. If you notice inequalities in power between characters in a work of literature, if you question how the class or educational background of an author affects his or her work, or if you believe that a certain type of literature—a Shakespearean sonnet, say, or a pulp Western novel— appeals more to readers of a particular social background, then you are, at least in part, engaging in Marxist criticism.

CULTURAL STUDIES

Cultural studies is the general name given to a wide variety of critical practices, some of which might seem on the surface to have little in common with one another. Perhaps the best way to understand cultural studies is to begin with the notion that certain texts are privileged in our society while others are dismissed or derided. Privileged texts are the so-called great works of literature one commonly finds in anthologies and on course syllabi. Indeed, when we hear the word *literature*, these are probably the works we imagine. All other writing—from pulp romance novels to the slogans on bumper-stickers—belong to a second category of texts, those generally overlooked by traditional literary critics.

One major trend in cultural studies is the attempt to broaden the **canon**—those texts read and taught again and again and held up as examples of the finest expressions of the human experience. Critics have pointed out that canonical authors—Shakespeare, Milton, Keats, Steinbeck—tend (with obvious exceptions) to be from a fairly narrow segment of society: they are usually middle to upper-middle class, well-educated, heterosexual white males. Some cultural critics, therefore, have sought out and celebrated the writing of historically disadvantaged groups such as African Americans or gay and lesbian authors. One very active branch of cultural studies is **postcolonial criticism**, which focuses on writing from former British (and other) colonies around the world, where local authors often display attitudes and tastes very different from those of their former colonial masters. Other branches of cultural studies turn their attention to the works of various social "outsiders," like prisoners, school children, or mental patients. This attempt at broadening the canon is designed to provide students and scholars alike with a more inclusive definition of what art and literature are all about.

Cultural critics seek to blur or erase the line separating "high" from "low" art in the minds of the literary establishment. Some cultural critics believe that all texts are to some extent artistic expressions of a culture, and that any text can therefore give us vital insights into the human experience. Rather than traditional literary objects, then, a cultural critic might choose to study such things as movies and television shows, advertisements, religious tracts, graffiti, and comic books. These texts—and virtually any other visual or verbal work you can imagine—are submitted to the same rigorous scrutiny as a sonnet or a classic novel. Some cultural critics suggest that English departments should become departments of cultural studies, in which a course on hiphop culture would be valued as much as a course on Victorian poetry.

HISTORICAL CRITICISM AND NEW HISTORICISM

If you have ever written a research paper that involved some background reading about the life and times of an author, you have already engaged in a form of **historical criticism**. Literary scholars have long read history books and various sorts of historical documents—from newspaper articles to personal letters—to gain insights into the composition and significance of a given work. The explanatory footnotes that often appear in literary reprints and anthologies are one obvious manifestation of this type of sleuthing. Indeed, a work of literature could be virtually inexplicable if we did not understand something of the times in which it was written and first read. If you did not know that Walt Whitman's "When Lilacs Last in the Dooryard Bloom'd" was an elegy written upon the assassination of Abraham Lincoln, it would be difficult to make any sense at all of the poem, since neither the president's name nor the cause of his death actually appear in the work.

Likewise, historians have long turned to literary works and the visual arts in order to gain insights into the periods they study. While archives and contemporary documents can teach us a lot about the broad sweep of history—wars, leaders, the controversies of the day—it is often difficult to see from these documents what life was like for ordinary people, whose interior lives were not often documented. We may be able to learn from parish burial records, for example, how common childhood mortality was at a particular time in English history, but only when we read Ben Jonson's poem "On My First Son" do we begin to understand how this mortality may have affected the parents who lost their children. Likewise, the few pages of James Joyce's story "Araby" may tell us more about how adolescent boys lived and thought in turn-of-the-century Dublin than several volumes of social history.

One school of historical criticism, known as **New Historicism**, takes account of both what history has to teach us about literature *and* what literature has to teach us about history. (New Historicism has been around since the 1960s, and as with New Criticism, the name of the school is no longer as accurate as it once was.) New Historicists are sometimes said to read literary and nonliterary texts *in parallel*, attempting to see how each illuminates the other. Typically, New Historicists will examine many different types of documents—government records, periodicals, private diaries, bills of sale—in order to re-create, as much as possible, the rich cultural context that surrounded both an author and that author's original audience. In doing so, they seek to give modern audiences a reading experience as rich and informed as the original readers of a literary work.

PSYCHOLOGICAL THEORIES

At the beginning of the twenty-first century, it is easy to underestimate the enormous influence that the theories of the psychoanalyst Sigmund Freud (1856–1939) have had on our understanding of human behavior and motivation. For many modern readers, Freud seems to have little to say; his work is too focused on sex and too thoroughly bound by the norms of the bourgeois Viennese society in which he lived. But if you have ever wondered what the buried significance of a dream was or whether someone had a subconscious motivation for an action, you have been affected by Freudian thinking. Freud popularized the notions that the mind can be divided into conscious and unconscious components and that we are often motivated most strongly by the unconscious. He taught us to think in terms of overt and covert desires (often referred to in Freudian language as *manifest* and *latent*) as the basis of human actions.

Like many intellectual movements of the twentieth century, psychology, and specifically Freudian psychology, has had a major influence on literary criticism. The most typical **psychological literary criticism** examines the internal mental states, the desires, and the motivations of literary characters. (In fact, Freud himself used Shakespeare's Hamlet as an example of a man whose life was ruled by what the psychiatrist called an Oedipal complex—man's unhealthy, but not uncommon, interest in his mother's sexuality.) Another subject of psychological criticism can be the author. A critic may examine the possible unconscious urges that drove an author to write a particular story or poem. Finally, a critic might examine the psychology of readers, trying to determine what draws us to or repels us from certain literary themes or forms. If any of these aspects of literature have ever interested you, you have engaged in psychological literary criticism.

Psychological critics often interpret literature as a psychologist might interpret a dream or a wish. Special attention is often paid to symbols as the manifest representation of a deeper, hidden meaning. Attention is also focused on the unstated motives and unconscious states of mind of characters, authors, or readers. Freud is not the only psychological theorist whose ideas are frequently used in literary analysis. Other important figures include Carl Jung (1875–1961), who gave us the notion of the collective unconscious and the influence of **archetypes** on our thinking, and Jacques Lacan (1901–1981), who had a special interest in the unconscious and the nature of language. You don't, however, need to be well-versed in the intricacies of psychoanalytic theory in order to be interested in the inner workings of the human mind or the ways in which they manifest themselves in literature.

READER-RESPONSE THEORIES

You no doubt have heard the old question: If a tree falls in the forest and nobody hears it, did the tree make a sound? Let us rephrase that question: If a book sits on a shelf and nobody reads it, what effect does the book have on the world? If you use **reader-response criticism**, your answer to that question will be a resounding *none*. Of course, the book exists as a physical object, a sheaf of paper bound in a cover and printed with symbols. But, say reader-response critics, as a work of art or a conduit for meaning, no text exists without a reader.

A text, according to the various theories of reader-response criticism, is not a container filled with meaning by its author but rather an interaction between an author and a reader, and it can never be complete unless readers bring to it their own unique insights. These insights come from a number of sources, including the reader's life experience as well as his or her beliefs, values, state of mind at the time of the reading, and, of course, previous reading experience. Reading is not a passive attempt to understand what lies within a text but an act of creation, no less so than the writing itself. Reader-response critics try to understand the process by which we make meaning out of words on a page. If you have ever wondered why a classmate or friend saw something entirely different than you did in a story or poem, then you have been a reader-response critic.

Two key terms associated with reader-response criticisms are *gaps* and *process*. Gaps are those things that a text doesn't tell us, that we need to fill in and work out for ourselves. Let us say, for instance, that you read a story told from the perspective of a child, but the author never explicitly mentions the child's age. How, then, do you imagine the narrator as you read? You pay attention to his or her actions and thoughts, and you compare this to your experience of real children you have known and others whose stories you have read. In doing so, you fill in a *gap* in the text and help solidify the text's meaning. Imagine, though, that as the story continues, new clues emerge and you need to adjust your assumptions about the child's age. This highlights the idea that reading is a *process*, that the meaning of the text is not fixed and complete but rather evolving as the text unfolds in the time it takes to read.

Some reader-response critics focus on the ways that meanings of a text change over time. To illustrate this idea, let us look at a specific example. Contemporary readers of Kate Chopin's short novel *The Awakening*, first published in 1899, tend to find the book's treatment of the heroine's sexuality subtle or even invisible. Such readers are often shocked or amused to learn that the book was widely condemned at the time of its publication as tasteless and overly explicit. Expectations and tastes change over time and place, and we can tell a lot about a society by examining how it responds to works of art. Reader-response critics, therefore, sometimes ask us to look at our own reactions to literature and to ask how, if at all, they match up with those of earlier readers. When we look at reactions to *The Awakening* at the end of the nineteenth century and then at the beginning of the twenty-first, we learn not only about Chopin's culture but also about our own.

STRUCTURALISM

Structuralism, as the name implies, is concerned with the structures that help us to understand and interpret literary texts. This may sound like a return to formalism, which, as we saw earlier, examines the formal and linguistic elements of a text. But the elements scrutinized by structuralist critics are of a different order entirely, being the structures that order our thinking rather than the interior architecture of poems, stories, and plays. Structuralist criticism actually derives from the work of anthropologists, linguists, and philosophers of the mid-twentieth century who sought to understand how humans thought and communicated.

The basic insight at the heart of the movement is the realization that we understand nothing in isolation but rather that every piece of our knowledge is part of a network of associations. Take, for instance, the question, "Is Jim a good father?" In order to form a simple yes or no answer to this question, we must consider, among other things, the spectrum of "good" and "bad," the expectations our culture holds for fathers, and all we know of Jim's relationship with his children.

For a structuralist literary critic, questions about literature are answered with the same sort of attention to context. Two different types of context are especially salient—the cultural and the literary. Cultural context refers to an understanding of all aspects of an author's (and a reader's) culture, including but not limited to the organizing structures of history, politics, religion, education, work, and family. Literary context refers to all related texts, literary and nonliterary, that affect our ability to interpret a text. What had the author read that might have affected the creation of the text? What have we read that might affect our interpretation? What are the norms of the textual genre, and how does this piece of literature conform to or break from those norms?

According to structuralist critics, then, we can only understand a text by placing it within the broader contexts of culture (that of both the reader and the author) and other texts (literary and nonliterary). To fully understand one of Shakespeare's love sonnets to the mysterious "dark lady," for example, we would need to understand the conventions of romantic love, the conceptions of dark versus fair women in culturally accepted standards of beauty, and the acceptable interactions between men and women in Shakespeare's England. We would also need to relate the sonnet to the history of love poems generally, to the development of the sonnet form specifically, and to the other works in Shakespeare's cycle of 154 sonnets.

POSTSTRUCTURALISM AND DECONSTRUCTION

Poststructuralism, it will come as no surprise, begins with the insights of structuralism but carries them one step further. If, as the structuralists insist, we can understand things only in terms of other things, then perhaps there is no center point of understanding but only an endlessly interconnected web of ideas leading to other ideas leading to still other ideas. This is the starting point of poststructuralist criticism, which posits that no text has a fixed or real meaning because no meaning exists outside of the network of other meanings to which it is connected. Meaning, then, including literary meaning, is forever shifting and altering as our understanding of the world changes. The best-known version of poststructuralism is **deconstruction**, a school of philosophy and literary criticism that first gained prominence in France and that seeks to overturn the very basis of Western philosophy by undermining the notion that reality has any stable existence.

At its worst, of course, this school of thought leads to the most slippery sort of relativism. What does it matter what I think of this poem or this play? I think what I want, you think what you want. Perhaps next week I will think something different. Who cares? Every interpretation is of equal value, and none has any real value at all. At its best, though, poststructuralist criticism can lead toward truly valuable insights into literature. It reminds us that meaning within a text is contingent on all sorts of exterior understandings; it allows for several interpretations, even contradictory interpretations, to exist simultaneously; and, by insisting that no text and no meaning is absolute, it allows for a playful approach to even the most "serious" of literary objects. Indeed, one of the recurrent themes of deconstructionist criticism is the French term *jouissance*, often translated as *bliss*, which refers to a free-spirited, almost sexual enjoyment of literary language.

Having thus briefly described deconstruction, we would do well to dispel a common misconception about the word. In recent years, many people, both within and outside of academia, have begun to use *deconstruct* as a synonym for *analyze*. You might hear, for instance, "We completely deconstructed that poem in class—I understand it much better now," or "The defense attorney deconstructed the prosecutor's argument." In both these cases, what the speaker likely means has little if anything to do with the literary critical practice of deconstruction. When we take apart a text or an argument and closely examine the parts, we are engaging not in deconstruction but in analysis.

By now you may be wondering what sort of literary critic you are. You may feel that you have been a formalist one day and a psychological critic the next. This is not surprising, and it should cause you no worry, as virtually none of these schools is mutually exclusive. Indeed, most professional critics mix and match the various schools in whatever way best suits their immediate needs. The close reading techniques of the New Critics, for instance, are frequently adopted by those who would fervently reject the New Critical stance that social and political context be excluded from consideration. If you wished to write about the social decline of Mme. Loisel in Guy de Maupassant's story "The Necklace," you might well find yourself in the position of a Marxist-feminist-New Historicist critic. That's fine. Writing with the knowledge that you are drawing from Marxism, feminism, and New Historicism, you will almost certainly write a better-organized, better-informed, and more thorough paper than you would have had you begun with no conscious basis in literary theory.

URSULA K. HEISE

The Hitchhiker's Guide to Ecocriticism

A professor of English at Stanford University, **Ursula K. Heise** is also a Guggenheim Fellow (2011–2012) and the past president of the Association for the Study of Literature and the Environment (ASLE). She has authored several books, including *Chronoschisms: Time, Narrative, and Postmodernism* (1997) and *Sense of Place and Sense of Planet: The Environmental Imagination of the Global* (2008). She is currently working on a book project entitled *Where the Wild Things Used to Be: Narrative, Database, and Biodiversity Loss*.

"The Hitchhiker's Guide to Ecocriticism" was first published in *PMLA* in March of 2006.

The first few frames of the Belgian comic-strip artist Raymond Macherot's work "Les Croquillards" (1957) provide a shorthand for some of the issues that concern environmentally oriented criticism, one of the most recent fields of research to have emerged from the rapidly diversifying matrix of literary and cultural studies in the 1990s. A heron is prompted to a lyrical reflection on the change of seasons by a leaf that gently floats down to the surface of his pond (see the next p.): "Ah! the poetry of autumn . . . dying leaves, wind, departing birds. . . ." This last thought jolts him back to reality: "But—I'm a migratory bird myself! . . . Good grief! What've I been thinking?" And off he takes on his voyage south, only to be hailed by the protagonists, the field rats Chlorophylle and Minimum (the latter under the spell of a bad cold), who hitch a ride to Africa with him. "Are you traveling on business?" he asks his newfound passengers. "No, for our health," they answer.

The scene unfolds around two conceptual turns relevant to ecocriticism. The speaking animal, a staple of comic strips, is credited with an aesthetic perception of nature that relies on the long Western tradition of associating beauty with ephemerality: autumn's appeal arises from its proximity to death, decay, and departure, a beauty the wind will carry away in an instant. But ironically this

Romantic valuation of nature separates the heron from his innate attunement to its rhythms: the falling leaf makes him sink into autumnal reverie and forget to seek out warmer latitudes. As soon as he takes flight, however, Macherot once again twists the idea of seasonal migration by turning the heron into a sort of jetliner on bird wings transporting what might be business or leisure travelers. What is (or should be) natural for the bird is not so for the rats, whose illness hints at another type of failure to adapt to seasonal rhythms. On one hand, this comic strip humorously raises the question whether an aesthetic appreciation of nature brings one closer to it or alienates one from it; on the other, it highlights the tension between bonds to nature that are established by innate instinct, those that arise through aesthetic valuation, and those that are mediated by modern-day travel. The heron's flight remains comically suspended between the vocabularies of nature, art, and international business. In what ways do highly evolved and self-aware beings relate to nature? What roles do language, literature, and art play in this relation? How have modernization and globalization processes transformed it? Is it possible to return to more ecologically attuned ways of inhabiting nature, and what would be the cultural prerequisites for such a change?

This is a sample of issues that are often raised in ecocriticism, a rapidly growing field in literary studies. The story of its institutional formation has been told in detail and from several perspectives (Cohen 9–14; Garrard 3– 15; Glotfelty, "Introduction" xvii–xviii, xxii–xxiv; Love 1–5; Branch and Slovic xiv–xvii):[1] scattered projects and publications involving the connection between literature and the environment in the 1980s led to the founding of ASLE, the Association for the Study of Literature and the Environment, during a convention of the Western Literature Association in 1992. In 1993 the journal *ISLE: Interdisciplinary Studies in Literature and Environment* was established, and in 1995 ASLE started holding biennial conferences. Seminal texts and anthologies such as Lawrence Buell's *The Environmental Imagination* (1995), Kate Soper's *What Is Nature?* (1995), and Cheryll Glotfelty and Harold Fromm's *Ecocriticism Reader* (1996) followed, as well as special journal issues (Murphy, *Ecology*; *Ecocriticism*). At the same time, newly minted ecocritics began to trace the origins of their intellectual concerns back to such seminal works in American and British literary studies as Henry Nash Smith's *Virgin Land* (1950), Leo Marx's *The Machine in the Garden* (1964), Roderick Nash's *Wilderness and the American Mind* (1967), Raymond Williams's *The Country and the City* (1973), Joseph Meeker's *The Comedy of Survival* (1974), and Annette Kolodny's *The Lay of the Land* (1975). ASLE membership grew rapidly, topping a thousand in the early years of the new century, and offspring organizations in Australia–New Zealand, Korea, Japan, India, and the United Kingdom were founded, as was, most recently, the independent European Association for the Study of Literature, Culture and Environment (EASLCE).

Given the steadily increasing urgency of environmental problems for ever more closely interconnected societies around the globe, the explosion of articles and books in the field may not strike one as particularly surprising. But what is remarkable about this burst of academic interest is that it took place at such a late date; most of the important social movements of the 1960s and 1970s left their marks on literary criticism long before environmentalism did, even though environmentalism succeeded in establishing a lasting presence in the political sphere. Why this delay?

The main reason lies no doubt in the development of literary theory between the late 1960s and the early 1990s. Under the influence of mostly French philosophies of language, literary critics during this period took a fresh look at questions of representation, textuality, narrative, identity, subjectivity, and historical discourse from a fundamentally skeptical perspective that emphasized the multiple disjunctures between forms of representation and the realities they purported to refer to. In this intellectual context, the notion of nature tended to be approached as a sociocultural construct that had historically often served to legitimize the ideological claims of specific social groups. From Roland Barthes's call in 1957 "always to strip down Nature, its 'laws' and its 'limits,' so as to expose History there, and finally to posit Nature as itself historical" (*Mythologies* 175; trans. mine) to Graeme Turner's claim in 1990 that "Cultural Studies defines itself in part . . . through its ability to explode the category of 'the natural'" (qtd. in Hochman 10), the bulk of cultural criticism was premised on an overarching project of denaturalization. This perspective obviously did not encourage connections with a social movement aiming to reground human cultures in natural systems and whose primary pragmatic goal was to rescue a sense of the reality of environmental degradation from the obfuscations of political discourse.

By the early 1990s, however, the theoretical panorama in literary studies had changed considerably. New historicism had shaded into American cultural studies, which styled itself antitheoretical as much as theoretical, signaling not so much the advent of a new paradigm as the transition of the discipline into a field of diverse specialties and methodologies no longer ruled by any dominant framework. Ecocriticism found its place among this expanding matrix of coexisting projects, which in part explains the theoretical diversity it has attained in a mere dozen years. But this diversity also results from its relation to the sociopolitical forces that spawned it. Unlike feminism or postcolonialism, ecocriticism did not evolve gradually as the academic wing of an influential political movement. It emerged when environmentalism had already turned into a vast field of converging and conflicting projects and given rise to two other humanistic subdisciplines, environmental philosophy and history. This diversity resonates in the different names by which the field has been identified: *ecocriticism* has imposed itself as a convenient shorthand for what some critics prefer to call *environmental criticism, literary-environmental studies, literary ecology, literary environmentalism,* or *green cultural studies* (see Buell, *Future* 11–12).

Changes in the perceived cultural relevance of biology also helped to open up the conceptual space for ecocriticism. Sociobiological approaches that had been rejected in the 1970s reentered debate in the 1990s as genetic research and biotechnologies began to shed new light on old questions about innate and acquired behavior. While many of these questions have remained intensely controversial among scientists and humanities scholars and while many ecocritics are highly critical of sociobiology and evolutionary psychology, there can be no doubt that the 1990s offered a climate very different from that of earlier decades for investigating the relation between nature and culture. This is not to say that the early 1990s marked an altogether welcoming moment for the articulation of an environmentalist perspective on culture. The so-called science wars, brewing since the 1980s, came to a head with Paul Gross and Norman Levitt's polemical repudiation of constructivist approaches to science in their book *Higher Superstition* (1994). The physicist Alan Sokal's faux-poststructuralist essay on quantum mechanics in the journal *Social Text* in 1996 took the confrontation between scientists and their critics to a new level of ferocity as well as public awareness. Ecocriticism, with its triple allegiance to the scientific study of nature, the scholarly analysis of cultural representations, and the political struggle for more sustainable ways of inhabiting the natural world, was born in the shadow of this controversy. Even though the grounds of the debate have shifted since then, the underlying issues of realism and representation that informed the science wars continue to pose challenges for ecocritical theory.

Because of the diversity of political and cross-disciplinary influences that went into its making, ecocriticism is not an easy field to summarize. Even if ecocritics, perhaps more than other academic scholars, still long for a sense of community and shared holistic ideals, the reality is that they diverge widely in their views. Recent vigorous critiques and ripostes are healthy signs of a rapidly expanding field. Somewhat like cultural studies, ecocriticism coheres more by virtue of a common political project than on the basis of shared theoretical and methodological assumptions, and the details of how this project should translate into the study of culture are continually subject to challenge and revision. For this reason, ecocriticism has also become a field whose complexities by now require the book-length introductions that have appeared over the last two years: Greg Garrard's *Ecocriticism* (2004), Buell's *The Future of Environmental Criticism* (2005), and, shorter and sketchier, Walter Rojas Pérez's *La ecocrítica hoy* (2004).

ENVIRONMENTALISM AND THE CRITIQUE
OF MODERNITY

Like feminism and critical race studies, ecocriticism started with a critical reconceptualization of modernist notions of human psychological identity and political subjecthood. The ecocritical attempt to think beyond conceptual dichotomies that modernity, the Enlightenment, and science were thought to have imposed on Western culture—the separation of subject and object, body and environment, nature and culture—articulated itself, as it did in other fields, through the combination of analytic modes of academic discourse with more experientially based forms of writing that Scott Slovic has called "narrative scholarship" ("Ecocriticism"). But ecocriticism in its first stage differed sharply from other forms of "postmodern" thought in that it sought to redefine the human subject not so much in relation to the human others that subjecthood had traditionally excluded as in relation to the nonhuman world. Environmentalism and ecocriticism aim their critique of modernity at its presumption to know the natural world scientifically, to manipulate it technologically and exploit it economically, and thereby ultimately to create a human sphere apart from it in a historical process that is usually labeled "progress." This domination strips nature of any value other than as a material resource and commodity and leads to a gradual destruction that may in the end deprive humanity of its basis for subsistence. Such domination empties human life of the significance it had derived from living in and with nature and alienates individuals and communities from their rootedness in place.

Projected alternatives to this kind of modernity extend from deep ecology to social ecology. Deep ecology foregrounds the value of nature in and of itself, the equal rights of other species, and the importance of small communities. Social ecology, by contrast, tends to value nature primarily in its human uses and has affinities with political philosophies ranging from anarchism and socialism to feminism. Deep ecology, associated often with a valuation of wild and rural spaces, self-sufficiency, a sense of place, and local knowledge and sometimes with an alternative spirituality, played an important part in the early stages of ecocriticism. Especially for Americanists, this philosophy resonated with writers from Thoreau (in a certain reading of his work) to Wendell Berry, Edward Abbey, and Gary Snyder. From the late 1990s on, however, the field gradually moved to the more social-ecological positions that dominate ecocriticism today (Buell, *Future* 97–98).

This shift was prompted in part by the sheer numerical expansion of the field, which led scholars from a wide variety of intellectual backgrounds to bring their interests to bear on environmental issues. In part it also emerged under the pressure of explicit challenges to the field: like other areas of cultural theory, ecocriticism saw its initial assumptions questioned for what they had socially excluded, historically erased, and textually forgotten (or refused) to account for.[2] The historicization of the wilderness concept by the environmental historian William Cronon is undoubtedly one of the most important critiques. Unlike ecological movements in other parts of the world, Cronon argues, environmentalism in the United States tends to hold up an ideal of landscapes untouched by human beings as the standard against which actual landscapes are measured. But this standard is problematic in its relation to past and future. It conceals the fact that the apparently transhistorical ideal of *wilderness* only acquired connotations of the sublime and sacred in the nineteenth century and that the cultural valuation of pristine and uninhabited areas led to the displacement of native inhabitants and in some cases to the creation of official parks. Far from being nature in its original state, such wildernesses were the product of cultural processes. The wilderness concept makes it difficult for a political program to conceptualize desirable forms of human inhabitation, relying as it does on the categorical separation of human beings from nature.

For ecocritics, who had often referred to statements such as Thoreau's "In wildness is the preservation of the world" as touchstones, Cronon's critique prompted a reexamination of established environmental authors as well as a broadening of the canon. Greater attention to women's and Native American literature shifted the emphasis to more communal engagements with a natural world conceived as always intertwined with human existence.[3] But greater inclusiveness also brought more challenges, since not all minority literatures proved as easy to assimilate into ecocritical concerns as Native American texts, many of whose authors had long been active in the environmental movement. African American literature, for example, as Michael Bennett and others have shown, is difficult to address with standard ecocritical vocabulary, since African American authors tend to associate rural life and sometimes even wild places with memories of slavery and persecution rather than with peaceful refuge (see Wallace and Armbruster). "[O]f what use is ecocriticism if the culture under consideration has a different relationship with pastoral space and wilderness than the ideal kinship that most nature writers and ecocritics assume and seek?" Bennett asks, and he emphasizes that "even the most inviting physical environment cannot be considered separately from the sociopolitical structures that shape its uses and abuses" (195, 201).

Critiques such as these led to increased emphasis on urban spaces (Bennett and Teague; Dixon; MacDonald) as well as on issues of social inequality that environmental problems often overlap. From the turn of the millennium, environmental-justice criticism increasingly influenced the field by drawing attention to social and racial inequalities in both access to natural resources and exposure to technological and ecological risk (Martínez-Alier; Adamson, Evans, and Stein). "Aesthetic appreciation of nature has not only been a class-coded activity, but the insulation of the middle and upper classes from the most brutal effects of industrialization has played a crucial role in environmental devastation," T. V. Reed argues in his call for an ecocriticism that fuses concerns for natural preservation with those for distributive justice (151). Along with the emergence of a fully poststructuralist ecocriticism (about which more later on), this critical agenda has opened up the full gamut of concepts and methods from cultural studies for environmental criticism.

The shift to a more in-depth engagement with the sociopolitical framing of environmental issues has also fundamentally, if not always explicitly, altered the way in which most ecocritics view the relation between modernity and nature. In earlier types of environmental scholarship, nature tended to be envisioned as a victim of modernization but also as its opposite and alternative; nature is now more often viewed as inextricably entwined with modernity— both as a concept and in the material shape in which we experience it today. More than that, environmentalists and ecocritics have begun to see how their search for a more authentic relation to nature is itself a product of modernization. The geographer David Harvey points out that

> the problem of authenticity is itself peculiarly modern. Only as modern industrialization separates us from the process of production and we encounter the environment as a finished commodity does it emerge. . . . The final victory of modernity . . . is not the disappearance of the non-modern world, but its artificial preservation and reconstruction. . . . The search for an authentic sense of community and of an authentic relation to nature among many radical and ecological movements is the cutting edge of exactly such a sensibility. (301–02)

Understanding itself in this way, as both derived from and resistant to modernity, may also help ecocriticism develop modes of critique of the modern that are less dependent than they have been so far on recourse to premodern forms of inhabitation and culture.

SCIENTIFIC INTERSECTIONS

Ecocriticism's engagement with modernization has been partly shaped by environmentalists' ambivalence toward scientific inquiry (see Heise). On one hand, science is viewed as a root cause of environmental deterioration, both in that it has cast nature as an object to be analyzed and manipulated and in that it has provided the means of exploiting nature more radically than was possible by premodern means. On the other hand, environmentalists are aware that the social legitimation of environmental politics and their own insights into the state of nature centrally depend on science. In ecocriticism, this ambivalence has translated into divergent perceptions of how the sciences should inform cultural inquiry.

At one end of the spectrum, a small number of ecocritics, such as Joseph Carroll and Glen Love, would like to make the life sciences in general and evolutionary theory in particular the foundation of literary study, following E. O. Wilson's idea of "consilience." Starting from the idea that culture is based on the human "adapted mind"— that is, "a biologically constrained set of cognitive and motivational characteristics" (Carroll vii)—this group seeks to explain cultural phenomena in terms of what they accomplish for human adaptation and survival. Many scholars in the humanities almost instinctively recoil in horror from such a sociobiological agenda, associating it with social Darwinism or Nietzschean ideology and the legitimations they have historically provided for various forms of political hegemony. But, in fairness, Darwinian theory should not simply be conflated with such ideological appropriations: Carroll categorically dismisses social Darwinism as a value-laden misinterpretation of evolutionary theory (xiv).

The more crucial question is what contribution an adaptationist approach, with its concept of human nature as a "universal, species-typical array of behavioral and cognitive characteristics" (vii), might be able to make to a discipline that has recently invested most of its theoretical capital in historical and cultural diversity. One answer is that there is no compelling reason why cultural inquiry has to focus on cultural differences rather than similarities. Fair enough— literary criticism certainly used to be more interested in universals than it has been in the last three decades. If the adaptationist approach can produce an analysis of cultural and literary universals that is descriptive rather than normative and that does not rely on the values of one particular culture dressed up as human nature (as was usually done in earlier attempts to define universals), it deserves to be heard as part of a full theory of culture. Obviously, an important part of such an analysis would have to be a careful examination of the terms used to describe the object of study: words such as *literature, aesthetics, narrative,* and *culture* itself have complex cultural histories and cannot be taken for granted in a biologically based approach.

What is less clear is how such an adaptationist understanding might inflect the vast areas of literary study that are concerned with historically and culturally specific phenomena. Human anatomy and physiology have not changed substantially over the last few thousand years, whereas cultural forms have varied enormously over the same time period. While a biological perspective might provide a general background, it seems at present unlikely to transform the study of such variations in the near future. In this sense, literary Darwinism offers not so much a competing theoretical approach as the outline of a different research area (culture, in its most abstract and universally human dimensions and evolutionary functions) that only partially overlaps with what most cultural scholars focus on to-day (cultures, in their historically and locally specific dimensions and social functions).

Most ecocritical work is shaped by science in a more indirect but no less important way. Ecology, for many environmentalists a countermodel against "normal" analytic science, has opened the way for a holistic understanding of how natural systems work as vast interconnected webs that, if left to themselves, tend toward stability, harmony, and self-regeneration. A fully mature ecosystem, the climax community of classical ecology, consists of a set of animals and plants ideally adapted to their environment. With such a standard in mind, science can be easily associated with a set of ideal values and a code of ethics: "Ecology . . . seemed to be a science that dealt with harmony, a harmony found in nature, offering a model for a more organic, cooperative human community" (Worster 363). Understood in this way, science can help determine what kinds of human interventions into the natural world are acceptable and what types of cultures are to be considered superior or inferior, and it can help ecocriticism evaluate texts that engage with nature. A powerful image behind an important social movement, the idea of holistic, self-regenerating ecosystems has catalyzed political, legal, and cultural changes that have unquestionably benefited the environment and human welfare (340–87).

But by the time ecocriticism emerged in the 1990s, this idea had already been exposed as no longer in accord with the state of knowledge in ecological science. Even by the 1960s, ecology had become a more analytic, empirical, and mathematical field than it was at its emergence in the late nineteenth century. Holistic notions of universal connectedness, stability, and harmony had lost much of their credibility among ecological scientists, for the most part engaged in specialized research (372–79). As environmental historians realized, ecology no longer offered a general foundation for "morality and causality": "Historians thought ecology was the rock upon which they could build environmental history; it turned out to be a swamp" (White 1113, 1114). The biologist Daniel Botkin's popular scientific book *Discordant Harmonies* (1990) brought such insights to a broader public by presenting a different and more complex image of ecosystems as dynamic, perpetually changing, and often far from stable or balanced: "We have tended to view nature as a Kodachrome still-life, much like a tourist-guide illustration . . . but nature is a moving picture show" (6).

This idea is taken up in the first book-length critique of ecocriticism, Dana Phillips's *The Truth of Ecology* (2003), which lambasts environmental scholars for adhering to an obsolete notion of ecological science and for transferring ecological terms to literary study by means of mere metaphor (42–82). Phillips is certainly right in cautioning ecocritics against undue metaphorization, moralization, or spiritualization of scientific concepts and in calling for more up-to-date scientific literacy—a literacy that, one should mention, would minimally require some training in quantitative methods that does not to date form part of cultural scholars' education. Yet a comprehensive alternative model for linking ecology and ecocriticism does not emerge from his analysis. Perhaps, given the varied and controversial nature of current connections between the humanities and sciences, such a model would be a rather tall order. Nevertheless, because of the importance of ecological science for environmentally oriented criticism, Garrard is surely right that defining their relation more clearly is one of the key challenges for ecocritical scholarship (178). Those ecocritics who situate their work at the poststructuralist end of the spectrum would go one step further than Phillips by not only criticizing particular ideas about the environment wrongly believed to derive from science but also exposing the concept of the environment itself as a cultural construct. In his study of antebellum American literature, for example, David Mazel emphasizes that his analysis

is not . . . about some myth *of* the environment, as if the environment were an ontologically stable, foundational entity we have a myth *about*. Rather, the environment is *itself* a myth, a "grand fable," a complex fiction, a widely shared, occasionally contested, and literally ubiquitous narrative. . . . [T]his study treats the environment as a discursive construction, something whose "reality" derives from the ways we write, speak, and think about it. (xii)

Mazel examines how early America's self-definition as "Nature's Nation" generates environmental discourses that end up bolstering conservative social agendas despite their professed progressive politics (xii). This resolutely constructivist and politically oriented argument is quite familiar from new historicism and cultural studies. To the extent that a scientific view of nature forms part of the analysis at all, it is to study science's role in the emergence of a socioculturally grounded conception of the environment. Most ecocritics have been reluctant to go as far as Mazel in reducing nature to a discursive reality, but he illustrates one extreme of the theoretical spectrum: while literary Darwinists subordinate cultural phenomena to scientific explanation, ecopoststructuralists subordinate material reality and its scientific explanation to cultural analysis. Ecocritical inquiry, most of which adopts a more dialectical perspective on the relation between culture and science, plays itself out in the tension between these two extremes.[4]

REALISMS: PERCEPTION AND REPRESENTATION

This tension between realist and constructivist approaches crucially involves questions about how our perception of the environment is culturally shaped and how that perception is mediated through language and literature. One strand of ecocriticism critical of modernist thought has tended to privilege philosophies and modes of writing that seek to transcend divisions between culture and nature, subject and object, and body and environment. The European phenomenological tradition has provided some of the most powerful impulses for thinking beyond such dichotomies. The German philosopher Martin Heidegger's notion of "dwelling" as part of human essence and as a form of existence that allows other forms of being to manifest themselves (160–64) has been interpreted as proto-environmentalist by some. The French phenomenologist Maurice Merleau-Ponty's emphasis on bodily experience, and especially the erotic metaphor that undergirds the "embrace of the flesh of the world," spelled out in his *Le visible et l'invisible*, (188–95, 302–04), has been taken up by some ecocritics as a way of envisioning the physical interrelatedness of body and habitat. The

Norwegian philosopher Arne Naess's "deep ecology," finally, itself influenced by Heidegger, portrays environmentalism as the realization of a self that encompasses both the individual and the cosmos (171–76).

The influence of these phenomenological approaches makes itself felt in numerous literary works and critical analyses that focus on the importance of a "sense of place," on "dwelling," "reinhabitation" (Snyder), or an "erotics of place" (T. Williams). Sometimes this cognitive, affective, and ethical attachment to place is envisioned in terms of epiphanic fusions with the environment: Edward Abbey describes in *Desert Solitaire* how after a prolonged solitary stay in the wilderness, he began to perceive a leaf when he looked at his hand (251); Snyder's "Second Shaman Song" and one of Aldo Leopold's sketches feature similar experiences of total immersion.[5] This emphasis on interrelatedness had led some ecocritics to revise assumptions of conventional rhetoric—for example, the pathetic fallacy, which "is a fallacy only to the ego clencher," as Neil Evernden puts it: "There is no such thing as an individual, only . . . individual as a component of place, defined by place" (101, 103). Since metaphor is a particularly easy way of establishing such connections between mind, body, and place, it is not surprising that ecocriticism has engaged poetry more than other schools of criticism have in recent decades.[6]

The interest in modes of thought and language that reduce or nullify the distance between the experiencing body and experienced environment has been productive for ecocriticism and set it apart from other theoretical approaches. Yet the difficulties of such a perspective are also quite obvious. In the pursuit of physical connectedness between body and environment, language and texts might initially function as mediating tools but can in the end be little more than obstacles—as they are for Macherot's lyrically minded waterfowl (see also Phillips 11–20). Physical closeness also usually refers to the individual's encounter with nature, but some feminist and indigenous perspectives understand this encounter as a fundamentally communal one. Phenomenological approaches tend not to offer clear models for mediated and collective experiences of nature; neither do they provide the means for explaining how the authenticity of natural encounters is itself culturally shaped. To the extent that this postulation of authenticity relies on the assumption that all modern subjects are alienated from nature, it is difficult to describe the particular forms of alienation suffered by socially disenfranchised groups.

This is not to say that attention to the real differences that class, gender, and race make in the experience of nature does not come with its own set of representational problems. As Buell has convincingly shown, many instances of "toxic discourse"—accounts of pollution, health threats, and the displacement of native inhabitants—that at first sight look realistic rely in fact on tropes and genres with long traditions in American literary history (*Writing* 35–54). The rhetorical power of such accounts derives precisely from their reliance on such traditions. To give one well-known example, Rachel Carson's influential indictment of pesticide overuse in *Silent Spring* (1962) skillfully uses tropes of the pastoral, biblical apocalypse, nuclear fear (in her comparisons of chemical contamination with radioactive fallout), and 1950s anti-Communism ("a grim specter has crept upon us almost unnoticed" [3]; Killingsworth and Palmer 27–32). Problems of textuality and literariness therefore surface at both ends of the ecocritical spectrum, in phenomenologically informed explorations of the encounter between body and environment as well as in politically oriented approaches to the disjunctions between body, community, and nature that result from environmental pollution and social oppression.

Poststructuralists circumvent such difficulties by presenting nature as a purely discursive construction. But like feminists and race theorists who emphasized the cultural rather than biological grounding of their objects of study, these critics must face the objection that such a view plays into the enemy's hand by obfuscating the material reality of environmental degradation. This problem may be a minor one for academic cultural theory, which surely stands to be enriched by the poststructuralist approach, as Mazel argues (xv), but it is serious for green politics. In the end, it seems likely that strong constructivist positions will be less convincing to ecocritics, many of whom are also green activists, than weak constructivist ones that analyze cultural constructions of nature with a view toward the constraints that the real environment imposes on them (see Hayles; Soper 151–55). This would also seem the most promising theoretical ground from which to pursue the analysis of environmental literature in its relation to cultural and rhetorical traditions, on one hand, and social as well as scientific realities, on the other.

THINKING GLOBALLY

Along with its theoretical diversity and interdisciplinarity, the rapid expansion of its analytic canon is one of the most striking features of ecocriticism. British Romanticism and twentieth-century American literature initially proved the most fertile fields of inquiry, as two cultural moments with a decisive influence on current conceptions of nature. Jonathan Bate's *Romantic Ecology* (1991) and *Song of the Earth* (2000) as well as Karl Kroeber's *Ecological Literary Criticism* (1994) blazed the environmental trail in studies of Romanticism; Slovic's *Seeking Awareness in American Nature Writing* (1992) and Buell's *Environmental Imagination* foregrounded the importance of nature writing for the American literary canon. Slovic's and Buell's efforts were accompanied by a multitude of other studies of American literature, often with a focus on nonfiction and nature poetry by such writers as Thoreau, Emerson, John Muir, Mary Austin, Robinson Jeffers, Edward Abbey, Gary Snyder, Wendell Berry, Annie Dillard, and Barry Lopez. A second wave of publications placed greater emphasis on women writers, from Willa Cather and Adrienne Rich to Terry Tempest Williams and Karen Tei Yamashita, and on Native American literature, from Leslie Marmon Silko to Simon Ortiz, Linda Hogan, and Joy Harjo. This shift in themes and authors was accompanied by a broadening of the generic horizon. Science fiction came into view as a genre with important environmental dimensions, as did film and computer games. At the same time, ecocritics have developed analyses of cultural institutions and practices outside the arts, from landscape architecture and green consumerism to various forms of tourism and the national park system.

Critics such as Patrick Murphy and Slovic have also made sustained efforts to spread ecocritical analysis to the study of other cultures and languages, though their success has been limited. Ecocriticism has achieved fairly good coverage of Australian, British, Canadian, and United States literatures, but ecocritical work on languages other than English is still scarce,[7] and some of it is not well connected to scholarship in English. Murphy's monumental anthology *Literature of Nature: An International Sourcebook* (1998) represents a first heroic effort to put ecocriticism on a truly comparatist and global basis. Yet its coverage remains uneven, not only because there are more essays on anglophone than on other literatures but also because essays on some countries cover several hundred years (India), others only one literary period (Taiwan), and yet others a single author (Brazil). The surprising selectiveness of the bibliographies in some of these essays is symptomatic of broader international disjunctures.[8] Works on British or American environmental literature tend to refer to one another but not to work like Jorge Marcone's and Candace Slater's on Latin American texts or Axel Goodbody's and Heather Sullivan's on German literature, even though much of this work is available in English. Critical anthologies are usually not received by anglophone ecocritics when their focus of study lies outside English-based literatures.[9] Ecocriticism is a good deal more international than cultural studies was initially, but its geographic scope is not evident in most of the published work. Obviously, part of the problem is linguistic: mono-lingualism is currently one of ecocriticism's most serious intellectual limitations. The environmentalist ambition is to think globally, but doing so in terms of a single language is inconceivable—even and especially when that language is a hegemonic one.

Precisely because ecocritical work encompasses many literatures and cultures, it would also stand to gain from a closer engagement with theories of globalization (Garrard 178).[10] To date, environmental-justice ecocriticism is the only branch of the field that has addressed globalization issues in any depth. To put it somewhat simplistically, this type of ecocriticism rejects economic globalization, which it understands to be dominated by transna-tional corporations, but welcomes cultural border crossings and alliances, especially when they are initiated by the disenfranchised in the current economic world order. The interdependencies of these two forms of globalization, however, deserve closer theoretical scrutiny. Ecological issues are situated at a complex intersection of politics, economy, technology, and culture; envisioning them in their global implications requires an engagement with a variety of theoretical approaches to globalization, especially, for ecocritics, those that focus on its cultural dimensions. With such a theoretical framework to link together the pieces of its international and in-terdisciplinary mosaic, ecocriticism promises to become one of the most intellectually exciting and politically urgent ventures in current literary and cultural studies.

Notes

1. See also the useful typology of ecocriticism in Reed 148–49.

2. See Cohen for a more chronological account of these challenges.

3. Space constraint makes it impossible for me to give a detailed account of the role of ecofeminism here, whose intellectual trajectory and complexity deserve an essay of their own.

4. As Levin sums it up, "Much recent [ecocritical] work can be divided into two competing critical camps: realists, who advocate a return to nature as a means of healing our modern/postmodern alienation, and social constructionists, who see that nature as a discursive strategy and adopt a more skeptical stance with regard to its alleged healing properties. . . . [T]he dialectical critics from the two different camps

appear to have more in common with each other than the more and less sophisticated representatives of the same camp" (175).

5. On Snyder, see Buell, *Environmental Imagination* 166–67; on Leopold, see Berthold-Bond 23–24.

6. Admittedly, the emphasis has been on fairly conventional forms of poetry from Romanticism to the present. More recently, however, experimental poetry has come into focus, from the founding of the journal *Ecopoetics*, in 2001, to Cooperman's work on Olson, Hart's on Eigner, and Fletcher's on Ashbery (175–224).

7. Research by Americanists outside the United States includes work by Hollm; Mayer; and Suberchicot. In her 2004 presidential address to the American Studies Association, Shelley Fisher Fishkin foregrounded the importance of more sustained attention to such research in American studies at large (35–40).

8. Even in single national traditions, some of the omissions are surprising: the essay on Brazil does not refer to Soares's critical anthology *Ecologia e literatura* (1991), and none of the four pieces on Japan in Murphy's anthology mentions Colligan-Taylor's *The Emergence of Environmental Literature in Japan* (1990).

9. For example, Larsen, Nøjgaard, and Petersen's *Nature: Literature and Its Otherness* (1997).

10. Guha's critique of American environmentalism and Guha and Martínez-Alier's *Varieties of Environmentalism* provide good starting points for such an inquiry.

Works Cited

Abbey, Edward. *Desert Solitaire: A Season in the Wilderness*. New York: Ballantine, 1968.

Adamson, Joni, Mei Mei Evans, and Rachel Stein, eds. *The Environmental Justice Reader: Politics, Poetics, and Pedagogy*. Tucson: U of Arizona P, 2002.

Armbruster, Karla, and Kathleen R. Wallace, eds. *Beyond Nature Writing: Exploring the Boundaries of Ecocriticism*. Charlottesville: U of Virginia P, 2001.

Barthes, Roland. *Mythologies*. Paris: Seuil, 1957.

Bate, Jonathan. *Romantic Ecology: Wordsworth and the Environmental Tradition*. London: Routledge, 1991.

———. *The Song of the Earth*. London: Picador, 2000.

Bennett, Michael. "Anti-pastoralism, Frederick Douglass, and the Nature of Slavery." Armbruster and Wallace 195–210.

Bennett, Michael, and David W. Teague, eds. *The Nature of Cities: Ecocriticism and Urban Environments*. Tucson: U of Arizona P, 1999.

Berthold-Bond, Daniel. "The Ethics of 'Place': Reflections on Bioregionalism." *Environmental Ethics* 22 (2000): 5–24.

Botkin, Daniel B. *Discordant Harmonies: A New Ecology for the Twenty-First Century*. New York: Oxford UP, 1990.

Branch, Michael P., and Scott Slovic, eds. *The ISLE Reader: Ecocriticism, 1993–2003*. Athens: U of Georgia P, 2003.

Buell, Lawrence. *The Environmental Imagination: Thoreau, Nature Writing, and the Formation of American Culture*. Cambridge: Harvard UP, 1995.

———. *The Future of Environmental Criticism: Environmental Crisis and Literary Imagination*. Oxford: Blackwell, 2005.

———. *Writing for an Endangered World: Literature, Culture, and Environment in the U.S. and Beyond*. Cambridge: Harvard UP, 2001.

Carroll, Joseph. *Literary Darwinism: Evolution, Human Nature, and Literature*. New York: Routledge, 2004.

Carson, Rachel. *Silent Spring*. Boston: Houghton, 1962.

Cohen, Michael P. "Blues in the Green: Ecocriticism under Critique." *Environmental History* 9 (2004): 9–36.

Colligan-Taylor, Karen. *The Emergence of Environmental Literature in Japan*. New York: Garland, 1990.

Cooperman, Matthew. "Charles Olson: Archaeologist of Morning, Ecologist of Evening." Tallmadge and Harrington 208–28.

Cronon, William. "The Trouble with Wilderness; or, Getting Back to the Wrong Nature." *Uncommon Ground: Rethinking the Human Place in Nature*. Ed. Cronon. New York: Norton, 1995. 69–90.

Dixon, Terrell, ed. *City Wilds: Essays and Stories about Urban Nature*. Athens: U of Georgia P, 2002.

Ecocriticism. Spec. issue of *New Literary History* 30.3 (1999): 505–716.

Evernden, Neil. "Beyond Ecology: Self, Place, and the Pathetic Fallacy." Glotfelty and Fromm 92–104.

Fishkin, Shelley Fisher. "Crossroads of Cultures: The Transnational Turn in American Studies." *American Quarterly* 57 (2005): 17–57.

Fletcher, Angus. *A New Theory for American Poetry: Democracy, the Environment, and the Future of Imagination*. Cambridge: Harvard UP, 2004.

Garrard, Greg. *Ecocriticism*. London: Routledge, 2004.

Glotfelty, Cheryll. "Introduction: Literary Studies in an Age of Environmental Crisis." Glotfelty and Fromm xv–xxxvii.

Glotfelty, Cheryll, and Harold Fromm, eds. *The Ecocriticism Reader: Landmarks in Literary Ecology*. Athens: U of Georgia P, 1996.

Goodbody, Axel. "Deutsche Ökolyrik: Comparative Observations on the Emergence and Expression of Environmental Consciousness in West and East German Poetry." *German Literature at a Time of Change, 1989–1990: German Unity and German Identity in Literary Perspective*. Ed. Arthur Williams, Stuart Parkes, and Roland Smith. Bern: Lang, 1991. 373–400.

———. "'Es stirbt das Land an seinen Zwecken': Writers, the Environment and the Green Movement in the GDR." *German Life and Letters* 47 (1994): 325–36.

Gross, Paul R., and Norman Levitt. *Higher Superstition: The Academic Left and Its Quarrels with Science.* Baltimore: Johns Hopkins UP, 1994.

Guha, Ramachandra. "Radical American Environmentalism and Wilderness Preservation: A Third World Critique." *Environmental Ethics* 11 (1989): 71–84.

Guha, Ramachandra, and Joan Martínez-Alier. *Varieties of Environmentalism: Essays North and South.* London: Earthscan, 1997.

Hart, George. "Postmodernist Nature/Poetry: The Example of Larry Eigner." Tallmadge and Harrington 315–32.

Harvey, David. *Justice, Nature and the Geography of Difference.* Oxford: Blackwell, 1996.

Hayles, N. Katherine. "Constrained Constructivism: Locating Scientific Inquiry in the Theater of Representation." *Realism and Representation: Essays on the Problem of Realism in Relation to Science, Literature, and Culture.* Ed. George Levine. Madison: U of Wisconsin P, 1993. 27–43.

Heidegger, Martin. "Bauen Wohnen Denken." *Vorträge und Aufsätze.* Ed. Friedrich-Wilhelm von Herrmann. Frankfurt am Main: Klostermann, 2000. 145–64.

Heise, Ursula K. "Science and Ecocriticism." *American Book Review* 18 (1997): 4–6.

Hochman, Jhan. *Green Cultural Studies: Nature in Film, Novel, and Theory.* Moscow: U of Idaho P, 1998.

Hollm, Jan. *Die angloamerikanische Ökotopie: Literarische Entwürfe einer grünen Welt.* Frankfurt am Main: Lang, 1998.

Killingsworth, M. Jimmie, and Jacqueline S. Palmer. "Millennial Ecology: The Apocalyptic Narrative from Silent Spring to Global Warming." *Green Culture: Environmental Rhetoric in Contemporary America.* Ed. Carl G. Herndl and Stuart C. Brown. Madison: U of Wisconsin P, 1996. 21–45.

Kolodny, Annette. *The Lay of the Land: Metaphor as History and Experience in American Life and Letters.* Chapel Hill: U of North Carolina P, 1975.

Kroeber, Karl. *Ecological Literary Criticism: Romantic Imagining and the Biology of Mind.* New York: Columbia UP, 1994.

Larsen, Svend Eric, Morten Nøjgaard, and Annelise Ballegard Petersen, eds. *Nature: Literature and Its Otherness / La littérature et son autre.* Odense, Den.: Odense UP, 1997.

Levin, Jonathan. "Beyond Nature? Recent Work in Ecocriticism." *Contemporary Literature* 43 (2002): 171–86.

Love, Glen A. *Practical Ecocriticism: Literature, Biology, and the Environment.* Charlottesville: U of Virginia P, 2003.

MacDonald, Scott. "Ten+ (Alternative) Films about American Cities." Branch and Slovic 217–39.

Macherot, Raymond. "Les croquillards." *Chlorophylle à Coquefredouille.* N.p.: Le Lombard, 1998. 7–52.

Marcone, Jorge. "De retorno a lo natural: La serpiente de oro, la 'novela de la selva' y la crítica ecológica." *Hispania* 81 (1998): 299–308.

———. "Jungle Fever: Primitivism in Environmentalism: Rómulo Gallegos's Canaima and the Romance of the Jungle." *Primitivism and Identity in Latin America: Essays on Art, Literature, and Culture.* Ed. Erik Camayd-Freixas and José Eduardo González. Tucson: U of Arizona P, 2000. 157–72.

Martínez-Alier, Joan. "'Environmental Justice' (Local and Global)." *The Cultures of Globalization.* Ed. Fredric Jameson and Masao Miyoshi. Durham: Duke UP, 1998. 312–26.

Marx, Leo. *The Machine in the Garden: Technology and the Pastoral Ideal in America.* New York: Oxford UP, 1964.

Mayer, Sylvia. *Naturethik und Neuengland-Regionalliteratur: Harriet Beecher Stowe, Rose Terry Cooke, Sarah Orne Jewett, Mary E. Wilkins Freeman.* Heidelberg: Winter, 2004.

Mazel, David. *American Literary Environmentalism.* Athens: U of Georgia P, 2000.

Meeker, Joseph. *The Comedy of Survival: Literary Ecology and a Play Ethic.* 3rd ed. Tucson: U of Arizona P, 1997.

Merleau-Ponty, Maurice. *Le visible et l'invisible: Suivi de notes de travail.* Ed. Claude Lefort. Paris: Gallimard, 1964.

Murphy, Patrick D., ed. *Ecology in Latin American and Caribbean Literature.* Spec. issue of *Hispanic Journal* 19.2 (1998): 199–342.

———, ed. *Literature of Nature: An International Sourcebook.* Chicago: Fitzroy Dearborn, 1998.

Naess, Arne. *Ecology, Community and Lifestyle: Outline of an Ecosophy.* Trans. David Rothenberg. Cambridge: Cambridge UP, 1989.

Nash, Roderick. *Wilderness and the American Mind.* New Haven: Yale UP, 1967.

Phillips, Dana. *The Truth of Ecology: Nature, Culture, and Literature in America.* Oxford: Oxford UP, 2003.

Reed, T. V. "Toward an Environmental Justice Ecocriticism." Adamson, Evans, and Stein 145–62.

Rojas Pérez, Walter. *La ecocrítica hoy.* San José, Costa Rica: Aire Moderno, 2004.

Slater, Candace. *Entangled Edens: Visions of the Amazon.* Berkeley: U of California P, 2002.

Slovic, Scott. "Ecocriticism: Storytelling, Values, Communication, Contact." *ASLE Related Conferences and Abstracts.* 7 Dec. 2005 <-http://www.asle.umn.edu/conf/other_conf/wla/1994/slovic.html>.

———. *Seeking Awareness in American Nature Writing: Henry Thoreau, Annie Dillard, Edward Abbey, Wendell Berry, Barry Lopez.* Salt Lake City: U of Utah P, 1992.

Smith, Henry Nash. *Virgin Land: The American West as Symbol and Myth*. Cambridge: Harvard UP, 1950.

Snyder, Gary. "Reinhabitation." *A Place in Space: Ethics, Aesthetics, and Watersheds*. Washington: Counterpoint, 1995. 183–91.

Soares, Angélica. *Ecologia e literatura*. Rio de Janeiro: Tempo Brazileiro, 1992.

Sokal, Alan D. "Transgressing the Boundaries: Toward a Transformative Hermeneutics of Quantum Gravity." *Social Text* 46–47 (1996): 217–52.

Soper, Kate. *What Is Nature? Culture, Politics and the Non-human*. Oxford: Blackwell, 1995.

Suberchicot, Alain. *Littérature américaine et écologie*. Paris: Harmattan, 2002.

Sullivan, Heather I. "Organic and Inorganic Bodies in the Age of Goethe: An Ecocritical Reading of Ludwig Tieck's 'Rune Mountain' and the Earth Sciences." *ISLE* 10.2 (2003): 21–46.

Tallmadge, John, and Henry Harrington, eds. *Reading under the Sign of Nature: New Essays in Ecocriticism*. Salt Lake City: U of Utah P, 2000.

Wallace, Kathleen R., and Karla Armbruster. "The Novels of Toni Morrison: 'Wild Wilderness Where There Was None.'" Armbruster and Wallace 211–30.

White, Richard. "Environmental History, Ecology, and Meaning." *Journal of American History* 76 (1990): 1111–16.

Williams, Raymond. *The Country and the City*. New York: Oxford UP, 1973.

Williams, Terry Tempest. "Yellowstone: The Erotics of Place." *An Unspoken Hunger: Stories from the Field*. New York: Pantheon, 1994. 81–87.

Wilson, Edward O. *Consilience: The Unity of Knowledge*. New York: Knopf, 1998.

Worster, Donald. *Nature's Economy: A History of Ecological Ideas*. 2nd ed. Cambridge: Cambridge UP, 1994.

[2006]

GEORGE ORWELL [1903–1950]

Shooting an Elephant

Born in India in 1903, Eric Blair was the son of an English civil servant in the British Raj, the rule of India by the British, as was his father. Educated in England, Blair was an Imperial policeman in India for five years but resigned and returned to England to pursue his dream of becoming a writer, complete with a pen name, **George Orwell**. Known best for his novels *Animal Farm* (1945) and *1984* (1949), Orwell's political concerns were expressed in nonfiction as well, in works such as his chronicle of life among the poor, *Down and Out in Paris and London* (1933). Because of his stands against economic injustice and totalitarianism, Orwell remains an influential figure, as the adjectivization of his pen name shows — *Orwellian* has entered the vernacular as a term to describe the violence done to language and common sense by totalitarianism. "Shooting an Elephant" tells the story of a moment early in Orwell's life when his sense of injustice surfaced.

In Moulmein, in Lower Burma, I was hated by large numbers of people — the only time in my life that I have been important enough for this to happen to me. I was sub-divisional police officer of the town, and in an aimless, petty kind of way anti-European feeling was very bitter. No one had the guts to raise a riot, but if a European woman went through the bazaars alone somebody would probably spit betel juice over her dress. As a police officer I was an obvious target and was baited whenever it seemed safe to do so. When a nimble Burman tripped me up on the football field and the referee (another Burman) looked the other way, the crowd yelled with hideous laughter. This happened more than once. In the end the sneering yellow faces of young men that met me everywhere, the insults hooted after me when I was at a safe distance, got badly on my nerves. The young Buddhist priests were the worst of all. There were several thousands of them in the town and none of them seemed to have anything to do except stand on street corners and jeer at Europeans.

All this was perplexing and upsetting. For at that time I had already made up my mind that imperialism was an evil thing and the sooner I chucked up my job and got out of it the better. Theoretically—and secretly, of course—I was all for the Burmese and all against their oppressors, the British. As for the job I was doing, I hated it more bitterly than I can perhaps make clear. In a job like that you see the dirty work of Empire at close quarters. The wretched prisoners huddling in the stinking cages of the lock-ups, the grey, cowed faces of the long-term convicts, the scarred buttocks of the men who had been flogged with bamboos—all these oppressed me with an intolerable sense of guilt. But I could get nothing into perspective. I was young and ill-educated and I had had to think out my problems in the utter silence that is imposed on every Englishman in the East. I did not even know that the British Empire is dying, still less did I know that it is a great deal better than the younger empires that are going to supplant it. All I knew was that I was stuck between my hatred of the empire I served and my rage against the evil-spirited little beasts who tried to make my job impossible. With one part of my mind I thought of the British Raj as an unbreakable tyranny, as something clamped down, in *saecula saeculorum* upon the will of prostrate peoples; with another part I thought that the greatest joy in the world would be to drive a bayonet into a Buddhist priest's guts. Feelings like these are the normal by-products of imperialism; ask any Anglo-Indian official, if you can catch him off duty.

One day something happened which in a roundabout way was enlightening. It was a tiny incident in itself, but it gave me a better glimpse than I had had before of the real nature of imperialism—the real motives for which despotic governments act. Early one morning the sub-inspector at a police station the other end of the town rang me up on the phone and said that an elephant was ravaging the bazaar. Would I please come and do something about it? I did not know what I could do, but I wanted to see what was happening and I got on to a pony and started out. I took my rifle, an old .44 Winchester and much too small to kill an elephant, but I thought the noise might be useful *in terrorem*. Various Burmans stopped me on the way and told me about the elephant's doings. It was not, of course, a wild elephant, but a tame one which had gone "must." It had been chained up, as tame elephants always are when their attack of "must" is due, but on the previous night it had broken its chain and escaped. Its mahout, the only person who could manage it when it was in that state, had set out in pursuit, but had taken the wrong direction and was now twelve hours' journey away, and in the morning the elephant had suddenly reappeared in the town. The Burmese population had no weapons and were quite helpless against it. It had already destroyed somebody's bamboo hut, killed a cow and raided some fruit-stalls and devoured the stock; also it had met the municipal rubbish van and, when the driver jumped out and took to his heels, had turned the van over and inflicted violences upon it.

The Burmese sub-inspector and some Indian constables were waiting for me in the quarter where the elephant had been seen. It was a very poor quarter, a labyrinth of squalid bamboo huts, thatched with palm-leaf, winding all over a steep hillside. I remember that it was a cloudy, stuffy morning at the beginning of the rains. We began questioning the people as to where the elephant had gone and, as usual, failed to get any definite information. That is invariably the case in the East; a story al-ways sounds clear enough at a distance, but the nearer you get to the scene of events the vaguer it becomes. Some of the people said that the elephant had gone in one direction, some said that he had gone in an-other, some professed not even to have heard of any elephant. I had al-most made up my mind that the whole story was a pack of lies, when we heard yells a little distance away. There was a loud, scandalized cry of "Go away, child! Go away this instant!" and an old woman with a switch in her hand came round the corner of a hut, violently shooing away a crowd of naked children. Some more women followed, clicking their tongues and exclaiming; evidently there was something that the children ought not to have seen. I rounded the hut and saw a man's dead body sprawling in the mud. He was an Indian, a black Dravidian coolie, al-most naked, and he could not have been dead many minutes. The people said that the elephant had come suddenly upon him round the corner of the hut, caught him with its trunk, put its foot on his back and ground him into the earth. This was the rainy season and the ground was soft, and his face had scored a trench a foot deep and a couple of yards long. He was lying on his belly with arms crucified and head sharply twisted to one side. His face was coated with mud, the eyes wide open, the teeth bared and grinning with an expression of unendurable agony. (Never tell me, by the way, that the dead look peaceful. Most of the corpses I have seen looked devilish.) The friction of the great beast's foot had stripped the skin from his back as neatly as one skins a rabbit. As soon as I saw the dead man I sent an orderly to a friend's house nearby to borrow an elephant rifle. I had already sent back the pony, not wanting it to go mad with fright and throw me if it smelt the elephant.

The orderly came back in a few minutes with a rifle and five car- 5 tridges, and meanwhile some Burmans had arrived and told us that the elephant was in the paddy fields below, only a few hundred yards away. As I started forward practically the whole population of the quarter flocked out of the houses and followed me. They had seen the rifle and were all shouting excitedly that I was going to shoot the elephant. They had not shown much interest in the elephant when he was merely ravaging their homes, but it was different now that he was going to be shot. It was a bit of fun to them, as it would be to an English crowd; besides they wanted the meat. It made me vaguely uneasy. I had no intention of shooting the elephant—I had merely sent for the rifle to defend myself if necessary—and it is always unnerving to have a crowd following you. I marched down the hill, looking and feeling a fool, with the rifle over my shoulder and an ever-growing army of people jostling at my heels. At the bottom, when you got away from the huts, there was a metalled road and beyond that a miry waste of paddy fields a thousand yards across, not yet ploughed but soggy from the first rains and dotted with coarse grass. The elephant was standing eight yards from the road, his left side towards us. He took not the slightest notice of the crowd's approach. He was tearing up bunches of grass, beating them against his knees to clean them and stuffing them into his mouth.

I had halted on the road. As soon as I saw the elephant I knew with perfect certainty that I ought not to shoot him. It is a serious matter to shoot a working elephant—it is comparable to destroying a huge and costly piece of machinery—and obviously one ought not to do it if it can possibly be avoided. And at that distance, peacefully eating, the elephant looked no more dangerous than a cow. I thought then and I think now that his attack of "must" was already passing off; in which case he would merely wander harmlessly about until the mahout came back and caught him. Moreover, I did not in the least want to shoot him. I decided that I would watch him for a little while to make sure that he did not turn savage again, and then go home.

But at that moment I glanced round at the crowd that had followed me. It was an immense crowd, two thousand at the least and growing every minute. It blocked the road for a long distance on either side. I looked at the sea of yellow faces above the garish clothes—faces all happy and excited over this bit of fun, all certain that the elephant was going to be shot. They were watching me as they would watch a conjurer about to perform a trick. They did not like me, but with the magical rifle in my hands I was momentarily worth watching. And suddenly I realized that I should have to shoot the elephant after all. The people expected it of me and I had got to do it; I could feel their two thousand wills pressing me forward, irresistibly. And it was at this moment, as I stood there with the rifle in my hands, that I first grasped the hollowness, the futility of the white man's dominion in the East. Here was I, the white man with his gun, standing in front of the unarmed native crowd—seemingly the leading actor of the piece; but in reality I was only an absurd puppet pushed to and fro by the will of those yellow faces behind. I perceived in this moment that when the white man turns tyrant it is his own freedom that he destroys. He becomes a sort of hollow, posing dummy, the conventionalized figure of a sahib. For it is the condition of his rule that he shall spend his life in trying to impress the "natives," and so in every crisis he has got to do what the "natives" expect of him. He wears a mask, and his face grows to fit it. I had got to shoot the elephant. I had committed myself to doing it when I sent for the rifle. A sahib has got to act like a sahib; he has got to appear resolute, to know his own mind and do definite things. To come all that way, rifle in hand, with two thousand people marching at my heels, and then to trail feebly away, having done nothing—no, that was impossible. The crowd would laugh at me. And my whole life, every white man's life in the East, was one long struggle not to be laughed at.

But I did not want to shoot the elephant. I watched him beating his bunch of grass against his knees, with that preoccupied grandmotherly air that elephants have. It seemed to me that it would be murder to shoot him. At that age I was not squeamish about killing animals, but I had never shot an elephant and never wanted to. (Somehow it always seems worse to kill a *large* animal.) Besides, there was the beast's owner to be considered. Alive, the elephant was worth at least a hundred pounds; dead, he would only be worth the value of his tusks, five pounds, possibly. But I had got to act quickly. I turned to some experienced-looking Burmans who had been there when we arrived, and asked them how the elephant had been behaving. They all said the same thing: he took no notice of you if you left him alone, but he might charge if you went too close to him.

It was perfectly clear to me what I ought to do. I ought to walk up to within, say, twenty-five yards of the elephant and test his behavior. If he charged, I could shoot; if he took no notice of me, it would be safe to leave him until the mahout came back. But also I knew that I was going to do no such thing. I was a poor shot with a rifle and the ground was soft mud into which one would sink at every step. If the elephant charged and I missed him, I should have about as much chance as a toad under a steam-roller. But even then I was not thinking particularly of my own skin, only of the watchful yellow faces behind. For at that moment, with the crowd watching me, I was not afraid in the ordinary sense, as I would have been if I had been alone. A white man mustn't be frightened in front of "natives"; and so, in general, he isn't frightened. The sole thought in my mind was that if anything went wrong those two thousand Burmans would see me pursued, caught, trampled on and reduced to a grinning corpse like that Indian up the hill. And if that happened it was quite probable that some of them would laugh. That would never do. There was only one alternative. I shoved the cartridges into the magazine and lay down on the road to get a better aim.

The crowd grew very still, and a deep, low, happy sigh, as of people who see the theatre curtain go up at last, breathed from innumerable throats. They were going to have their bit of fun after all. The rifle was a beautiful German thing with cross-hair sights. I did not then know that in shooting an elephant one would shoot to cut an imaginary bar running from ear-hole to ear-hole. I ought, therefore, as the elephant was sideways on, to have aimed straight at his ear-hole; actually I aimed several inches in front of this, thinking the brain would be further forward.

When I pulled the trigger I did not hear the bang or feel the kick—one never does when a shot goes home—but I heard the devilish roar of glee that went up from the crowd. In that instant, in too short a time, one would have thought, even for the bullet to get there, a mysterious, terrible change had come over the elephant. He neither stirred nor fell, but every line of his body had altered. He looked suddenly stricken, shrunken, immensely old, as though the frightful impact of the bullet had paralysed him without knocking him down. At last, after what seemed a long time—it might have been five seconds, I dare say—he sagged flabbily to his knees. His mouth slobbered. An enormous senility seemed to have settled upon him. One could have imagined him thousands of years old. I fired again into the same spot. At the second shot he did not collapse but climbed with desperate slowness to his feet and stood weakly upright, with legs sagging and head drooping. I fired a third time. That was the shot that did for him. You could see the agony of it jolt his whole body and knock the last remnant of strength from his legs. But in falling he seemed for a moment to rise, for as his hind legs collapsed beneath him he seemed to tower upward like a huge rock toppling, his trunk reaching skywards like a tree. He trumpeted, for the first and only time. And then down he came, his belly towards me, with a crash that seemed to shake the ground even where I lay.

I got up. The Burmans were already racing past me across the mud. It was obvious that the elephant would never rise again, but he was not dead. He was breathing very rhythmically with long rattling gasps, his great mound of a side painfully rising and falling. His mouth was wide open—I could see far down into caverns of pale pink throat. I waited a long time for him to die, but his breathing did not weaken. Finally I fired my two remaining shots into the spot where I thought his heart must be. The thick blood welled out of him like red velvet, but still he did not die. His body did not even jerk when the shots hit him, the tortured breathing continued without a pause. He was dying, very slowly and in great

76

agony, but in some world remote from me where not even a bullet could damage him further. I felt that I had got to put an end to that dreadful noise. It seemed dreadful to see the great beast lying there, powerless to move and yet powerless to die, and not even to be able to finish him. I sent back for my small rifle and poured shot after shot into his heart and down his throat. They seemed to make no impression. The tortured gasps continued as steadily as the ticking of a clock.

In the end I could not stand it any longer and went away. I heard later that it took him half an hour to die. Burmans were bringing dahs and baskets even before I left, and I was told they had stripped his body almost to the bones by the afternoon.

Afterwards, of course, there were endless discussions about the shooting of the elephant. The owner was furious, but he was only an Indian and could do nothing. Besides, legally I had done the right thing, for a mad elephant has to be killed, like a mad dog, if its owner fails to control it. Among the Europeans opinion was divided. The older men said I was right, the younger men said it was a damn shame to shoot an elephant for killing a coolie, because an elephant was worth more than any damn Coringhee coolie. And afterwards I was very glad that the coolie had been killed; it put me legally in the right and it gave me a sufficient pretext for shooting the elephant. I often wondered whether any of the others grasped that I had done it solely to avoid looking a fool.

[1950]

N. SCOTT MOMADAY [b. 1934]

The Way to Rainy Mountain

A poet, novelist, autobiographer, playwright, teacher, visual artist, and environmentalist, **N. Scott Momaday** is a foremost Native American voice. He was born in 1934 in Lawton, Oklahoma, and raised on a reservation in New Mexico. His first novel, *House Made of Dawn* (1968), won a Pulitzer Prize, and his autobiographical *The Way to Rainy Mountain* (1969) is still widely read today.

This excerpt from *The Way to Rainy Mountain* demonstrates well Momaday's use of the Kiowa oral tradition. The folktales and legends lend both poetry and wisdom to Momaday's exploration of his family's past and his culture's history. As you read, consider how his identity is tied to the place where he was born and raised. How true is that for you?

A single knoll rises out of the plain in Oklahoma, north and west of the Wichita Range. For my people, the Kiowas, it is an old landmark, and they gave it the name Rainy Mountain. The hardest weather in the world is there. Winter brings blizzards, hot tornadic winds arise in the spring, and in summer the prairie is an anvil's edge. The grass turns brittle and brown, and it cracks beneath your feet. There are green belts along the rivers and creeks, linear groves of hickory and pecan, willow and witch hazel. At a distance in July or August the steaming foliage seems almost to writhe in fire. Great green and yellow grasshoppers are everywhere in the tall grass, popping up like corn to sting the flesh, and tortoises crawl about on the red earth, going nowhere in the plenty of time. Loneliness is an aspect of the land. All things in the plain are isolate; there is no confusion of objects in the eye, but *one* hill or *one* tree or *one* man. To look upon that landscape in the early morning, with the sun at your back, is to lose the sense of proportion. Your imagination comes to life, and this, you think, is where Creation was begun.

I returned to Rainy Mountain in July. My grandmother had died in the spring, and I wanted to be at her grave. She had lived to be very old and at last infirm. Her only living daughter was with her when she died, and I was told that in death her face was that of a child.

I like to think of her as a child. When she was born, the Kiowas were living the last great moment of their history. For more than a hundred years they had controlled the open range from the Smoky Hill River to the Red, from the headwaters of the Canadian to the fork of the Arkansas and Cimarron. In alliance with the Comanches, they had ruled the whole of the southern Plains. War was their sacred business, and they were among the finest horsemen the world has ever known. But warfare for the Kiowas was preeminently a matter of disposition rather than of survival, and they never understood the grim, unrelenting advance of the U.S. Cavalry. When at last, divided and ill-provisioned, they were driven onto the Staked Plains in the cold rains of autumn, they fell into panic. In Palo Duro Canyon they abandoned their crucial stores to pillage and had nothing then but their lives. In order to save themselves, they surrendered to the soldiers at Fort Sill and were imprisoned in the old stone corral that now stands as a military museum. My grandmother was spared the humiliation of those high gray walls by eight or ten years, but she must have known from birth the affliction of defeat, the dark brooding of old warriors.

Her name was Aho, and she belonged to the last culture to evolve in North America. Her forebears came down from the high country in western Montana nearly three centuries ago. They were a mountain people, a mysterious tribe of hunters whose language has never been positively classified in any major group. In the late seventeenth century they began a long migration to the south and east. It was a journey toward the dawn, and it led to a golden age. Along the way the Kiowas were befriended by the Crows, who gave them the culture and religion of the Plains. They acquired horses, and their ancient nomadic spirit was suddenly free of the ground. They acquired Tai-me, the sacred Sun Dance doll, from that moment the object and symbol of their worship, and so shared in the divinity of the sun. Not least, they acquired the sense of destiny, therefore courage and pride. When they entered upon the southern Plains they had been transformed. No longer were they slaves to the simple necessity of survival; they were a lordly and dangerous society of fighters and thieves, hunters and priests of the sun. According to their origin myth, they entered the world through a hollow log. From one point of view, their migration was the fruit of an old prophecy, for indeed they emerged from a sunless world.

Although my grandmother lived out her long life in the shadow of 5 Rainy Mountain, the immense landscape of the continental interior lay like memory in her blood. She could tell of the Crows, whom she had never seen, and of the Black Hills, where she had never been. I wanted to see in reality what she had seen more perfectly in the mind's eye, and traveled fifteen hundred miles to begin my pilgrimage.

79

Yellowstone, it seemed to me, was the top of the world, a region of deep lakes and dark timber, canyons and waterfalls. But, beautiful as it is, one might have the sense of confinement there. The skyline in all directions is close at hand, the high wall of the woods and deep cleavages of shade. There is a perfect freedom in the mountains, but it belongs to the eagle and the elk, the badger and the bear. The Kiowas reckoned their stature by the distance they could see, and they were bent and blind in the wilderness.

Descending eastward, the highland meadows are a stairway to the plain. In July the inland slope of the Rockies is luxuriant with flax and buckwheat, stonecrop and larkspur. The earth unfolds and the limit of the land recedes. Clusters of trees, and animals grazing far in the distance, cause the vision to reach away and wonder to build upon the mind. The sun follows a longer course in the day, and the sky is immense beyond all comparison. The great billowing clouds that sail upon it are the shadows that move upon the grain like water, dividing light. Farther down, in the land of the Crows and Blackfeet, the plain is yellow. Sweet clover takes hold of the hills and bends upon itself to cover and seal the soil. There the Kiowas paused on their way; they had come to the place where they must change their lives. The sun is at home on the plains. Precisely there does it have the certain character of a god. When the Kiowas came to the land of the Crows, they could see the dark lees of the hills at dawn across the Bighorn River, the profusion of light on the grain shelves, the oldest deity ranging after the solstices. Not yet would they veer southward to the caldron of the land that lay below; they must wean their blood from the northern winter and hold the mountains a while longer in their view. They bore Tai-me in procession to the east.

A dark mist lay over the Black Hills, and the land was like iron. At the top of a ridge I caught sight of Devil's Tower upthrust against the gray sky as if in the birth of time the core of the earth had broken through its crust and the motion of the world was begun. There are things in nature that engender an awful quiet in the heart of man; Devil's Tower is one of them. Two centuries ago, because they could not do otherwise, the Kiowas made a legend at the base of the rock. My grandmother said:

Eight children were there at play, seven sisters and their brother. Suddenly the boy was struck dumb; he trembled and began to run upon his hands and feet. His fingers became claws, and his body was covered with fur. Directly there was a bear where the boy had been. The sisters were terrified; they ran, and the bear after them. They came to the stump of a great tree, and the tree spoke to them. It bade them climb upon it, and as they did so it began to rise into the air. The bear came to kill them, but they were just beyond its reach. It reared against the tree and scored the bark all around with its claws. The seven sisters were borne into the sky, and they became the stars of the Big Dipper.

From that moment, and so long as the legend lives, the Kiowas have kinsmen in the night sky. Whatever they were in the mountains, they could be no more. However tenuous their well-being, however much they had suffered and would suffer again, they had found a way out of the wilderness.

My grandmother had a reverence for the sun, a holy regard that now is all but gone out of mankind. There was a wariness in her, and an ancient awe. She was a Christian in her later years, but she had come a long way about, and she never forgot her birthright. As a child she had been to the Sun Dances; she had taken part in those annual rites, and by them she had learned the restoration of her people in the presence of Tai-me. She was about seven when the last Kiowa Sun Dance was held in 1887 on the Washita River above Rainy Mountain Creek. The buffalo were gone. In order to consummate the ancient sacrifice—to impale the head of a buffalo bull upon the medicine tree—a delegation of old men journeyed into Texas, there to beg and barter for an animal from the Goodnight herd. She was ten when the Kiowas came together for the last time as a living Sun Dance culture. They could find no buffalo; they had to hang an old hide from the sacred tree. Before the dance could begin, a company of soldiers rode out from Fort Sill under orders to disperse the tribe. Forbidden without cause the essential act of their faith, having seen the wild herds slaughtered and left to rot upon the ground, the Kiowas backed away forever from the medicine tree. That was July 20, 1890, at the great bend of the Washita. My grandmother was there. Without bitterness, and for as long as she lived, she bore a vision of deicide.

Now that I can have her only in memory, I see my grandmother in the several postures that were peculiar to her: standing at the wood stove on a winter morning and turning meat in a great iron skillet; sitting at the south window, bent above her beadwork, and afterwards, when her vision failed, looking down for a long time into the fold of her hands; going out upon a cane, very slowly as she did when the weight of age came upon her; praying. I remember her most often at prayer. She made long, rambling prayers out of suffering and hope, having seen many things. I was never sure that I had the right to hear, so exclusive were they of all mere custom and company. The last time I saw her she prayed standing by the side of her bed at night, naked to the waist, the light of a kerosene lamp moving upon her dark skin. Her long, black hair, always drawn and braided in the day, lay upon her shoulders and against her breasts like a shawl. I do not speak Kiowa, and I never understood her

10

prayers, but there was something inherently sad in the sound, some merest hesitation upon the syllables of sorrow. She began in a high and descending pitch, exhausting her breath to silence; then again and again — and always the same intensity of effort, of something that is, and is not, like urgency in the human voice. Transported so in the dancing light among the shadows of her room, she seemed beyond the reach of time. But that was illusion; I think I knew then that I should not see her again.

Houses are like sentinels in the plain, old keepers of the weather watch. There, in a very little while, wood takes on the appearance of great age. All colors wear soon away in the wind and rain, and then the wood is burned gray and the grain appears and the nails turn red with rust. The windowpanes are black and opaque; you imagine there is nothing within, and indeed there are many ghosts, bones given up to the land. They stand here and there against the sky, and you approach them for a longer time than you expect. They belong in the distance; it is their domain.

Once there was a lot of sound in my grandmother's house, a lot of coming and going, feasting and talk. The summers there were full of excitement and reunion. The Kiowas are a summer people; they abide the cold and keep to themselves, but when the season turns and the land becomes warm and vital they cannot hold still; an old love of going returns upon them. The aged visitors who came to my grandmother's house when I was a child were made of lean and leather, and they bore themselves upright. They wore great black hats and bright ample shirts that shook in the wind. They rubbed fat upon their hair and wound their braids with strips of colored cloth. Some of them painted their faces and carried the scars of old and cherished enmities. They were an old council of warlords, come to remind and be reminded of who they were. Their wives and daughters served them well. The women might indulge themselves; gossip was at once the mark and compensation of their servitude. They made loud and elaborate talk among themselves, full of jest and gesture, fright and false alarm. They went abroad in fringed and flowered shawls, bright beadwork and German silver. They were at home in the kitchen, and they prepared meals that were banquets.

There were frequent prayer meetings, and great nocturnal feasts. When I was a child I played with my cousins outside, where the lamplight fell upon the ground and the singing of the old people rose up around us and carried away into the darkness. There were a lot of good things to eat, a lot of laughter and surprise. And afterwards, when the quiet returned, I lay down with my grandmother and could hear the frogs away by the river and feel the motion of the air.

Now there is a funeral silence in the rooms, the endless wake of some final word. The walls have closed in upon my grandmother's house.

When I returned to it in mourning, I saw for the first time in my life how small it was. It was late at night, and there was a white moon, nearly full. I sat for a long time on the stone steps by the kitchen door. From there I could see out across the land; I could see the long row of trees by the creek, the low light upon the rolling plains, and the stars of the Big Dipper. Once I looked at the moon and caught sight of a strange thing. A cricket had perched upon the handrail, only a few inches away from me. My line of vision was such that the creature filled the moon like a fossil. It had gone there, I thought, to live and die, for there, of all places, was its small definition made whole and eternal. A warm wind rose up and purled like the longing within me.

The next morning I awoke at dawn and went out on the dirt road to 15 Rainy Mountain. It was already hot, and the grasshoppers began to fill the air. Still, it was early in the morning, and the birds sang out of the shadows. The long yellow grass on the mountain shone in the bright light, and a scissortail hied above the land. There, where it ought to be, at the end of a long and legendary way, was my grandmother's grave. Here and there on the dark stones were ancestral names. Looking back once, I saw the mountain and came away.

[1969]

ROBERT FROST [1874–1963]

Stopping by Woods on a Snowy Evening

Robert Frost (1874–1963) was born in San Francisco and lived there until he was eleven. When his father died, the family moved to Massachusetts, where Robert did well in school, especially in the classics, but later dropped out of both Dartmouth College and Harvard University. He went unrecognized as a poet until 1913, when he was first published in England, where he had moved with his wife and four children. Upon returning to the States, Frost quickly achieved success with more publications and became the most celebrated poet in mid-twentieth-century America. He held a teaching position at Amherst College and received many honorary degrees as well as an invitation to recite a poem at John F. Kennedy's inauguration. Although his work is principally associated with the life and landscape of New England, and although he was a poet of traditional verse forms and meters, he is also considered a quintessentially modern poet for his adherence to language as it is actually spoken, the psychological complexity of his portraits, and the degree to which his work is infused with layers of ambiguity and irony.

Whose woods these are I think I know.
His house is in the village, though;
He will not see me stopping here
To watch his woods fill up with snow.

My little horse must think it queer   5
To stop without a farmhouse near
Between the woods and frozen lake
The darkest evening of the year.

He gives his harness bells a shake
To ask if there is some mistake.   10
The only other sound's the sweep
Of easy wind and downy flake.

The woods are lovely, dark, and deep,
But I have promises to keep,
And miles to go before I sleep,   15
And miles to go before I sleep.

[1923]

RACHEL CARSON [1907–1964]

Fable for Tomorrow

Ecologist, scientist, and nature writer **Rachel Carson** is considered a
founder of the modern environmental movement. Originally from
Springdale, Pennsylvania, Carson graduated from Pennsylvania College
for Women (now Chatham College) in 1929, Woods Hole Marine Biological Laboratory, and Johns Hopkins University, where she received her
M.A in zoology in 1932. After receiving her degrees, Carson worked for
the U.S. Bureau of Fisheries, first as a writer and finally as editor-in-
chief of publications. As a naturalist and conservationist, Carson shared
her understanding of ocean life and her concern for the environment
through her clear and accessible writing. Her works include *Under the
Sea-Wind* (1941); *The Sea around Us* (1951), a National Book Award winner and the basis for an Oscar-winning documentary; *The Edge of the Sea*
(1955); and *The Sense of Wonder* (published posthumously in 1965). She
was also the winner of many honorary degrees and awards for her con-
servation efforts and writing. Carson died of cancer in 1964.

The following piece is the first chapter of *Silent Spring*, Carson's
1962 book that argued, radically for its time, that pesticides were tox-
ins polluting the environment and destroying wildlife.

There was once a town in the heart of America where all life seemed to live
in harmony with its surroundings. The town lay in the midst of a checker-
board of prosperous farms, with fields of grain and hillsides of orchards
where, in spring, white clouds of bloom drifted above the green fields. In
autumn, oak and maple and birch set up a blaze of color that flamed and
flickered across a backdrop of pines. Then foxes barked in the hills and
deer silently crossed the fields, half hidden in the mists of the fall mornings.

Along the roads, laurel, viburnum, and alder, great ferns and wild-
flowers delighted the traveler's eye through much of the year. Even in
winter the roadsides were places of beauty, where countless birds came
to feed on the berries and on the seed heads of the dried weeds rising
above the snow. The countryside was, in fact, famous for the abundance
and variety of its bird life, and when the flood of migrants was pouring

through in spring and fall people traveled from great distances to observe them. Others came to fish the streams, which flowed clear and cold out of the hills and contained shady pools where trout lay. So it had been from the days many years ago when the first settlers raised their houses, sank their wells, and built their barns.

Then a strange blight crept over the area and everything began to change. Some evil spell had settled on the community: mysterious maladies swept the flocks of chickens; the cattle and sheep sickened and died. Everywhere was a shadow of death. The farmers spoke of much illness among their families. In the town the doctors had become more and more puzzled by new kinds of sickness appearing among their patients. There had been several sudden and unexplained deaths, not only among adults but even among children, who would be stricken suddenly while at play and die within a few hours.

There was a strange stillness. The birds, for example—where had they gone? Many people spoke of them, puzzled and disturbed. The feeding stations in the backyards were deserted. The few birds seen anywhere were moribund; they trembled violently and could not fly. It was a spring without voices. On the mornings that had once throbbed with the dawn chorus of robins, catbirds, doves, jays, wrens, and scores of other bird voices there was now no sound; only silence lay over the fields and woods and marsh.

On the farms the hens brooded, but no chicks hatched. The farmers 5 complained that they were unable to raise any pigs—the litters were small and the young survived only a few days. The apple trees were coming into bloom but no bees droned among the blossoms, so there was no pollination and there would be no fruit.

The roadsides, once so attractive, were now lined with browned and withered vegetation as though swept by fire. These, too, were silent, deserted by all living things. Even the streams were now lifeless. Anglers no longer visited them, for all the fish had died.

In the gutters under the eaves and between the shingles of the roofs, a white granular powder still showed a few patches; some weeks before it had fallen like snow upon the roofs and the lawns, the fields and streams.

No witchcraft, no enemy action had silenced the rebirth of new life in this stricken world. The people had done it themselves.

This town does not actually exist, but it might easily have a thousand counterparts in America or elsewhere in the world. I know of no community that has experienced all the misfortunes I describe. Yet every one of these disasters has actually happened somewhere, and many real communities have already suffered a substantial number of them. A grim specter has crept upon us almost unnoticed, and this imagined tragedy may easily become a stark reality we all shall know.

ANNIE DILLARD [b. 1945]

Seeing

Born in 1945 in Pittsburgh, **Annie Dillard** is best known as a nature writer. *Pilgrim at Tinker Creek* (1974) won a Pulitzer Prize and established her as a writer whose nature walks lead not just into the woods but also upward, to spiritual considerations. In her nonfiction, fiction, and poetry, including her autobiographical *An American Childhood* (1987), she has continued to describe the world around her in close detail and then to leap off into the metaphysical. Dillard teaches creative writing at Wesleyan University in Connecticut.

In "Seeing," from *Pilgrim at Tinker Creek*, Dillard uses specific details and precisely crafted imagery to share her appreciation for the gifts nature sometimes reveals to the fortunate observer. To see such beauties in nature, she writes, "I try to keep my eyes open." She prizes the fleeting moments when "the world [is] unraveled from reason," when visions powerful and sublime rise out of muddy silt, shoot through the heavens, or transfigure a simple tree. Dillard closes her essay by noting that "the vision comes and goes, mostly goes, but I live for it, for the moment when the mountains open and a new light roars in spate through the crack, and the mountains slam."

When I was six or seven years old, growing up in Pittsburgh, I used to take a penny of my own and hide it for someone else to find. It was a curious compulsion; sadly, I've never been seized by it since. For some reason I always "hid" the penny along the same stretch of sidewalk up the street. I'd cradle it at the roots of a maple, say, or in a hole left by a chipped-off piece of sidewalk. Then I'd take a piece of chalk and, starting at either end of the block, draw huge arrows leading up to the penny from both directions. After I learned to write I labeled the arrows "SURPRISE AHEAD" or "MONEY THIS WAY." I was greatly excited, during all this arrowdrawing, at the thought of the first lucky passerby who would receive in this way, regardless of merit, a free gift from the universe. But I never lurked about. I'd go straight home and not give the matter another thought, until, some months later, I would be gripped by the impulse to hide another penny.

There are lots of things to see, unwrapped gifts and free surprises. The world is fairly studded and strewn with pennies cast broadside from a generous hand. But — and this is the point — who gets excited by a mere penny? If you follow one arrow, if you crouch motionless on a bank to watch a tremulous ripple thrill on the water, and are rewarded by the sight of a muskrat kit paddling from its den, will you count that sight a chip of copper only, and go your rueful way? It is very dire poverty indeed for a man to be so malnourished and fatigued that he won't stoop to pick up a penny. But if you cultivate a healthy poverty and simplicity, so that finding a penny will make your day, then, since the world is in fact planted in pennies, you have with your poverty bought a lifetime of days. What you see is what you get.

Unfortunately, nature is very much a now-you-see-it, now-you-don't affair. A fish flashes, then dissolves in the water before my eyes like so much salt. Deer apparently ascend bodily into heaven; the brightest oriole fades into leaves. These disappearances stun me into stillness and concentration; they say of nature that it conceals with a grand nonchalance, and they say of vision that it is a deliberate gift, the revelation of a dancer who for my eyes only flings away her seven veils.

For nature does reveal as well as conceal: now-you-don't-see-it, now-you-do. For a week this September migrating red-winged blackbirds were feeding heavily down by Tinker Creek at the back of the house. One day I went out to investigate the racket; I walked up to a tree, an Osage orange, and a hundred birds flew away. They simply materialized out of the tree. I saw a tree, then a whisk of color, then a tree again. I walked closer and another hundred blackbirds took flight. Not a branch, not a twig budged: the birds were apparently weightless as well as invisible. Or, it was as if the leaves of the Osage orange had been freed from a spell in the form of red-winged blackbirds; they flew from the tree, caught my eye in the sky, and vanished. When I looked again at the tree, the leaves had reassembled as if nothing had happened. Finally I walked directly to the trunk of the tree and a final hundred, the real diehards, appeared, spread, and vanished. How could so many hide in the tree without my seeing them? The Osage orange, unruffled, looked just as it had looked from the house, when three hundred red-winged blackbirds cried from its crown. I looked upstream where they flew, and they were gone. Searching, I couldn't spot one. I wandered upstream to force them to play their hand, but they'd crossed the creek and scattered. One show to a customer. These appearances catch at my throat; they are the free gifts, the bright coppers at the roots of trees.

It's all a matter of keeping my eyes open. Nature is like one of those line 5 drawings that are puzzles for children: Can you find hidden in the tree a duck, a house, a boy, a bucket, a giraffe, and a boot? Specialists can find the most incredibly hidden things. A book I read when I was young recommended an easy way to find caterpillars: you simply find some fresh caterpillar droppings, look up, and there's your caterpillar. More recently an author advised me to set my mind at ease about those piles of cut stems on the ground in grassy fields. Field mice make them; they cut the grass down by degrees to reach the seeds at the head. It seems that when the grass is tightly packed, as in a field of ripe grain, the blade won't topple at a single cut through the stem; instead, the cut stem simply drops vertically, held in the crush of grain. The mouse severs the bottom again and again, the stem keeps dropping an inch at a time, and finally the head is low enough for the mouse to reach the seeds. Meanwhile the mouse is positively littering the field with its little piles of cut stems into which, presumably, the author is constantly stumbling.

If I can't see these minutiae, I still try to keep my eyes open. I'm always on the lookout for ant lion traps in sandy soil, monarch pupae near milkweed, skipper larvae in locust leaves. These things are utterly common, and I've not seen one. I bang on hollow trees near water, but so far no flying squirrels have appeared. In flat country I watch every sunset in hopes of seeing the green ray. The green ray is a seldom-seen streak of light that rises from the sun like a spurting fountain at the moment of sunset; it throbs into the sky for two seconds and disappears. One more reason to keep my eyes open. A photography professor at the University of Florida just happened to see a bird die in midflight; it jerked, died, dropped, and smashed on the ground.

I squint at the wind because I read Stewart Edward White: "I have always maintained that if you looked closely enough you could see the wind—the dim, hardly-made-out, fine débris fleeing high in the air." White was an excellent observer, and devoted an entire chapter of *The Mountains* to the subject of seeing deer: "As soon as you can forget the naturally obvious and construct an artificial obvious, then you too will see deer."

But the artificial obvious is hard to see. My eyes account for less than 1 percent of the weight of my head; I'm bony and dense; I see what I expect. I just don't know what the lover knows; I can't see the artificial obvious that those in the know construct. The herpetologist asks the native. "Are there snakes in that ravine?" "No, sir." And the herpetologist comes home with, yessir, three bags full. Are there butterflies on that mountain? Are the bluets in bloom? Are there arrowheads here, or fossil ferns in the shale?

Peeping through my keyhole I see within the range of only about 30 percent of the light that comes from the sun; the rest is infrared and some little ultraviolet, perfectly apparent to many animals, but invisible to me.

A nightmare network of ganglia, charged and firing without my knowledge, cuts and splices what I do see, editing it for my brain. Donald E. Carr points out that the sense impressions of one-celled animals are not edited for the brain: "This is philosophically interesting in a rather mournful way, since it means that only the simplest animals perceive the universe as it is."

A fog that won't burn away drifts and flows across my field of vision. 10 When you see fog move against a backdrop of deep pines, you don't see the fog itself, but streaks of clearness floating across the air in dark shreds. So I see only tatters of clearness through a pervading obscurity. I can't distinguish the fog from the overcast sky; I can't be sure if the light is direct or reflected. Everywhere darkness and the presence of the unseen appalls. We estimate now that only one atom dances alone in every cubic meter of intergalactic space. I blink and squint. What planet or power yanks Halley's Comet out of orbit? We haven't seen it yet; it's a question of distance, density, and the pallor of reflected light. We rock, cradled in the swaddling band of darkness. Even the simple darkness of night whispers suggestions to the mind. This summer, in August, I stayed at the creek too late.

Where Tinker Creek flows under the sycamore log bridge to the tear-shaped island, it is slow and shallow, fringed thinly in cattail marsh. At this spot an astonishing bloom of life supports vast breeding populations of insects, fish, reptiles, birds, and mammals. On windless summer evenings I stalk along the creek bank or straddle the sycamore log in absolute stillness, watching for muskrats. The night I stayed too late I was hunched on the log staring spellbound at spreading, reflected stains of lilac on the water. A cloud in the sky suddenly lighted as if turned on by a switch; its reflection just as suddenly materialized on the water upstream, flat and floating, so that I couldn't see the creek bottom, or life in the water under the cloud. Downstream, away from the cloud on the water, water turtles smooth as beans were gliding down with the current in a series of easy, weightless push-offs, as men bound on the moon. I didn't know whether to trace the progress of one turtle I was sure of, risking sticking my face in one of the bridge's spider webs made invisible by the gathering dark, or take a chance on seeing the carp, or scan the mudbank in hope of seeing a muskrat, or follow the last of the swallows who caught at my heart and trailed it after them like streamers as they appeared from directly below, under the log, flying upstream with their tails forked, so fast.

But shadows spread and deepened and stayed. After thousands of years we're still strangers to darkness, fearful aliens in an enemy camp with our arms crossed over our chests. I stirred. A land turtle on the bank, startled, hissed the air from its lungs and withdrew to its shell. An uneasy pink here, an unfathomable blue there, gave great suggestion of lurking beings. Things were going on. I couldn't see whether that rustle I heard was a distant rattle-snake, slit-eyed, or a nearby sparrow kicking in the dry flood debris slung at the foot of a willow. Tremendous action roiled the water everywhere I looked, big action, inexplicable. A tremor welled up beside a gaping muskrat burrow in the bank and I caught my breath, but no muskrat appeared. The ripples continued to fan upstream with a steady, powerful thrust. Night was knitting an eyeless mask over my face, and I still sat transfixed. A distant airplane, a delta wing out of nightmare, made a gliding shadow on the creek's bottom that looked like a stingray cruising upstream. At once a black fin slit the pink cloud on the water, shearing it in two. The two halves merged together and seemed to dissolve before my eyes. Darkness pooled in the cleft of the creek and rose, as water collects in a well. Untamed, dreaming lights flickered over the sky. I saw hints of hulking underwater shadows, two pale splashes out of the water, and round ripples rolling close together from a blackened center.

At last I stared upstream where only the deepest violet remained of the cloud, a cloud so high its underbelly still glowed, its feeble color reflected from a hidden sky lighted in turn by a sun halfway to China. And out of that violet, a sudden enormous black body arced over the water. Head and tail, if there was a head and tail, were both submerged in cloud. I saw only one ebony fling, a headlong dive to darkness; then the waters closed, and the lights went out.

I walked home in a shivering daze, up hill and down. Later I lay open-mouthed in bed, my arms flung wide at my sides to steady the whirling darkness. At this latitude I'm spinning 836 miles an hour round the earth's axis; I feel my sweeping fall as a breakneck arc like the dive of dolphins, and the hollow rushing of wind raises the hairs on my neck and the side of my face. In orbit around the sun I'm moving 64,800 miles an hour. The solar system as a whole, like a merry-go-round unhinged, spins, bobs, and blinks at the speed of 43,200 miles an hour along a course set east of Hercules. Someone has piped, and we are dancing a tarantella until the sweat pours. I open my eyes and I see dark, muscled forms curl out of water, with flapping gills and flattened eyes. I close my eyes and I see stars, deep stars giving way to deeper stars, deeper stars bowing to deepest stars at the crown of an infinite cone.

"Still," wrote Van Gogh in a letter, "a great deal of light falls on every- 15 thing." If we are blinded by darkness, we are also blinded by light. Sometimes here in Virginia at sunset low clouds on the southern or northern horizon are completely invisible in the lighted sky. I only know one is there because I can see its reflection in still water. The first time I discovered this mystery I looked from cloud to no-cloud in bewilderment, checking my bearings over and over, thinking maybe the ark of the covenant was just passing by south of Dead Man Mountain. Only much later did I learn the explanation: polarized light from the sky is very much weakened by reflection, but the light in clouds isn't polarized. So invisible clouds pass among visible clouds, till all slide over the mountains; so a greater light extinguishes a lesser as though it didn't exist.

In the great meteor shower of August, the Perseid, I wail all day for the shooting stars I miss. They're out there showering down committing hara-kiri in a flame of fatal attraction, and hissing perhaps at last into the ocean. But at dawn what looks like a blue dome clamps down over me like a lid on a pot. The stars and planets could smash and I'd never know. Only a piece of ashen moon occasionally climbs up or down the inside of the dome, and our local star without surcease explodes on our heads. We have really only that one light, one source for all power, and yet we must turn away from it by universal decree. Nobody here on the planet seems aware of this strange, powerful taboo, that we all walk about carefully averting our faces, this way and that, lest our eyes be blasted forever.

Darkness appalls and light dazzles; the scrap of visible light that doesn't hurt my eyes hurts my brain. What I see sets me swaying. Size and distance and the sudden swelling of meanings confuse me, bowl me over. I straddle the sycamore log bridge over Tinker Creek in the summer. I look at the lighted creek bottom: snail tracks tunnel the mud in quavering curves. A crayfish jerks, but by the time I absorb what has happened, he's gone in a billowing smoke screen of silt. I look at the water; minnows and shiners. If I'm thinking minnows, a carp will fill my brain till I scream. I look at the water's surface: skaters, bubbles, and leaves sliding down. Suddenly, my own face, reflected, startles me witless. Those snails have been tracking my face! Finally, with a shuddering wrench of the will, I see clouds, cirrus clouds. I'm dizzy, I fall in.

This looking business is risky. Once I stood on a humped rock on nearby Purgatory Mountain, watching through binoculars the great autumn hawk migration below, until I discovered that I was in danger of joining the hawks on a vertical migration of my own. I was used to binoculars, but not, apparently, to balancing on humped rocks while looking through them. I reeled. Everything advanced and receded by turns; the world was full of unexplained foreshortenings and depths. A distant huge object, a hawk the size of an elephant, turned out to be the browned bough of a nearby loblolly pine. I followed a sharp-shinned hawk against a featureless sky, rotating my head unawares as it flew, and when I lowered the glass a glimpse of my own looming shoulder sent me staggering. What prevents the men at Palomar from falling, voiceless and blinded, from their tiny, vaulted chairs?

I reel in confusion: I don't understand what I see. With the naked eye I can see two million light-years to the Andromeda galaxy. Often I slop some creek water in a jar, and when I get home I dump it in a white china bowl. After the silt settles I return and see tracings of minute snails on the bottom, a planarian or two winding round the rim of water, roundworms shimmying, frantically, and finally, when my eyes have adjusted to these dimensions, amoebae. At first the amoebae look like *muscae volitantes*, those curled moving spots you seem to see in your eyes when you stare at a distant wall. Then I see the amoebae as drops of water congealed, bluish, translucent, like chips of sky in the bowl. At length I choose one individual and give myself over to its idea of an evening. I see it dribble a grainy foot before it on its wet, unfathomable way. Do its unedited sense impressions include the fierce focus of my eyes? Shall I take it outside and show it Andromeda, and blow its little endoplasm? I stir the water with a finger, in case it's running out of oxygen. Maybe I should get a tropical aquarium with motorized bubblers and lights, and keep this one for a pet. Yes, it would tell its fissioned descendants, the universe is two feet by five, and if you listen closely you can hear the buzzing music of the spheres.

Oh, it's mysterious, lamplit evenings here in the galaxy, one after the 20 other. It's one of those nights when I wander from window to window looking for a sign. But I can't see. Terror and a beauty insoluble are a riband of blue woven into the fringe of garments of things both great and small. No culture explains, no bivouac offers real haven or rest. But it could be that we are not seeing something. Galileo thought comets were an optical illusion. This is fertile ground: since we are certain that they're not, we can look at what our scientists have been saying with fresh hope. What if there are *really* gleaming, castellated cities hung upside down over the desert sand? What limpid lakes and cool date palms have our caravans always passed untried? Until, one by one, by the blindest of leaps, we light on the road to these places, we must stumble in darkness and hunger. I turn from the window. I'm blind as a bat, sensing only from every direction the echo of my own thin cries.

I chanced on a wonderful book called *Space and Sight*, by Marius Von Senden. When Western surgeons discovered how to perform safe cataract operations, they ranged across Europe and America operating on dozens of men and women of all ages who had been blinded by cataracts since birth. Von Senden collected accounts of such cases; the histories are fascinating. Many doctors had tested their patients' sense perceptions and ideas of space both before and after the operations. The vast majority of patients, of both sexes and all ages, had, in Von Senden's opinion, no idea of space whatsoever. Form, distance, and size were so many meaningless syllables. A patient "had no idea of depth, confusing it with roundness." Before the operation a doctor would give a blind patient a cube and a sphere; the patient would tongue it or feel it with his hands and name it correctly. After the operation the doctor would show the same objects to the patient without letting him touch them; now he had no clue whatsoever to what he was seeing. One patient called lemonade "square" because it pricked on his tongue as a square shape pricked on the touch of his hands. Of another post-operative patient the doctor writes, "I have found in her no notion of size, for example, not even within the narrow limits which she might have encompassed with the aid of touch. Thus when I asked her to show me how big her mother was, she did not stretch out her hands, but set her two index fingers a few inches apart."

For the newly sighted, vision is pure sensation unencumbered by meaning. When a newly sighted girl saw photographs and paintings, she asked, "'Why do they put those dark marks all over them?' 'Those aren't dark marks,' her mother explained, 'those are shadows. That is one of the ways the eye knows that things have shape. If it were not for shadows, many things would look flat.' 'Well, that's how things do look,' Joan answered. 'Everything looks flat with dark patches.'"

In general the newly sighted see the world as a dazzle of "color-patches." They are pleased by the sensation of color, and learn quickly to name the colors, but the rest of seeing is tormentingly difficult. Soon after his operation a patient "generally bumps into one of these colour-patches and observes them to be substantial, since they resist him as tactual objects do. In walking about it also strikes him — or can if he pays attention — that he is continually passing in between the colours he sees, that he can go past a visual object that a part of it then steadily disappears from view; and that in spite of this, however he twists and turns — whether entering the room from the door, for example, or returning back to it — he always has a visual space in front of him. Thus he gradually comes to realize that there is also a space behind him, which he does not see."

The mental effort involved in these reasonings proves overwhelming for many patients. It oppresses them to realize that they have been visible to people all along, perhaps unattractively so, without their knowledge or consent. A disheartening number of them refuse to use their new vision, continuing to go over objects with their tongues, and lapsing into apathy and despair.

On the other hand, many newly sighted people speak well of the world, and teach us how dull our own vision is. To one patient, a human 25

95

hand, unrecognized, is "something bright and then holes." Shown a bunch of grapes, a boy calls out, "It is dark, blue and shiny....It isn't smooth, it has bumps and hollows." A little girl visits a garden. "She is greatly astonished, and can scarcely be persuaded to answer, stands speechless in front of the tree, which she only names on taking hold of it, and then as 'the tree with the lights in it.'" Another patient, a twenty-two-year-old girl, was dazzled by the world's brightness and kept her eyes shut for two weeks. When at the end of that time she opened her eyes again, she did not recognize any objects, but "the more she now directed her gaze upon everything about her, the more it could be seen how an expression of gratification and astonishment overspread her features; she repeatedly exclaimed: 'Oh God! How beautiful!'"

I saw color-patches for weeks after I read this wonderful book. It was summer; the peaches were ripe in the valley orchards. When I woke in the morning, color-patches wrapped round my eyes, intricately, leaving not one unfilled spot. All day long I walked among shifting color-patches that parted before me like the Red Sea and closed again in silence, transfigured, wherever I looked back. Some patches swelled and loomed while others vanished utterly, and dark marks flitted at random over the whole dazzling sweep. But I couldn't sustain the illusion of flatness. I've been around for too long. Form is condemned to an eternal danse macabre with meaning: I couldn't unpeach the peaches. Nor can I remember ever having seen without understanding; the color-patches of infancy are lost. My brain then must have been smooth as any balloon. I'm told I reached for the moon; many babies do. But the color-patches of infancy swelled as meaning filled them; they arrayed themselves in solemn ranks down distance which unrolled and stretched before me like a plain. The moon rocketed away. I live now in a world of shadows that shape and distance color, a world where space makes a kind of terrible sense. What Gnosticism is this, and what physics? The fluttering patch I saw in my nursery window—silver and green and shape-shifting blue—is gone; a row of Lombardy poplars takes its place, mute, across the distant lawn. That humming oblong creature pale as light that stole along the walls of my room at night, stretching exhilaratingly around the corners, is gone too, gone the night I ate of the bittersweet fruit, put two and two together and puckered forever my brain. Martin Buber tells this tale: "Rabbi Mendel once boasted to his teacher Rabbi Elimelekh that evenings he saw the angel who rolls away the light before the darkness, and morning the angel who rolls away the darkness before the light. 'Yes,' said Rabbi Elimelekh, 'in my youth I saw that too. Later on you don't see these things anymore.'"

Why didn't someone hand those newly sighted people paints and brushes from the start, when they still didn't know what anything was?

Then maybe we all could see color-patches too, the world unraveled from reason, Eden before Adam gave names. The scales would drop from my eyes; I'd see trees like men walking; I'd run down the road against all orders, hallooing and leaping.

Seeing is of course very much a matter of verbalization. Unless I call my attention to what passes before my eyes, I simply won't see it. If Tinker Mountain erupted, I'd be likely to notice. But if I want to notice the lesser cataclysms of valley life, I have to maintain in my head a running description of the present. It's not that I'm observant; it's just that I talk too much. Otherwise, especially in a strange place, I'll never know what's happening. Like a blind man at the ball game, I need a radio.

When I see this way I analyze and pry. I hurl over logs and roll away stones; I study the bank a square foot at a time, probing and tilting my head. Some days when a mist covers the mountains, when the muskrats won't show and the microscope's mirror shatters, I want to climb up the blank blue dome as a man would storm the inside of a circus tent, wildly, dangling, and with a steel knife claw a rent in the top, peep, and, if I must, fall.

But there is another kind of seeing that involves a letting go. When I 30 see this way I sway transfixed and emptied. The difference between the two ways of seeing is the difference between walking with and without a camera. When I walk with a camera I walk from shot to shot, reading the light on a calibrated meter. When I walk without a camera, my own shutter opens, and the moment's light prints on my own silver gut. When I see this second way I am above all an unscrupulous observer.

It was sunny one evening last summer at Tinker Creek; the sun was low in the sky, upstream. I was sitting on the sycamore log bridge with the sunset at my back, watching the shiners the size of minnows who were feeding over the muddy sand in skittery schools. Again and again, one fish, then another, turned for a split second across the current and flash! the sun shot out from its silver side. I couldn't watch for it. It was always just happening somewhere else, and it drew my vision just as it disappeared: flash! like a sudden dazzle of the thinnest blade, a sparking over a dun and olive ground at chance intervals from every direction. Then I noticed white specks, some sort of pale petals, small, floating from under my feet on the creek's surface, very slow and steady. So I blurred my eyes and gazed toward the brim of my hat and saw a new world. I saw the pale white circles roll up, roll up, like the world's turning, mute and perfect, and I saw the linear flashes, gleaming silver, like stars being born at random down a rolling scroll of time. Something broke and something opened. I filled up like a new wineskin. I breathed an air like light; I saw a light like water. I was the lip of a fountain the creek filled forever; I was ether, the leaf in the zephyr; I was flesh-flake, feather, bone.

When I see this way I see truly. As Thoreau says, I return to my senses. I am the man who watches the baseball game in silence in an empty stadium. I see the game purely; I'm abstracted and dazed. When it's all over and the white-suited players lope off the green field to their shadowed dugouts, I leap to my feet, I cheer and cheer.

But I can't go out and try to see this way. I'll fail, I'll go mad. All I can do is try to gag the commentator, to hush the noise of useless interior babble that keeps me from seeing just as surely as a newspaper dangled before my eyes. The effort is really a discipline requiring a lifetime of dedicated struggle; it marks the literature of saints and monks of every order east and west, under every rule and no rule, discalced and shod. The world's spiritual geniuses seem to discover universally that the mind's muddy river, this ceaseless flow of trivia and trash, cannot be dammed, and that trying to dam it is a waste of effort that might lead to madness. Instead you must allow the muddy river to flow unheeded in the dim channels of consciousness; you raise your sights; you look along it, mildly, acknowledging its presence without interest and gazing beyond it into the realm of the real where subjects and objects act and rest purely, without utterance. "Launch into the deep," says Jacques Ellul, "and you shall see."

The secret of seeing, then, is the pearl of great price. If I thought he could teach me to find it and keep it forever I would stagger barefoot across a hundred deserts after any lunatic at all. But although the peace may be found, it may not be sought. The literature of illumination reveals this above all: although it comes to those who wait for it, it is always, even to the most practiced and adept, a gift and a total surprise. I return from one walk knowing where the killdeer nests in the field by the creek and the hour the laurel blooms. I return from the same walk a day later scarcely knowing my own name. Litanies hum in my ears; my tongue flaps in my mouth, *Alim non*, alleluia! I cannot cause light; the most I can do is try to put myself in the path of its beam. It is possible, in deep space, to sail on solar wind. Light, be it particle or wave, has force: you rig a giant sail and go. The secret of seeing is to sail on solar wind. Hone and spread your spirit till you yourself are a sail, whetted, translucent, broadside to the merest puff.

When her doctor took her bandages off and led her into the garden, 35 the girl who was no longer blind saw "the tree with the lights in it." It was for this tree I searched through the peach orchards of summer, in the forests of fall and down winter and spring for years. Then one day I was walking along Tinker Creek thinking of nothing at all and I saw the tree with the lights in it. I saw the backyard cedar where the mourning doves roost charged and transfigured, each cell buzzing with flame. I stood on the grass with the lights in it, grass that was wholly fire, utterly focused and utterly dreamed. It was less like seeing than like being for the first time seen, knocked breathless by a powerful glance. The flood of fire abated, but I'm still spending the power. Gradually the lights went out in the cedar, the colors died, the cells unflamed and disappeared. I was still ringing. I had been my whole life a bell, and never knew it until at that moment I was lifted and struck. I have since only very rarely seen the tree with the lights in it. The vision comes and goes, mostly goes, but I live for it, for the moment when the mountains open and a new light roars in spate through the crack, and the mountains slam.

GARRETT KAORU HONGO [b. 1951]

Yellow Light

Born in Volcano, Hawaii, **Garrett Kaoru Hongo** (b. 1951) grew up on
Oahu and in Los Angeles, and did graduate work in Japanese language
and literature at the University of Michigan. Hongo has published several books of poetry, including *The River of Heaven* (1988), the Lamont
Poetry Selection of the Academy of American Poets and a finalist for
the Pulitzer Prize. He has also written *Volcano: A Memoir of Hawai'i*
(1995) and edited collections of Asian American verse. He currently
teaches at the University of Oregon, Eugene, where he directed the creative writing program from 1989 to 1993. His work often comments
through rich textures and sensuous detail on conditions endured by
Japanese Americans during World War II and thereafter.

One arm hooked around the frayed strap
of a tar-black, patent-leather purse,
the other cradling something for dinner:
fresh bunches of spinach from a J-Town *yaoya*,°   *vegetable stand or seller*
sides of split Spanish mackerel from Alviso's,   5
maybe a loaf of Langendorf;° she steps
off the hissing bus at Olympic and Fig,
begins the three-block climb up the hill,
passing gangs of schoolboys playing war,
Japs against Japs, Chicanas chalking sidewalks   10
with the holy double-yoked crosses of hopscotch,
and the Korean grocer's wife out for a stroll
around this neighborhood of Hawaiian apartments
just starting to steam with cooking
and the anger of young couples coming home   15
from work, yelling at kids, flicking on
TV sets for the Wednesday Night Fights.

If it were May, hydrangeas and jacaranda
flowers in the streetside trees would be

6. **Langendorf:** A well-known bakery in California.

blooming through the smog of late spring.   20
Wisteria in Masuda's front yard would be
shaking out the long tresses of its purple hair.
Maybe mosquitoes, moths, a few orange butterflies
settling on the lattice of monkey flowers
tangled in chain-link fences by the trash.   25

But this is October, and Los Angeles
seethes like a billboard under twilight.
From used-car lots and the movie houses uptown,
long silver sticks of light probe the sky.
From the Miracle Mile, whole freeways away,   30
a brilliant fluorescence breaks out
and makes war with the dim squares
of yellow kitchen light winking on
in all the side streets of the Barrio.

She climbs up the two flights of flagstone   35
stairs to 201-B, the spikes of her high heels
clicking like kitchen knives on a cutting board,
props the groceries against the door,
fishes through memo pads, a compact,
empty packs of chewing gum, and finds her keys.   40

The moon then, cruising from behind
a screen of eucalyptus across the street,
covers everything, everything in sight,
in a heavy light like yellow onions.

[1982]

HENRY DAVID THOREAU [1817–1862]

The Battle of the Ants

Henry David Thoreau was born in 1817 and raised in Concord, Massachusetts, living there for most of his life. Along with Ralph Waldo Emerson, Thoreau was one of the most important thinkers of his time in America and is still widely read today. *Walden* (1854), the work for which he is best known, is drawn from the journal he kept during his two-year-long stay in a cabin on Walden Pond. In *Walden*, Thoreau explores his interests in naturalism, individualism, and self-sufficiency. He is also remembered for his essay "Civil Disobedience" (1849), an early, influential statement of this tactic of protest later practiced by Mahatma Gandhi and, under the leadership of Martin Luther King Jr., many in the civil rights movement.

In "The Battle of the Ants," from *Walden*, Thoreau writes about stumbling upon a battle-in-miniature between opposing armies of red and black ants. Likening the tiny warriors' feats to those of Achilles, Thoreau wonders at the complexity and sheer numbers enlisted in the epic battle on his woodpile. Awed by nature's daunting display and not one to trivialize the natural world, he writes, "I never learned which party was victorious, nor the cause of the war, but I felt for the rest of that day as if I had my feelings excited and harrowed by witnessing the struggle, the ferocity and carnage, of a human battle before my door." He goes on to situate the battle of the ants as if it is a true human battle, relating it to political events of the day.

One day when I went out to my wood-pile, or rather my pile of stumps, I observed two large ants, the one red, the other much larger, nearly half an inch long, and black, fiercely contending with one another. Having once got hold they never let go, but struggled and wrestled and rolled on the chips incessantly. Looking farther, I was surprised to find that the chips were covered with such combatants, that it was not a *duellum*, but a *bellum*, a war between two races of ants, the red always pitted against the black, and frequently two red ones to one black. The legions of these Myrmidons covered all the hills and vales in my wood-yard, and the ground was already strewn with the dead and dying, both red and black. It was the only battle which I have ever witnessed, the only battle-field I ever trod while the battle was raging; internecine war; the red republicans on the one hand, and the black imperialists on the other. On every side they were engaged in deadly combat, yet without any noise that I could hear, and human soldiers never fought so resolutely. I watched a couple that were fast locked in each other's embraces, in a little sunny valley amid the chips, now at noonday prepared to fight till the sun went down, or life went out. The smaller red champion had fastened himself like a vice to his adversary's front, and through all the tumblings on that field never for an instant ceased to gnaw at one of his feelers near the root, having already caused the other to go by the board; while the stronger black one dashed him from side to side, and, as I saw on looking nearer, had already divested him of several of his members. They fought with more pertinacity than bulldogs. Neither manifested the least disposition to retreat. It was evident that their battle-cry was "Conquer or die." In the meanwhile there came along a single red ant on the hillside of this valley, evidently full of excitement, who either had despatched his foe, or had not yet taken part in the battle; probably the latter, for he had lost none of his limbs; whose mother had charged him to return with his shield or upon it. Or perchance he was some Achilles, who had nourished his wrath apart, and had now come to avenge or rescue his Patroclus. He saw this unequal combat from afar—for the blacks were nearly twice the size of the red—he drew near with rapid pace till he stood on his guard within half an inch of the combatants; then, watching his opportunity, he sprang upon the black warrior, and commenced his operations near the root of his right fore leg, leaving the foe to select among his own members; and so there were three united for life, as if a new kind of attraction had been invented which put all other locks and cements to shame. I should not have wondered by this time to find that they had their respective musical bands stationed on some eminent chip, and playing their national airs the while, to excite the slow and cheer the dying combatants. I was myself excited somewhat even as if they had been men. The more you think of it, the less the difference. And certainly there is not the fight recorded in Concord history, at least, if in the history of America, that will bear a moment's comparison with this, whether for the numbers engaged in it, or for the patriotism and heroism displayed. For numbers and for carnage it was an Austerlitz or Dresden. Concord Fight! Two killed on the patriots' side, and Luther Blanchard wounded! Why here every ant was a Buttrick—"Fire! for God's sake fire!"—and thousands shared the fate of Davis and Hosmer. There was not one hireling there. I have no doubt that it was a principle they fought for, as much as our ancestors, and not to avoid a three-penny tax on their tea; and the results of this battle will be as important and memorable to those whom it concerns as those of the battle of Bunker Hill, at least.

I took up the chip on which the three I have particularly described were struggling, carried it into my house, and placed it under a tumbler on my window-sill, in order to see the issue. Holding a microscope to the first-mentioned red ant, I saw that, though he was assiduously gnawing at the near fore leg of his enemy, having severed his remaining feeler, his own breast was all torn away, exposing what vitals he had there to the jaws of the black warrior, whose breastplate was apparently too thick for him to pierce; and the dark carbuncles of the sufferer's eyes shone with ferocity such as war only could excite. They struggled half an hour longer under the tumbler, and when I looked again the black soldier had severed the heads of his foes from their bodies, and the still living heads were hanging on either side of him like ghastly trophies at his saddle-bow, still apparently as firmly fastened as ever, and he was endeavoring with feeble struggles, being without feelers, and with only the remnant of a leg, and I know not how many other wounds, to divest himself of them; which at length, after half an hour more, he accomplished. I raised the glass, and he went off over the window-sill in that crippled state. Whether he finally survived that combat, and spent the remainder of his days in some Hôtel des Invalides, I do not know; but I thought that his industry would not be worth much thereafter. I never learned which party was victorious, nor the cause of the war, but I felt for the rest of that day as if I had my feelings excited and harrowed by witnessing the struggle, the ferocity and carnage, of a human battle before my door.

Kirby and Spence tell us that the battle of ants have long been celebrated and the date of them recorded, though they say that Huber is the only modern author who appears to have witnessed them. "Aeneas Sylvius," say they, "after giving a very circumstantial account of one contested with great obstinacy by a great and small species on the trunk of a pear tree," adds that "'this action was fought in the pontificate of Eugenius the Fourth, in the presence of Nicholas Pistoriensis, an eminent lawyer, who related the whole history of the battle with the greatest fidelity.' A similar engagement between great and small ants is recorded by Olaus Magnus, in which the small ones, being victorious, are said to have buried the bodies of their own soldiers, but left those of their giant enemies a prey to the birds. This event happened previous to the expulsion of the tyrant Christiern the Second from Sweden." The battle which I witnessed took place in the Presidency of Polk, five years before the passage of Webster's Fugitive-Slave Bill.

ELIZABETH BISHOP   [1911–1979]

The Fish

Born in Worcester, Massachusetts, **Elizabeth Bishop** (1911–1979) was raised in Nova Scotia by her grandparents after her father died and her mother was committed to an asylum. She attended Vassar College intending to study medicine but was encouraged by Marianne Moore to be a poet. From 1935 to 1937 she traveled in France, Spain, northern Africa, Ireland, and Italy. She settled in Key West, Florida, for four years and then in Rio de Janeiro for almost twenty. She wrote slowly and carefully, producing a small body of technically sophisticated, formally varied, witty, and thoughtful poetry, revealing in precise, true-to-life images her impressions of the physical world. She served as Consultant in Poetry at the Library of Congress from 1949 to 1950.

I caught a tremendous fish
and held him beside the boat
half out of water, with my hook
fast in a corner of his mouth.
He didn't fight.   5
He hadn't fought at all.
He hung a grunting weight,
battered and venerable
and homely. Here and there
his brown skin hung in strips   10
like ancient wallpaper,
and its pattern of darker brown
was like wallpaper:
shapes like full-blown roses
stained and lost through age.   15
He was speckled with barnacles,
fine rosettes of lime,
and infested
with tiny white sea-lice,
and underneath two or three   20
rags of green weed hung down.

While his gills were breathing in
the terrible oxygen
— the frightening gills,
fresh and crisp with blood,   25
that can cut so badly —
I thought of the coarse white flesh
packed in like feathers,
the big bones and the little bones,
the dramatic reds and blacks   30
of his shiny entrails,
and the pink swim-bladder
like a big peony.
I looked into his eyes
which were far larger than mine   35
but shallower, and yellowed,
the irises backed and packed
with tarnished tinfoil
seen through the lenses
of old scratched isinglass.°   *transparent sheet of mica* 40
They shifted a little, but not
to return my stare.
— It was more like the tipping
of an object toward the light.
I admired his sullen face,   45
the mechanism of his jaw,
and then I saw
that from his lower lip
— if you could call it a lip —
grim, wet, and weaponlike,   50
hung five old pieces of fish-line,
or four and a wire leader
with the swivel still attached,
with all their five big hooks
grown firmly in his mouth.   55
A green line, frayed at the end
where he broke it, two heavier lines,
and a fine black thread
still crimped from the strain and snap
when it broke and he got away.   60
Like medals with their ribbons
frayed and wavering,
a five-haired beard of wisdom
trailing from his aching jaw.

I stared and stared   65
and victory filled up
the little rented boat,
from the pool of bilge
where oil had spread a rainbow
around the rusted engine   70
to the bailer rusted orange,
the sun-cracked thwarts,
the oarlocks on their strings,
the gunnels—until everything
was rainbow, rainbow, rainbow!   75
And I let the fish go.

[1946]

DIANE ACKERMAN   [b. 1956]

We Are All a Part of Nature

Hailing from Waukegan, Illinois, writer and naturalist **Diane Ackerman** received her B.A. from Penn State and an M.A., M.F.A. and Ph.D. from Cornell University. The author of numerous collections of poetry and prose, Ackerman is best known for *A Natural History of the Senses* (1990), upon which PBS television based a five-hour series that she hosted. Ackerman has been awarded a Guggenheim Fellowship, the John Burroughs Nature Award, and the Lavan Poetry Prize, and has been named a Literary Lion by the New York Public Library. Represented widely in leading literary journals and anthologies, Ackerman's nature writing is also regularly published in the *New York Times*, the *New Yorker*, *National Geographic*, and other well-known periodicals. Ackerman has taught at Cornell, Columbia, and the University of Richmond, and she has been granted the unusual honor of having a molecule named after her: dianeackerone.

In "We Are All a Part of Nature," originally appearing in *Parade* magazine in 2004, Ackerman celebrates nature and her place within it. Lyrical and joyous, her lush writing reminds us what a great privilege it is to be alive, we, the far distant offspring of algae, on this complex and comical, daunting, and delicious planet.

A film starts running across my mind's eye, accompanied by the sound of heartbeats and birdsong. It contains my whole experience of Earth, including all the oceans I've floated on or swum under, the skies I've flown through, the lands I've walked upon, the humans and other animals I've known, lots of nature I've never witnessed firsthand but glimpsed in documentaries or read about, and the Earth seen from space.

Naturally, that film would take lifetimes to explore, because nature means the full sum of creation, from the Big Bang to the whole shebang. It includes: spring moving north at about 13 miles a day; afternoon tea and cookies; snow forts; pepper-pot stew; pink sand and confetti-colored cottages; moths with fake eyes on their hind wings; emotions both savage and blessed; tidal waves; pogo-hopping sparrows; blushing octopuses; scientists bloodhounding the truth; memory's wobbling aspic; the harvest moon rising like slow thunder; fat rainbows beneath spongy clouds; tiny tassels of worry on a summer day; the night sky's distant leak of suns; an aging father's voice so husky it could pull a sled; the courtship pantomimes of cardinals whistling in the spring with "what cheer, what cheer, what cheer!"

Sometimes we forget that nature also means us. Termites build mounds; we build cities. All of our being—juices, flesh and spirit—is nature.

Nature surrounds, permeates, effervesces in and includes us. At the end of our days, it deranges and disassembles us like old toys banished to the basement. There, once living beings, we return to our nonliving elements, but we still and forever remain a part of nature. Not everyone agrees with me. Many people harbor an us-against-them mentality in which nature is the enemy and the kingdom of animals doesn't really include us. Then we can attribute to animals all the things about ourselves that we can't stand.

True, we build more elaborate habitats than other animals who, to the 5 best of my knowledge, don't require anything like electric cow-milk frothing machines, beeswax on a flaming string, or vaporized flower essence mixed with musk from the anal sac of civets to encourage breeding. But I could be wrong. Maybe the wren's liquid melody is equally fantastic. And I'm reluctant to hazard a guess about the necking and petting of alligators, whose cheeks are studded with exquisitely sensitive pleasure nodes. Even at our most domesticated and tame, we're like pet zebras or grizzly bears—dangerous to anger, always flirting with a tantrum just under the well-behaved surface. We're remarkable animals, erudite and loving, but, like circus lions, we will always be wild and fiercely unpredictable.

Each day, I wake startled to be alive on a planet packed with so much life. No gasp of sunlight goes unused. Life homesteads every pore and crevice, including deep dark ocean trenches. Life's rule seems to be variations on every possible theme: And so we have tree frogs with sticky feet, marsupial frogs, poisonous frogs, toe-tapping frogs, frogs that go peep and many more.

The leafy green abundance we usually think of as nature began with Earth's earliest life-forms, blue-green algae. Their gift was the cell, a microscopic circus that still is the basis of a cougar, bombardier beetle, and one's nephew. Their genius was inventing photosynthesis. Around 2.4 billion years ago, they began building solar power plants under their walls, digesting their surroundings and, in the process, excreting oxygen, a poisonous gas.

Over time, the algae sheathed the planet, and oxygen fizzed through the oceans, saturating them. Then the bubbles rose, breathing life into a slaggy sky, whose cloudbanks thinned as the blues appeared. Hydrogen ballooned away into space, while heavier oxygen stayed home. Earth became a planet rich in poisonous, flammable oxygen.

Meanwhile, evolution tinkered with creatures immune to oxygen, including some willing to pool their DNA. Complex animals evolved. And the rest is history. In every flake of skin, we still resemble those one-celled pioneers. If they didn't excrete oxygen, we wouldn't be here. So, no matter how politely one puts it, we owe our existence to the flatulence of blue-green algae. That should humble us and remind us that we share our origins and future with the rest of life on Earth. We need a healthy environment if we hope to stay healthy.

Most days, I make time to play outside, usually in the garden or on   10
a bike or taking a walk. I live in the country, but nature also means the manicured wilderness of a large city, where flimsy blades of grass crack through cement and fragile snowflakes halt traffic. What feats of strength! A city park lures countless animals from miles away to its bustling green oasis. Surrounded by trees and sky, it's easier to feel a powerful sense of belonging to the pervasive mystery of nature, of being molded by unseen forces older than our daily concerns. Without that, life would feel flat as a postage stamp.

But nature also means comfort, heritage, and seasoned home. In-doors, a sensuous activity I heartily recommend is what I think of as "spanieling." Find a shaft of sunlight pouring through a window on a cold day, curl up in the puddle of warmth it creates, relish the breath of sun on your skin, and nap with doglike dereliction. If you have trouble turning off your mind-theater, picture yourself as a squirrel, bear, or cocker spaniel enjoying a simple sunbath.

Steep yourself in nature. The world will wait.

BARBARA EHRENREICH   [b. 1941]

Cultural Baggage

A renowned social critic and prolific essayist, **Barbara Ehrenreich** was born in Butte, Montana, in 1941. In 1963 she graduated with a B.A. in physics from Reed College and went on to earn a Ph.D. in cell biology from Rockefeller University. Initially she had no intention of becoming a writer, but she found herself attracted to a career in social activism rather than research science and began writing investigative articles for small newsletters. Her articles have appeared in the *New York Times,* *Ms.,* the *Atlantic Monthly, In These Times,* and *The New Republic,* among others. From 1991 to 1997 Ehrenreich was a regular columnist for *Time* magazine and is currently a regular columnist for *The Progressive.* Her national best seller, *Nickel and Dimed* (2001), narrates her efforts to survive on low-income wages and her follow-up book, *Bait and Switch* (2005), recounts her undercover efforts to find a white-collar job in corporate America.

In "Cultural Baggage," Ehrenreich appraises her diverse ethnic and religious heritage and wonders just how much significance she can allot to any one set of traditions. At first despairing of her rootlessness, she concludes that living by her parent's greatest tenets — "Think for yourself" and "Try new things" — are all the cultural roots she needs.

An acquaintance was telling me about the joys of rediscovering her ethnic and religious heritage. "I know exactly what my ancestors were doing 2,000 years ago," she said, eyes gleaming with enthusiasm, "and *I can do the same things now.*" Then she leaned forward and inquired politely, "And what is your ethnic background, if I may ask?"

"None," I said, that being the first word in line to get out of my mouth. Well, not "none," I backtracked. Scottish, English, Irish — that was something, I supposed. Too much Irish to qualify as a WASP; too much of the hated English to warrant a "Kiss Me, I'm Irish" button; plus there are a number of dead ends in the family tree due to adoptions, missing records, failing memories and the like. I was blushing by this time. Did "none" mean I was rejecting my heritage out of Anglo-Celtic self-hate? Or was I revealing a hidden ethnic chauvinism in which the Britannically

Barbara Ehrenreich, "Cultural Baggage" from *The New York Times Magazine*, April 5, 1992. Copyright © 1992 The New York Times. Reprinted by permission.

111

derived serve as a kind of neutral standard compared with the ethnic "others"?

Throughout the 60's and 70's, I watched one group after another— African-Americans, Latinos, Native Americans—stand up and proudly reclaim their roots while I just sank back ever deeper into my seat. All this excitement over ethnicity stemmed, I uneasily sensed, from a past in which their ancestors had been trampled upon by *my* ancestors, or at least by people who looked very much like them. In addition, it had begun to seem almost un-American not to have some sort of hyphen at hand, linking one to more venerable times and locales.

But the truth is, I was raised with none. We'd eaten ethnic foods in my childhood home, but these were all borrowed, like the pasties, or Cornish meat pies, my father had picked up from his fellow miners in Butte, Mont. If my mother had one rule, it was militant ecumenism in all matters of food and experience. "Try new things," she would say, meaning anything from sweetbreads to clams, with an emphasis on the "new."

As a child, I briefly nourished a craving for tradition and roots. I 5 immersed myself in the works of Sir Walter Scott. I pretended to believe that the bagpipe was a musical instrument. I was fascinated to learn from a grandmother that we were descended from certain Highland clans and longed for a pleated skirt in one of their distinctive tartans.

But in "Ivanhoe," it was the dark-eyed "Jewess" Rebecca I identified with, not the flaxen-haired bimbo Rowena. As for clans: Why not call them "tribes," those bands of half-clad peasants and warriors whose idea of cuisine was stuffed sheep gut washed down with whisky? And then there was the sting of Disraeli's remark— which I came across in my early teens—to the effect that his ancestors had been leading orderly, literate lives when my ancestors were still rampaging through the Highlands daubing themselves with blue paint.

Motherhood put the screws on me, ethnicity-wise. I had hoped that by marrying a man of Eastern European-Jewish ancestry I would acquire for my descendants the ethnic genes that my own forebears so sadly lacked. At one point, I even subjected the children to a seder of my own design, including a little talk about the flight from Egypt and its relevance to modern social issues. But the kids insisted on buttering their matzohs and snickering through my talk. "Give me a break, Mom," the older one said. "You don't even believe in God."

After the tiny pagans had been put to bed, I sat down to brood over Elijah's wine. What had I been thinking? The kids knew that their Jewish grandparents were secular folks who didn't hold seders themselves. And if ethnicity eluded me, how could I expect it to take root in my children, who are not only Scottish-English-Irish, but Hungarian-Polish-Russian to boot?

But, then, on the fumes of Manischewitz, a great insight took form in my mind. It was true, as the kids said, that I didn't "believe in God." But this could be taken as something very different from an accusation—a reminder of a genuine heritage. My parents had not believed in God either, nor had my grandparents or any other progenitors going back to the great-great level. They had become disillusioned with Christianity generations ago—just as, on the in-law side, my children's other ancestors had shaken their Orthodox Judaism. This insight did not exactly furnish me with an "identity," but it was at least something to work with: we are the kind of people, I realized—whatever our distant ancestors' religions—who do *not* believe, who do not carry on traditions, who do not do things just because someone has done them before.

The epiphany went on: I recalled that my mother never introduced a 10 procedure for cooking or cleaning by telling me, "Grandma did it this way." What did Grandma know, living in the days before vacuum cleaners and disposable toilet mops! In my parents' general view, new things were better than old, and the very fact that some ritual had been performed in the past was a good reason for abandoning it now. Because what was the past, as our forebears knew it? Nothing but poverty, superstition and grief. "Think for yourself," Dad used to say. "Always ask why."

In fact, this may have been the ideal cultural heritage for my particular ethnic strain—bounced as it was from the Highlands of Scotland across the sea, out to the Rockies, down into the mines and finally spewed out into high-tech, suburban America. What better philosophy, for a race of migrants, than "Think for yourself"? What better maxim, for a people whose whole world was rudely inverted every 30 years or so, than "Try new things"?

The more tradition-minded, the newly enthusiastic celebrants of Purim and Kwanzaa and Solstice, may see little point to survival if the survivors carry no cultural freight—religion, for example, or ethnic tradition. To which I would say that skepticism, curiosity and wide-eyed ecumenical tolerance are also worthy elements of the human tradition and are at least as old as such notions as "Serbian" or "Croatian," "Scottish" or "Jewish." I make no claims for my personal line of progenitors except that they remained loyal to the values that may have induced all of our ancestors, long, long ago, to climb down from the trees and make their way into the open plains.

A few weeks ago, I cleared my throat and asked the children, now mostly grown and fearsomely smart, whether they felt any stirrings of ethnic or religious identity, etc., which might have been, ahem, insufficiently nourished at home. "None," they said, adding firmly, "and the world would be a better place if nobody else did, either." My chest swelled with pride, as would my mother's, to know that the race of "none" marches on.

NATALIE ANGIER   [b. 1958]

Men, Women, Sex, and Darwin

Born in New York, **Natalie Angier** graduated with high honors from
Barnard College in 1978 having studied English, physics, and astron-
omy. A founding staff member of *Discover* magazine in 1980, Angier
has also been a science writer for *Time* magazine, a professor in the
Graduate Program in Science and Environmental Reporting at New
York University, and a contributing writer for *Atlantic, Parade, Reader's
Digest*, and the *Washington Monthly*, among others. Since 1990, Angier
has been a science writer on staff at the *New York Times*. In 1991 she
won a Pulitzer Prize for Beat Reporting, recognized for a variety of
science-based feature stories. Her book, *Natural Obsessions* (1988) was
named *New York Times* Notable Book of the Year and the American
Association for the Advancement of Science (AAAS) Notable Book of
the Year. Angier has also authored *The Beauty of the Beastly* (1995) and
Woman: An Intimate Geography (2000). Further honors include the
Lewis Thomas Award for distinguished writing in the life sciences and
the General Motors International Award for writing about cancer.

In "Men, Women, Sex, and Darwin," from *Woman: An Intimate Geography*, Angier refutes evolutionary psychologists' assertions that the
innate sexual desires and mate selection criteria of men and women
are dramatically different as well as inflexibly hardwired. Based on
"feeble and amusingly contradictory data"—primarily the perceived
sexual differences between gay men and lesbians—the findings of evolutionary psychologists, Angier attests, are too narrowly conceived and
essentially flawed. In her analysis of the evolution of the nuclear marriage, Angier highlights numerous social and environmental influences that affected mate selectivity and the frequency of promiscuity
in *both* men and women, thereby contesting evolutionary psychology's
views.

Life is short but jingles are forever. None more so, it seems, than the
familiar ditty, variously attributed to William James, Ogden Nash and

Dorothy Parker: "Hoggamus, higgamus, / Men are polygamous, / Higgamus, hoggamus, / Women monogamous."

Lately the pith of that jingle has found new fodder and new fans, through the explosive growth of a field known as evolutionary psychology. Evolutionary psychology professes to have discovered the fundamental modules of human nature, most notably the essential nature of man and of woman. It makes sense to be curious about the evolutionary roots of human behavior. It's reasonable to try to understand our impulses and actions by applying Darwinian logic to the problem. We're animals. We're not above the rude little prods and jests of natural and sexual selection. But evolutionary psychology as it has been disseminated across mainstream consciousness is a cranky and despotic Cyclops, its single eye glaring through an overwhelmingly masculinist lens. I say "masculinist" rather than "male" because the view of male behavior promulgated by hard-core evolutionary psychologists is as narrow and inflexible as their view of womanhood is.

I'm not interested in explaining to men what they really want or how they should behave. If a fellow chooses to tell himself that his yen for the fetching young assistant in his office and his concomitant disgruntlement with his aging wife make perfect Darwinian sense, who am I to argue with him? I'm only proposing here that the hard-core evolutionary psychologists have got a lot about women wrong—about some of us, anyway—and that women want more and deserve better than the cartoon *Olive Oyl* handed down for popular consumption.

The cardinal premises of evolutionary psychology of interest to this discussion are as follows: 1. Men are more promiscuous and less sexually reserved than women are. 2. Women are inherently more interested in a stable relationship than men are. 3. Women are naturally attracted to high-status men with resources. 4. Men are naturally attracted to youth and beauty. 5. Humankind's core preferences and desires were hammered out long, long ago, a hundred thousand years or more, in the legendary Environment of Evolutionary Adaptation, or E.E.A., also known as the ancestral environment, also known as the Stone Age, and they have not changed appreciably since then, nor are they likely to change in the future.

In sum: Higgamus, hoggamus, Pygmalionus, *Playboy* magazine, *eternitas*. Amen. 5

Hard-core evolutionary psychology types go to extremes to argue in favor of the yawning chasm that separates the innate desires of women and men. They declare ringing confirmation for their theories even in the face of feeble and amusingly contradictory data. For example: Among the cardinal principles of the evo-psycho set is that men are by nature more polygamous than women are, and much more accepting of casual, even anonymous, sex. Men can't help themselves, they say: they are always hungry for sex, bodies, novelty and nubility. Granted, men needn't act on such desires, but the drive to sow seed is there nonetheless, satiric and relentless, and women cannot fully understand its force. David Buss, a professor of psychology at the University of Texas at Austin and one of the most outspoken of the evolutionary psychologists, says that asking a man not to lust after a pretty young woman is like telling a carnivore not to like meat.

At the same time, they recognize that the overwhelming majority of men and women get married, and so their theories must extend to different innate mate preferences among men and women. Men look for the hallmarks of youth, like smooth skin, full lips and perky breasts; they want a mate who has a long child-bearing career ahead of her. Men also want women who are virginal and who seem as though they'll be faithful and not make cuckolds of them. The sexy, vampy types are fine for a Saturday romp, but when it comes to choosing a marital partner, men want modesty and fidelity.

Women want a provider, the theory goes. They want a man who seems rich, stable and ambitious. They want to know that they and their children will be cared for. They want a man who can take charge, maybe dominate them just a little, enough to reassure them that the man is genotypically, phenotypically, eternally, a king. Women's innate preference for a well-to-do man continues to this day, the evolutionary psychologists insist, even among financially independent and professionally successful women who don't need a man as a provider. It was adaptive in the past to look for the most resourceful man, they say, and adaptations can't be willed away in a generation or two of putative cultural change.

And what is the evidence for these male-female verities? For the difference in promiscuity quotas, the hard-cores love to raise the example of the differences between gay men and lesbians. Homosexuals are seen as a revealing population because they supposedly can behave according to the innermost impulses of their sex, untempered by the need to adjust to the demands and wishes of the opposite sex, as heterosexuals theoretically are. What do we see in this ideal study group? Just look at how gay men carry on! They are perfectly happy to have hundreds, thousands, of sexual partners, to have sex in bathhouses, in bathrooms, in Central Park. By contrast, lesbians are sexually sedate. They don't cruise sex clubs. They couple up and stay coupled, and they like cuddling and hugging more than they do serious, genitally based sex.

In the hard-core rendering of inherent male-female discrepancies in promiscuity, gay men are offered up as true men, real men, men set free to be men, while lesbians are real women, ultra-women, acting out every woman's fantasy of love and commitment. Interestingly, though, in many

10

neurobiology studies gay men are said to have somewhat feminized brains, with hypothalamic nuclei that are closer in size to a woman's than to a straight man's, and spatial-reasoning skills that are modest and ladylike rather than manfully robust. For their part, lesbians are posited to have somewhat masculinized brains and skills—to be sportier, more mechanically inclined, less likely to have played with dolls or tea sets when young—all as an ostensible result of exposure to prenatal androgens. And so gay men are sissy boys in some contexts and Stone Age manly men in others, while lesbians are battering rams one day and flower into the softest and most sexually divested girlish girls the next.

On the question of mate preferences, evo-psychos rely on surveys, most of them compiled by David Buss. His surveys are celebrated by some, derided by others, but in any event they are ambitious—performed in 37 countries, he says, on six continents. His surveys, and others emulating them, consistently find that men rate youth and beauty as important traits in a mate, while women give comparatively greater weight to ambition and financial success. Surveys show that surveys never lie. Lest you think that women's mate preferences change with their own mounting economic clout, surveys assure us that they do not. Surveys of female medical students, according to John Marshall Townsend, of Syracuse University, indicate that they hope to marry men with an earning power and social status at least equal to and preferably greater than their own.

Perhaps all this means is that men can earn a living wage better, even now, than women can. Men make up about half the world's population, but they still own the vast majority of the world's wealth—the currency, the minerals, the timber, the gold, the stocks, the amber fields of grain. In her superb book *Why So Slow?* Virginia Valian, a professor of psychology at Hunter College, lays out the extent of lingering economic discrepancies between men and women in the United States. In 1978 there were two women heading Fortune 1000 companies; in 1994, there were still two; in 1996, the number had jumped all the way to four. In 1985, 2 percent of the Fortune 1000's senior-level executives were women; by 1992, that number had hardly budged, to 3 percent. A 1990 salary and compensation survey of 799 major companies showed that of the highest-paid officers and directors, less than one-half of 1 percent were women. Ask, and he shall receive. In the United States the possession of a bachelor's degree adds $28,000 to a man's salary but only $9,000 to a woman's. A degree from a high-prestige school contributes $11,500 to a man's income but *subtracts* $2,400 from a woman's. If women continue to worry that they need a man's money, because the playing field remains about as level as the surface of Mars, then we can't conclude anything about innate preferences. If women continue to suffer from bag-lady syndrome even as they become prosperous, if they still see their wealth as provisional and capsizable, and if they still hope to find a man with a dependable income to supplement their own, then we can credit women with intelligence and acumen, for inequities abound.

There's another reason that smart, professional women might respond on surveys that they'd like a mate of their socioeconomic status or better. Smart, professional women are smart enough to know that men can be tender of ego—is it genetic?—and that it hurts a man to earn less money than his wife, and that resentment is a noxious chemical in a marriage and best avoided at any price. "A woman who is more successful than her mate threatens his position in the male hierarchy," Elizabeth Cashdan, of the University of Utah, has written. If women could be persuaded that men didn't mind their being high achievers, were in fact pleased and proud to be affiliated with them, we might predict that the women would stop caring about the particulars of their mates' income. The anthropologist Sara Blaffer Hrdy writes that "when female status and access to resources do not depend on her mate's status, women will likely use a range of criteria, not primarily or even necessarily prestige and wealth, for mate selection." She cites a 1996 *New York Times* story about women from a wide range of professions— bankers, judges, teachers, journalists—who marry male convicts. The allure of such men is not their income, for you can't earn much when you make license plates for a living. Instead, it is the men's gratitude that proves irresistible. The women also like the fact that their husbands' fidelity is guaranteed. "Peculiar as it is," Hrdy writes, "this vignette of sex-reversed claustration makes a serious point about just how little we know about female choice in breeding systems where male interests are not paramount and patrilines are not making the rules."

Do women love older men? Do women find gray hair and wrinkles attractive on men—as attractive, that is, as a fine, full head of pigmented hair and a vigorous, firm complexion? The evolutionary psychologists suggest yes. They believe that women look for the signs of maturity in men because a mature man is likely to be a comparatively wealthy and resourceful man. That should logically include baldness, which generally comes with age and the higher status that it often confers. Yet, as Desmond Morris points out, a thinning hairline is not considered a particularly attractive state.

Assuming that women find older men attractive, is it the men's alpha status? Or could it be something less complimentary to the male, something like the following—that an older man is appealing not because he is powerful but because in his maturity he has lost some of his power, has become less marketable and desirable and potentially more grateful and gracious, more likely to make a younger woman feel that there is a

15

118

balance of power in the relationship? The rude little calculation is simple: He is male, I am female—advantage, man. He is older, I am younger—advantage, woman. By the same token, a woman may place little value on a man's appearance because she values something else far more: room to breathe. Who can breathe in the presence of a handsome young man, whose ego, if expressed as a vapor, would fill Biosphere II? Not even, I'm afraid, a beautiful young woman.

In the end, what is important to question, and to hold to the fire of alternative interpretation, is the immutability and adaptive logic of the discrepancy, its basis in our genome rather than in the ecological circumstances in which a genome manages to express itself. Evolutionary psychologists insist on the essential discordance between the strength of the sex drive in males and females. They admit that many nonhuman female primates gallivant about rather more than we might have predicted before primatologists began observing their behavior in the field—more, far more, than is necessary for the sake of reproduction. Nonetheless, the credo of the coy female persists. It is garlanded with qualifications and is admitted to be an imperfect portrayal of female mating strategies, but then, that little matter of etiquette attended to, the credo is stated once again.

"Amid the great variety of social structure in these species, the basic theme...stands out, at least in minimal form: males seem very eager for sex and work hard to find it; females work less hard," Robert Wright says in *The Moral Animal.* "This isn't to say the females don't like sex. They love it, and may initiate it. And, intriguingly, the females of the species most closely related to humans—chimpanzees and bonobos—seem particularly amenable to a wild sex life, including a variety of partners. Still, female apes don't do what male apes do: search high and low, risking life and limb, to find sex, and to find as much of it, with as many different partners, as possible; it has a way of finding them." In fact female chimpanzees do search high and low and take great risks to find sex with partners other than the partners who have a way of finding them. DNA studies of chimpanzees in West Africa show that half the offspring in a group of closely scrutinized chimpanzees turned out not to be the offspring of the resident males. The females of the group didn't rely on sex "finding" its way to them; they proactively left the local environs, under such conditions of secrecy that not even their vigilant human observers knew they had gone, and became impregnated by outside males. They did so even at the risk of life and limb—their own and those of their offspring. Male chimpanzees try to control the movements of fertile females. They'll scream at them and hit them if they think the females aren't listening. They may even kill an infant they think is not their own. We don't know why the females take such risks to philander, but they do, and to say that female chimpanzees "work less hard" than males do at finding sex does not appear to be supported by the data.

Evo-psychos pull us back and forth until we might want to sue for whiplash. On the one hand we are told that women have a lower sex drive than men do. On the other hand we are told that the madonna-whore dichotomy is a universal stereotype. In every culture, there is a tendency among both men and women to adjudge women as either chaste or trampy. The chaste ones are accorded esteem. The trampy ones are consigned to the basement, a notch or two below goats in social status. A woman can't sleep around without risking terrible retribution, to her reputation, to her prospects, to her life. "Can anyone find a single culture in which women with unrestrained sexual appetites *aren't* viewed as more aberrant than comparably libidinous men?" Wright asks rhetorically.

Women are said to have lower sex drives than men, yet they are universally punished if they display evidence to the contrary—if they disobey their "natural" inclination toward a stifled libido. Women supposedly have a lower sex drive than men do, yet it is not low enough. There is still just enough of a lingering female infidelity impulse that cultures everywhere have had to gird against it by articulating a rigid dichotomy with menacing implications for those who fall on the wrong side of it. There is still enough lingering female infidelity to justify infibulation, purdah, claustration. Men have the naturally higher sex drive, yet all the laws, customs, punishments, shame, strictures, mystiques and antimystiques are aimed with full hominid fury at that tepid, sleepy, hypoactive creature, the female libido.

"It seems premature...to attribute the relative lack of female interest [20] in sexual variety to women's biological nature alone in the face of overwhelming evidence that women are consistently beaten for promiscuity and adultery," the primatologist Barbara Smuts has written. "If female sexuality is muted compared to that of men, then why must men the world over go to extreme lengths to control and contain it?"

Why indeed? Consider a brief evolutionary apologia for President Clinton's adulteries written by Steven Pinker, of the Massachusetts Institute of Technology. "Most human drives have ancient Darwinian rationales," he wrote. "A prehistoric man who slept with 50 women could have sired 50 children, and would have been more likely to have descendants who inherited his tastes. A woman who slept with fifty men would have no more descendants than a woman who slept with one. Thus, men should seek quantity in sexual partners; women, quality." And isn't it so, he says, everywhere and always so? "In our society," he continues, "most young men tell researchers that they would like eight sexual partners in the next two years; most women say that they would like one." Yet would a man find the prospect of a string of partners so appealing if the following rules were applied: that no matter how much he may like a particular woman and be pleased by her performance and want to sleep with her again, he will have no say in the matter and will be dependent on her mood and good graces for all future contact; that each act of casual sex will cheapen his status and make him increasingly less attractive to other women; and that society will not wink at his randiness but rather sneer at him and think him pathetic, sullied, smaller than life? Until men are subjected to the same severe standards and threat of censure as women are, and until they are given the lower hand in a so-called casual encounter from the start, it is hard to insist with such self-satisfaction that, hey, it's natural, men like a lot of sex with a lot of people and women don't.

Reflect for a moment on Pinker's philandering caveman who slept with 50 women. Just how good a reproductive strategy is this chronic, random shooting of the gun? A woman is fertile only five or six days a month. Her ovulation is concealed. The man doesn't know when she's fertile. She might be in the early stages of pregnancy when he gets to her; she might still be lactating and thus not ovulating. Moreover, even if our hypothetical Don Juan hits a day on which a woman is ovulating, the chances are around 65 percent that his sperm will fail to fertilize her egg; human reproduction is complicated, and most eggs and sperm are not up to the demands of proper fusion. Even if conception occurs, the resulting embryo has about a 30 percent chance of miscarrying at some point in gestation. In sum, each episode of fleeting sex has a remarkably small probability of yielding a baby—no more than 1 or 2 percent at best.

And because the man is trysting and running, he isn't able to prevent any of his casual contacts from turning around and mating with other men. The poor fellow. He has to mate with many scores of women for his wham-bam strategy to pay off. And where are all these women to be found, anyway? Population densities during that purportedly all-powerful psyche shaper the "ancestral environment" were quite low, and long-distance travel was dangerous and difficult.

There are alternatives to wantonness, as a number of theorists have emphasized. If, for example, a man were to spend more time with one woman rather than dashing breathlessly from sheet to sheet, if he were to feel compelled to engage in what animal behaviorists call mate guarding, he might be better off, reproductively speaking, than the wild Lothario, both because the odds of impregnating the woman would increase and because he'd be monopolizing her energy and keeping her from the advances of other sperm bearers. It takes the average couple three to four months of regular sexual intercourse to become pregnant.

121

That number of days is approximately equal to the number of partners our hypothetical libertine needs to sleep with to have one encounter result in a "fertility unit," that is, a baby. The two strategies, then, shake out about the same. A man can sleep with a lot of women—the quantitative approach—or he can sleep with one woman for months at a time, and be madly in love with her—the qualitative tactic.

It's possible that these two reproductive strategies are distributed in 25 discrete packets among the male population, with a result that some men are born philanderers and can never attach, while others are born romantics and perpetually in love with love; but it's also possible that men teeter back and forth from one impulse to the other, suffering an internal struggle between the desire to bond and the desire to retreat, with the circuits of attachment ever there to be toyed with, and their needs and desires difficult to understand, paradoxical, fickle, treacherous and glorious. It is possible, then, and for perfectly good Darwinian reason, that casual sex for men is rarely as casual as it is billed.

It needn't be argued that men and women are exactly the same, or that humans are meta-evolutionary beings, removed from nature and slaves to culture, to reject the perpetually regurgitated model of the coy female and the ardent male. Conflicts of interest are always among us, and the outcomes of those conflicts are interesting, more interesting by far than what the ultra-evolutionary psychology line has handed us. Patricia Gowaty, of the University of Georgia, sees conflict between males and females as inevitable and pervasive. She calls it sexual dialectics. Her thesis is that females and males vie for control over the means of reproduction. Those means are the female body, for there is as yet no such beast as the parthenogenetic man.

Women are under selective pressure to maintain control over their reproduction, to choose with whom they will mate and with whom they will not—to exercise female choice. Men are under selective pressure to make sure they're chosen or, barring that, to subvert female choice and coerce the female to mate against her will. "But once you have this basic dialectic set in motion, it's going to be a constant push-me, pull-you," Gowaty says. "That dynamism cannot possibly result in a unitary response, the caricatured coy woman and ardent man. Instead there are going to be some coy, reluctantly mating males and some ardent females, and any number of variations in between.

"A female will choose to mate with a male whom she believes, consciously or otherwise, will confer some advantage on her and her offspring. If that's the case, then her decision is contingent on what she brings to the equation." For example, she says, "the 'good genes' model leads to oversimplified notions that there is a 'best male' out there, a top-of-the-line hunk whom all females would prefer to mate with if they had the wherewithal. But in the viability model, a female brings her own genetic complement to the equation, with the result that what looks good genetically to one woman might be a clash of colors for another."

Maybe the man's immune system doesn't complement her own, for example, Gowaty proposes. There's evidence that the search for immune variation is one of the subtle factors driving mate selection, which may be why we care about how our lovers smell; immune molecules may be volatilized and released in sweat, hair, the oil on our skin. We are each of us a chemistry set, and each of us has a distinctive mix of reagents. "What pleases me might not please somebody else," Gowaty says. "There is no one-brand great male out there. We're not all programmed to look for the alpha male and only willing to mate with the little guy or the less aggressive guy because we can't do any better. But the propaganda gives us a picture of the right man and the ideal woman, and the effect of the propaganda is insidious. It becomes self-reinforcing. People who don't fit the model think, I'm weird, I'll have to change my behavior." It is this danger, that the ostensible "discoveries" of evolutionary psychology will be used as propaganda, that makes the enterprise so disturbing.

Variation and flexibility are the key themes that get set aside in the 30 breathless dissemination of evolutionary psychology. "The variation is tremendous, and is rooted in biology," Barbara Smuts said to me. "Flexibility itself is the adaptation." Smuts has studied olive baboons, and she has seen males pursuing all sorts of mating strategies. "There are some whose primary strategy is dominating other males, and being able to gain access to more females because of their fighting ability," she says. "Then there is the type of male who avoids competition and cultivates long-term relationships with females and their infants. These are the nice, affiliative guys. There's a third type, who focuses on sexual relationships. He's the consorter. . . . And as far as we can tell, no one reproductive strategy has advantages over the others."

Women are said to need an investing male. We think we know the reason. Human babies are difficult and time consuming to raise. Stone Age mothers needed husbands to bring home the bison. Yet the age-old assumption that male parental investment lies at the heart of human evolution is now open to serious question. Men in traditional foraging cultures do not necessarily invest resources in their offspring. Among the Hadza of Africa, for example, the men hunt, but they share the bounty of that hunting widely, politically, strategically. They don't deliver it straight to the mouths of their progeny. Women rely on their senior female kin to help feed their children. The women and their children in a gathering-hunting society clearly benefit from the meat that hunters bring back to the group. But they benefit as a group, not as a collection of nuclear family units, each beholden to the father's personal pound of wildeburger.

This is a startling revelation, which upends many of our presumptions about the origins of marriage and what women want from men and men from women. If the environment of evolutionary adaptation is not defined primarily by male parental investment, the bedrock of so much of evolutionary psychology's theories, then we can throw the door wide open and ask new questions, rather than endlessly repeating ditties and calling the female coy long after she has run her petticoats through the Presidential paper shredder.

For example: Nicholas Blurton Jones, of the University of California at Los Angeles, and others have proposed that marriage developed as an extension of men's efforts at mate guarding. If the cost of philandering becomes ludicrously high, the man might be better off trying to claim rights to one woman at a time. Regular sex with a fertile woman is at least likely to yield offspring at comparatively little risk to his life, particularly if sexual access to the woman is formalized through a public ceremony—a wedding. Looked at from this perspective, one must wonder why an ancestral woman bothered to get married, particularly if she and her female relatives did most of the work of keeping the family fed from year to year. Perhaps, Blurton Jones suggests, to limit the degree to which she was harassed. The cost of chronic male harassment may be too high to bear. Better to agree to a ritualized bond with a male and to benefit from whatever hands-off policy that marriage may bring, than to spend all of her time locked in one sexual dialectic or another.

Thus marriage may have arisen as a multifaceted social pact: between man and woman, between male and male and between the couple and the tribe. It is a reasonable solution to a series of cultural challenges that arose in concert with the expansion of the human neocortex. But its roots may not be what we think they are, nor may our contemporary mating behaviors stem from the pressures of an ancestral environment as it is commonly portrayed, in which a woman needed a mate to help feed and clothe her young. Instead, our "deep" feelings about marriage may be more pragmatic, more contextual and, dare I say it, more egalitarian than we give them credit for being.

If marriage is a social compact, a mutual bid between man and woman to contrive a reasonably stable and agreeable microhabitat in a community of shrewd and well-armed members, then we can understand why, despite rhetoric to the contrary, men are as eager to marry as women are. A raft of epidemiological studies have shown that marriage adds more years to the life of a man than it does to that of a woman. Why should that be, if men are so "naturally" ill suited to matrimony?

What do women want? None of us speak for all women, or for more than one woman, really, but we can hazard a mad guess that a desire for emotional parity is widespread and profound. It doesn't go away, although it often hibernates under duress, and it may be perverted by the restrictions of habitat or culture into something that looks like its opposite. The impulse for liberty is congenital. It is the ultimate manifestation of selfishness, which is why we can count on its endurance.

Mannie Garcia, *Barack Obama*, 2006, and Shepard Fairey, *Hope*, 2008. Artist Shepard Fairey created the poster image of Barack Obama used in the 2008 presidential campaign based on a photograph by Mannie Garcia. (AP Photo/Mannie Garcia/Shepard Fairey.)

LINDA CHAVEZ   [b. 1947]

Demystifying Multiculturalism

Born in Albuquerque, New Mexico (1947), **Linda Chavez** earned a B.A. from the University of Colorado in 1970. For most of the 1970s, Chavez was allied with Democratic politics and served as an advocate for liberal causes. After an appointment to the U.S. Commission on Civil Rights, she began to rethink government policy on civil rights and, in 1985, she changed her political affiliation to enter the Republican Party. At the appointment of President Reagan, Chavez served as director of the White House Office of Public Liaison, the highest ranking woman in the administration. In 1986, Chavez was the Republican nominee for the Senate in Maryland. Later, in 1992, she was elected to serve a four-year term as U.S. Expert for the U.N. Sub-Commission on the Prevention of Discrimination and Protection of Minorities. In each role, Chavez has pursued a conservative agenda, advocating the rapid assimilation of immigrants into mainstream American culture and seeking legislation for the adoption of English as the national language. Chavez's ideology is embodied in her writings, including a memoir, *An Unlikely Conservative: The Transformation of an Ex-Liberal* (2002) and *Out of the Barrio: Toward a New Politics of Hispanic Assimilation* (1991). Chavez remains active in politics and serves as an analyst to the Fox News Channel.

Multiculturalism is on the advance, everywhere from President Clinton's cabinet to corporate boardrooms to public-school classrooms. If you believe the multiculturalists' propaganda, whites are on the verge of becoming a minority in the United States. The multiculturalists predict that this demographic shift will fundamentally change American culture— indeed destroy the very idea that America *has* a single, unified culture. They aren't taking any chances, however. They have enlisted the help of government, corporate leaders, the media, and the education establishment in waging a cultural revolution. But has America truly become a

Linda Chavez, "Demystifying Multiculturalism" from *National Review*, February 21, 1994. Copyright © 1994 by National Review, Inc. Reprinted by permission of National Review.

multicultural nation? And if not, will those who capitulate to these demands create a self-fulfilling prophecy?

At the heart of the argument is the assumption that the white population is rapidly declining in relation to the non-white population. A 1987 Hudson Institute report helped catapult this claim to national prominence. The study, *Workforce 2000*, estimated that by the turn of the century only 15 percent of new workers would be white males. The figure was widely interpreted to mean that whites were about to become a minority in the workplace—and in the country.

In fact, white males will still constitute about 45 percent—a plurality—of the workforce in the year 2000. The proportion of white men in the workforce *is* declining—it was nearly 51 percent in 1980—but primarily because the proportion of white women is growing. They will make up 39 percent of the workforce within ten years, according to government projections, up from 36 percent in 1980. Together, white men and women will account for 84 percent of all workers by 2000—hardly a minority share.

But the business world is behaving as if a demographic tidal wave is about to hit. A whole new industry of "diversity professionals" has emerged to help managers cope with the expected deluge of nonwhite workers. These consultants are paid as much as $10,000 a day to train managers to "value diversity," a term so ubiquitous that it has appeared in more than seven hundred articles in major newspapers in the last three years. According to Heather MacDonald in *The New Republic*, about half of Fortune 500 corporations now employ someone responsible for "diversity."

What precisely does valuing diversity mean? The underlying assumptions seem to be that non-whites are so different from whites that employers must make major changes to accommodate them, and that white workers will be naturally resistant to including non-whites in their ranks. Public-opinion polls don't bear out the latter. They show that support among whites for equal job opportunity for blacks is extraordinarily high, exceeding 90 percent as early as 1975. As for accommodating different cultures, the problem is not culture—or race, or ethnicity—but education. Many young people, in particular, are poorly prepared for work, and the problem is most severe among those who attended inner-city schools, most of them blacks and Hispanics.

Nevertheless, multiculturalists insist on treating race and ethnicity as if they were synonymous with culture. They presume that skin color and national origin, which are immutable traits, determine values, mores, language, and other cultural attributes, which, of course, are learned. In the multiculturalists' world view, African-Americans, Puerto Ricans, or

128

Chinese-Americans living in New York City have more in common with persons of their ancestral group living in Lagos or San Juan or Hong Kong than they do with other New Yorkers who are white. Culture becomes a fixed entity, transmitted, as it were, in the genes, rather than through experience. Thus, "Afrocentricity," a variant of multiculturalism, is "a way of being," its exponents claim. According to a leader of the Afrocentric education movement, Molefi Kete Asante, there is "one African Cultural System manifested in diversities," whether one speaks of Afro-Brazilians, Cubans, or Nigerians (or, presumably, African-Americans). Exactly how this differs from the traditional racist notion that all blacks (Jews, Mexicans, Chinese, etc.) think alike is unclear. What is clear is that the multiculturalists have abandoned the ideal that all persons should be judged by the content of their character, not the color of their skin. Indeed, the multiculturalists seem to believe that a person's character is *determined* by the color of his skin and by his ancestry.

Such convictions lead multiculturalists to conclude that, again in the words of Asante, "[T]here is no common American culture." The logic is simple, but wrong-headed: Since Americans (or more often, their forebears) hail from many different places, each of which has its own specific culture, the argument goes, America must be multicultural. And it is becoming more so every day as new immigrants bring their cultures with them.

Indeed, multiculturalists hope to ride the immigrant wave to greater power and influence. They have certainly done so in education. Some 2.3 million children who cannot speak English well now attend public school, an increase of 1 million in the last seven years. Multicultural advocates cite the presence of such children to demand bilingual education and other multicultural services. The Los Angeles Unified School District alone currently offers instruction in Spanish, Armenian, Korean, Cantonese, Tagalog, Russian, and Japanese. Federal and state governments now spend literally billions of dollars on these programs.

Ironically, the multiculturalists' emphasis on education undercuts their argument that culture is inextricable from race or national origin. They are acutely aware just how fragile cultural identification is; why else are they so adamant about reinforcing it? Multiculturalists insist on teaching immigrant children in their native language, instructing them in the history and customs of their native land and imbuing them with reverence for their ancestral heroes, lest these youngsters be seduced by American culture. Far from losing faith in the power of assimilation, they seem to believe that without a heavy dose of multicultural indoctrination, immigrants won't be able to resist it. And they're right, though it remains to be seen whether anything, including the multiculturalists' crude methods, will ultimately detour immigrants from the assimilation path.

The urge to assimilate has traditionally been overpowering in the United   10
States, especially among the children of immigrants. Only groups that
maintain strict rules against intermarriage with persons outside the group,
such as Orthodox Jews and the Amish, have ever succeeded in preserving
distinct, full-blown cultures within American society. (It is interesting to
note that religion seems to be a more effective deterrent to full assimilation
than the secular elements of culture, including language.) Although many
Americans worry that Hispanic immigrants, for example, are not learning
English and will therefore fail to assimilate into the American mainstream,
little evidence supports the case. By the third generation in the United
States, a majority of Hispanics, like other ethnic groups, speak only
English and are closer to other Americans on most measures of social and
economic status than they are to Hispanic immigrants. On one of the most
rigorous gauges of assimilation—intermarriage—Hispanics rank high.
About one-third of young third-generation Hispanics marry non-Hispanic
whites, a pattern similar to that of young Asians. Even for blacks, exogamy
rates, which have been quite low historically, are going up; about 3 percent
of blacks now marry outside their group.

The impetus for multiculturalism is not coming from immigrants, but
from their more affluent and assimilated native-born counterparts. The
proponents are most often the elite—the best educated and most successful members of their respective racial and ethnic groups. College
campuses, where the most radical displays of multiculturalism take place,
are fertile recruiting grounds. Last May, for example, a group of Mexican-
American students at UCLA, frustrated that the university would not ele-
vate the school's 23-year-old Chicano-studies program to full department
status, stormed the faculty center, breaking windows and furniture and
causing half a million dollars in damage. The same month, a group of
Asian-American students at UC Irvine went on a hunger strike to pressure
administrators into hiring more professors of Asian-American studies.
These were not immigrants, or even, by and large, disadvantaged students, but middle-class beneficiaries of their parents' or grandparents'
successful assimilation to the American mainstream.

The protestors' quest had almost nothing to do with any effort to
maintain their ethnic identity. For the most part, such students probably
never thought of themselves as anything but American before they
entered college. A recent study of minority students at the University of
California at Berkeley found that most Hispanic and Asian students "discovered" their ethnic identity after they arrived on campus—when they
also discovered that they were victims of systematic discrimination. As
one Mexican-American freshman summed it up, she was "unaware of
the things that have been going on with our people, all the injustice

we've suffered, how the world really is. I thought racism didn't exist and here, you know, it just comes to light." The researchers added that "students of color" had difficulty pinpointing exactly what constituted this "subtle form of the new racism.... There was much talk about certain facial expressions, or the way people look, and how white students 'take over the class' and speak past you.'"

Whatever their new-found victim status, these students look amazingly like other Americans on most indices. For example, the median family income of Mexican-American students at Berkeley in 1989 was $32,500, slightly above the national median for all Americans that year, $32,191; and 17 percent of those students came from families that earned more than $75,000 a year, even though they were admitted to the university under affirmative-action programs (presumably because they suffered some educational disadvantage attributed to their ethnicity).

Affirmative-action programs make less and less sense as discrimination diminishes in this society—which it indisputably has—and as minorities improve their economic status. Racial and ethnic identity, too, might wane if there weren't such aggressive efforts to ensure that this not happen. The multiculturalists know they risk losing their constituency if young blacks, Hispanics, Asians, and others don't maintain strong racial and ethnic affiliations. Younger generations must be *trained* to think of themselves as members of oppressed minority groups entitled to special treatment. And the government provides both the incentives and the money to ensure that this happens. Meanwhile, the main beneficiaries are the multicultural professionals, who often earn exorbitant incomes peddling identity.

One particularly egregious example occurred in the District of   15 Columbia last fall. The school system paid $250,000 to a husband-and-wife consultant team to produce an Afrocentric study guide to be used in a single public elementary school. Controversy erupted after the two spent three years and produced only a five-page outline. Although the husband had previously taught at Howard University, the wife's chief credential was a master's degree from an unaccredited "university" which she and her husband had founded. When the *Washington Post* criticized the school superintendent for his handling of the affair, he called a press conference to defend the couple, who promptly claimed they were the victims of a racist vendetta.

D.C. students rank lowest in the nation in math and fourth-lowest in verbal achievement; one can only wonder what $250,000 in tutoring at one school might have done. Instead, the students were treated to bulletin boards in the classrooms proclaiming on their behalf: "We are the sons and daughters of The Most High. We are the princes and princesses of African kings and queens. We are the descendants of our black ancestors.

We are black and we are proud." This incident is not unique. Thousands of consultants with little or no real expertise sell feel-good programs to school systems across the nation.

Multiculturalism is not a grassroots movement. It was created, nurtured, and expanded through government policy. Without the expenditure of vast sums of public money, it would wither away and die. That is not to say that ethnic communities would disappear from the American scene or that groups would not retain some attachment to their ancestral roots. American assimilation has always entailed some give and take, and American culture has been enriched by what individual groups brought to it. The distinguishing characteristic of American culture is its ability to incorporate so many disparate groups, creating a new whole from the many parts. What could be more American, for example, than jazz and film, two distinctive art forms created, respectively, by blacks and immigrant Jews but which all Americans think of as their own? But in the past, government—especially public schools—saw it as a duty to try to bring newcomers into the fold by teaching them English, by introducing them to the great American heroes as their own, by instilling respect for American institutions. Lately, we have nearly reversed course, treating each group, new and old, as if what is most important is to preserve its separate identity and space.

It is easy to blame the ideologues and radicals who are pushing the disuniting of America, to use Arthur Schlesinger's phrase, but the real culprits are those who provide multiculturalists the money and the access to press their cause. Without the acquiescence of policy-makers and ordinary citizens, multiculturalism would be no threat. Unfortunately, most major institutions have little stomach for resisting the multicultural impulse—and many seem eager to comply with whatever demands the multiculturalists make. Americans should have learned by now that policy matters. We have only to look at the failure of our welfare and crime policies to know that providing perverse incentives can change the way individuals behave—for the worse. Who is to say that if we pour enough money into dividing Americans we won't succeed?

SHERMAN ALEXIE [b. 1966]

Postcards to Columbus

Of Spokane/Coeur d'Alene Native American descent, **Sherman Alexie** (b. 1966) was born on the Spokane Indian Reservation in Wellpinit, Washington. He earned his B.A. from Washington State University in Pullman. He has published eight books of poetry and several novels and collections of short fiction, including *The Lone Ranger and Tonto Fistfight in Heaven* (1993). He based the script for the film *Smoke Signals* on one of his short stories. "Postcards to Columbus" reflects Alexie's concern for the devaluation of his native culture.

Beginning at the front door of the White House, travel west
for 500 years, pass through small towns and house fires, ignore
hitchhikers and stranded motorists, until you find yourself
back at the beginning of this journey, this history and country

folded over itself like a Mobius strip. Christopher Columbus   5
where have you been? Lost between Laramie and San Francisco
or in the reservation HUD house, building a better mousetrap?
Seymour saw you shooting free throws behind the Tribal School

in a thunderstorm. Didn't you know lightning strikes the earth
800 times a second? But, Columbus, how could you ever imagine   10
how often our lives change? *Electricity is lightning pretending*
to be permanent and when the Indian child pushes the paper clip

into the electrical outlet, it's applied science, insane economics
of supply and demand, the completion of a 20th century circuit.
Christopher Columbus, you are the most successful real estate agent   15
who ever lived, sold acres and acres of myth, a house built on stilts

above the river salmon travel by genetic memory. Beneath the burden
of 15,000 years my tribe celebrated this country's 200th birthday
by refusing to speak English and we'll honor the 500th anniversary
of your invasion, Columbus, by driving blindfolded cross-country   20

naming the first tree we destroy *America*. We'll make the first guardrail we crash through our national symbol. Our flag will be a white sheet stained with blood and piss. Columbus, can you hear me over white noise of your television set? Can you hear ghosts of drums approaching?

[1993]

William McFarlane Notman, *Sitting Bull and Buffalo Bill,* **1885.** A promotional image for Buffalo Bill Cody's Wild West Show features Cody, who made his reputation as an Indian fighter, posing with Sitting Bull, who led the Sioux to victory over General George Custer's troops at the Battle of Little Bighorn in 1876. After years of exile in Canada, Sitting Bull returned to the United States and, for a few months, was a paid attraction in Cody's show. (Library of Congress Prints and Photographs Division, LC# USZ62-21207.)

JANE TOMPKINS

"Indians": Textualism, Morality, and the Problem of History

Jane Tompkins earned degrees from Bryn Mawr (B.A. magna cum laude) and Yale University (M.A. and Ph.D.). For years, she followed a traditional academic career path, holding teaching positions at Columbia University, the University of California, and Duke University. In mid-career, Tompkins encountered a personal crisis that precipitated a transformation in her lifestyle and thinking. She began to explore Buddhist meditation, karate, and the philosophy of revolutionary educational thinkers such as Paulo Freire, the radical Brazilian pedagogue. In response, Tompkins embraced an essentially student-centered pedagogy, encouraging students to plan their own syllabi, lead discussions, and determine their own grades. Tompkins describes her philosophy in *A Life in School: What the Teacher Learned* (1997), a work which has garnered both criticism and praise from her colleagues. Her earlier works include *Sensational Designs: The Cultural Work of American Fiction, 1770–1986* (1985) and *West of Everything: The Inner Life of Westerns* (1992). Tompkins' essay "'Indians': Textualism, Morality, and the Problem of History" examines the biases of historians and the impact of ideology on the construction of history.

When I was growing up in New York City, my parents used to take me to an event in Inwood Park at which Indians—real American Indians dressed in feathers and blankets — could be seen and touched by children like me. This event was always a disappointment. It was more fun to imagine that you *were* an Indian in one of the caves in Inwood Park than to shake the hand of an old man in a headdress who was not overwhelmed at the opportunity of meeting you. After staring at the Indians for a while, we would take a walk in the woods where the caves were, and once I asked my mother if the remains of a fire I had seen in one of them might have been left by the original inhabitants. After that, wandering up some stone steps cut into the side of the hill, I imagined I was a princess in a rude castle. My Indians, like my princesses, were creatures totally of the imagination, and I did not care to have any real exemplars interfering with what I already knew.

I already knew about Indians from having read about them in school. Over and over we were told the story of how Peter Minuit had bought Manhattan Island from the Indians for twenty-four dollars' worth of glass beads. And it was a story we didn't mind hearing because it gave us the rare pleasure of having someone to feel superior to, since the poor Indians had not known (as we eight-year-olds did) how valuable a piece of property Manhattan Island would become. Generally, much was made of the Indian presence in Manhattan; a poem in one of our readers began: "Where we walk to school today/Indian children used to play," and we were encouraged to write poetry on this topic ourselves. So I had a fairly rich relationship with Indians before I ever met the unprepossessing people in Inwood Park. I felt that I had a lot in common with them. They, too, liked animals (they were often named after animals); they, too, made mistakes—they liked the brightly colored trinkets of little value that the white men were always offering them; they were handsome, warlike, and brave and had led an exciting, romantic life in the forest long ago, a life such as I dreamed of leading myself. I felt lucky to be living in one of the places where they had definitely been. Never mind where they were or what they were doing now.

My story stands for the relationship most non-Indians have to the people who first populated this continent, a relationship characterized by narcissistic fantasies of freedom and adventure, of a life lived closer to nature and to spirit than the life we lead now. As Vine Deloria, Jr., has pointed out, the American Indian Movement in the early seventies couldn't get people to pay attention to what was happening to Indians who were alive in the present, so powerful was this country's infatuation with people who wore loincloths, lived in tepees, and roamed the plains and forests long ago.[1] The present essay, like these fantasies, doesn't have much to do with actual Indians, though its subject matter is the histories of European-Indian relations in seventeenth-century New England. In a sense, my encounter with Indians as an adult doing "research" replicates the childhood one, for while I started out to learn about Indians, I ended up preoccupied with a problem of my own.

This essay enacts a particular instance of the challenge poststructuralism poses to the study of history. In simpler language, it concerns the difference that point of view makes when people are giving accounts of events, whether at first or second hand. The problem is that if all accounts of events are determined through and through by the observer's frame of reference, then one will never know, in any given case, what really happened.

I encountered this problem in concrete terms while preparing to teach a 5
course in colonial American literature. I'd set out to learn what I could
about the Puritans' relations with American Indians. All I wanted was a
general idea of what had happened between the English settlers and the
natives in seventeenth-century New England; poststructuralism and its
dilemmas were the furthest thing from my mind. I began, more or less
automatically, with Perry Miller, who hardly mentions the Indians at all,
then proceeded to the work of historians who had dealt exclusively with
the European-Indian encounter. At first, it was a question of deciding
which of these authors to believe, for it quickly became apparent that
there was no unanimity on the subject. As I read on, however, I discovered
that the problem was more complicated than deciding whose version of
events was correct. Some of the conflicting accounts were not simply contradictory, they were completely incommensurable, in that their assumptions about what counted as a valid approach to the subject, and what the
subject itself was, diverged in fundamental ways. Faced with an array of
mutually irreconcilable points of view, points of view which determined
what was being discussed as well as the terms of the discussion, I decided
to turn to primary sources for clarification, only to discover that the primary sources reproduced the problem all over again. I found myself, in
other words, in an epistemological quandary, not only unable to decide
among conflicting versions of events but also unable to believe that any
such decision could, in principle, be made. It was a moral quandary as
well. Knowledge of what really happened when the Europeans and the
Indians first met seemed particularly important, since the result of that
encounter was virtual genocide. This was the kind of past "mistake"
which, presumably, we studied history in order to avoid repeating. If
studying history couldn't put us in touch with actual events and their
causes, then what was to prevent such atrocities from happening again?

For a while, I remained at this impasse. But through analyzing the
process by which I had reached it, I eventually arrived at an understanding
which seemed to offer a way out. This essay records the concrete experience
of meeting and solving the difficulty I have just described (as an abstract
problem, I thought I had solved it long ago). My purpose is not to throw
new light on antifoundationalist epistemology—the solution I reached is
not a new one—but to dramatize and expose the troubles antifoundational-
ism gets you into when you meet it, so to speak, in the road.

◆◆◆

My research began with Perry Miller. Early in the preface to *Errand
into the Wilderness,* while explaining how he came to write his history of
the New England mind, Miller writes a sentence that stopped me dead.

He says that what fascinated him as a young man about his country's history was "the massive narrative of the movement of European culture into the vacant wilderness of America."[2] "Vacant?" Miller, writing in 1956, doesn't pause over the word "vacant," but to people who read his preface thirty years later, the word is shocking. In what circumstances could someone proposing to write a history of colonial New England *not* take account of the Indian presence there?

The rest of Miller's preface supplies an answer to this question, if one takes the trouble to piece together its details. Miller explains that as a young man, jealous of older compatriots who had had the luck to fight in World War I, he had gone to Africa in search of adventure. "The adventures that Africa afforded," he writes, "were tawdry enough, but it became the setting for a sudden epiphany" (p. vii). "It was given to me," he writes, "disconsolate on the edge of a jungle of central Africa, to have thrust upon me the mission of expounding what I took to be the innermost propulsion of the United States, while supervising, in that barbaric tropic, the unloading of drums of case oil flowing out of the inexhaustible wilderness of America" (p. viii). Miller's picture of himself on the banks of the Congo furnishes a key to the kind of history he will write and to his mental image of a vacant wilderness; it explains why it was just there, under precisely these conditions, that he should have had his epiphany.

The fuel drums stand, in Miller's mind, for the popular misconception of what this country is about. They are "tangible symbols of [America's] appalling power," a power that everyone but Miller takes for the ultimate reality (p. ix). To Miller, "the mind of man is the basic factor in human history," and he will plead, all unaccommodated as he is among the fuel drums, for the intellect — the intellect for which his fellow historians, with their chapters on "stoves or bathtubs, or tax laws," "the Wilmot Proviso" and "the chain store," "have so little respect" (p. viii, ix). His preface seethes with a hatred of the merely physical and mechanical, and this hatred, which is really a form of moral outrage, explains not only the contempt with which he mentions the stoves and bathtubs but also the nature of his experience in Africa and its relationship to the "massive narrative" he will write.

Miller's experiences in Africa are "tawdry," his tropic is barbaric 10 because the jungle he stands on the edge of means nothing to him, no more, indeed something less, than the case oil. It is the nothingness of Africa that precipitates his vision. It is the barbarity of the "dark continent," the obvious (but superficial) parallelism between the jungle at Matadi and America's "vacant wilderness" that releases in Miller the desire to define and vindicate his country's cultural identity. To the young Miller, colonial Africa and colonial America are—but for

139

the history he will bring to light — mirror images of one another. And what he fails to see in the one landscape is the same thing he overlooks in the other: the human beings who people it. As Miller stood with his back to the jungle, thinking about the role of mind in human history, his failure to see that the land into which European culture had moved was not vacant but already occupied by a varied and numerous population, is of a piece with his failure, in his portrait of himself at Matadi, to notice *who* was carrying the fuel drums he was supervising the unloading of.

The point is crucial because it suggests that what is invisible to the historian in his own historical moment remains invisible when he turns his gaze to the past. It isn't that Miller didn't "see" the black men, in a literal sense, any more than it's the case that when he looked back he didn't "see" the Indians, in the sense of not realizing they were there. Rather, it's that neither the Indians nor the blacks *counted* for him, in a fundamental way. The way in which Indians can be seen but not counted is illustrated by an entry in Governor John Winthrop's journal, three hundred years before, when he recorded that there had been a great storm with high winds "yet through God's great mercy it did no hurt, but only killed one Indian with the fall of a tree."[3] The juxtaposition suggests that Miller shared with Winthrop a certain colonial point of view, a point of view from which Indians, though present, do not finally matter.

A book entitled *New England Frontier: Puritans and Indians, 1620–1675*, written by Alden Vaughan and published in 1965, promised to rectify Miller's omission. In the outpouring of work on the European-Indian encounter that began in the early sixties, this book is the first major landmark, and to a neophyte it seems definitive. Vaughan acknowledges the absence of Indian sources and emphasizes his use of materials which catch the Puritans "off guard."[4] His announced conclusion that "the New England Puritans followed a remarkably humane, considerate, and just policy in their dealings with the Indians" seems supported by the scope, documentation, and methodicalness of his project (*NEF*, p. vii). The author's fair-mindedness and equanimity seem everywhere apparent, so that when he asserts "the history of interracial relations from the arrival of the Pilgrims to the outbreak of King Philip's War is a credit to the integrity of both peoples," one is positively reassured (*NEF*, p. viii).

But these impressions do not survive an admission that comes late in the book, when, in the course of explaining why works like Helen Hunt Jackson's *Century of Dishonor* had spread misconceptions about Puritan treatment of the Indians, Vaughan finally lays his own cards on the table.

The root of the misunderstanding [about Puritans and Indians] . . . lie[s] in a failure to recognize the nature of the two societies that met in seventeenth century New England. One was unified, visionary, disciplined, and dynamic. The other was divided, self-satisfied, undisciplined, and static. It would be unreasonable to expect that such societies could live side by side indefinitely with no penetration of the more fragmented and passive by the more consolidated and active. What resulted, then, was not—as many have held—a clash of dissimilar ways of life, but rather the expansion of one into the areas in which the other was lacking. [*NEF,* p. 323]

From our present vantage point, these remarks seem culturally biased to an incredible degree, not to mention inaccurate: was Puritan society unified? If so, how does one account for its internal dissensions and obsessive need to cast out deviants? Is "unity" necessarily a positive culture trait? From what standpoint can one say that American Indians were neither disciplined nor visionary, when both these characteristics loom so large in the ethnographies? Is it an accident that ways of describing cultural strength and weakness coincide with gender stereotypes—active/ passive, and so on? Why is one culture said to "penetrate" the other? Why is the "other" described in terms of "lack"?

Vaughan's fundamental categories of apprehension and judgment will not withstand even the most cursory inspection. For what looked like evenhandedness when he was writing *New England Frontier* does not look that way anymore. In his introduction to *New Directions in American Intellectual History,* John Higham writes that by the end of the sixties

> the entire conceptual foundation on which [this sort of work] rested [had] crumbled away. . . . Simultaneously, in sociology, anthropology, and history, two working assumptions . . . came under withering attack: first, the assumption that societies tend to be integrated, and second, that a shared culture maintains that integration. . . . By the late 1960s all claims issued in the name of an "American mind". . . were subject to drastic skepticism.[5]

"Clearly," Higham continues, "the sociocultural upheaval of the sixties created the occasion" for this reaction.[6] Vaughan's book, it seemed, could only have been written before the events of the sixties had sensitized scholars to questions of race and ethnicity. It came as no surprise, therefore, that ten years later there appeared a study of European-Indian relations which reflected the new awareness of social issues the sixties had engendered. And it offered an entirely different picture of the European-Indian encounter.

Francis Jennings's *The Invasion of America* (1975) rips wide open the idea that the Puritans were humane and considerate in their dealings with the Indians. In Jennings's account, even more massively documented than Vaughan's, the early settlers lied to the Indians, stole from them, murdered them, scalped them, captured them, tortured them, raped them, sold them into slavery, confiscated their land, destroyed their crops, burned their homes, scattered their possessions, gave them alcohol, undermined their systems of belief, and infected them with diseases that wiped out ninety percent of their numbers within the first hundred years after contact.[7]

Jennings mounts an all-out attack on the essential decency of the Puritan leadership and their apologists in the twentieth century. The Pequot War, which previous historians had described as an attempt on the part of Massachusetts Bay to protect itself from the fiercest of the New England tribes, becomes, in Jennings's painstakingly researched account, a deliberate war of extermination, waged by whites against Indians. It starts with trumped-up charges, is carried on through a series of increasingly bloody reprisals, and ends in the massacre of scores of Indian men, women, and children, all so that Massachusetts Bay could gain political and economic control of the southern Connecticut Valley. When one reads this and then turns over the page and sees a reproduction of the Bay Colony seal, which depicts an Indian from whose mouth issue the words "Come over and help us," the effect is shattering.[8]

But even so powerful an argument as Jennings's did not remain unshaken by subsequent work. Reading on, I discovered that if the events of the sixties had revolutionized the study of European-Indian relations, the events of the seventies produced yet another transformation. The American Indian Movement, and in particular the founding of the Native American Rights Fund in 1971 to finance Indian litigation, and a court decision in 1975 which gave the tribes the right to seek redress for past injustices in federal court, created a climate within which historians began to focus on the Indians themselves. "Almost simultaneously," writes James Axtell, "frontier and colonial historians began to discover the necessity of considering the American natives as real determinants of history and the utility of ethnohistory as a way of ensuring parity of focus and impartiality of judgment."[9] In Miller, Indians had been simply beneath notice; in Vaughan, they belonged to an inferior culture; and in Jennings, they were the more or less innocent prey of power-hungry whites. But in the most original and provocative of the ethnohistories, Calvin Martin's *Keepers of the Game*, Indians became complicated, purposeful human beings, whose lives were spiritually motivated to a high degree.[10] Their relationship to the animals they hunted, to the natural environment, and to the whites with whom they traded became intelligible within a system of beliefs that formed the basis for an entirely new perspective on the European-Indian encounter.

Within the broader question of why European contact had such a devastating effect on the Indians, Martin's specific aim is to determine why Indians participated in the fur trade which ultimately led them to the brink of annihilation. The standard answer to this question had always been that once the Indian was introduced to European guns, copper kettles, woolen blankets, and the like, he literally couldn't keep his hands off them. In order to acquire these coveted items, he decimated the animal populations on which his survival depended. In short, the Indian's motivation in participating in the fur trade was assumed to be the same as the white European's—a desire to accumulate material goods. In direct opposition to this thesis, Martin argues that the reason why Indians ruthlessly exploited their own resources had nothing to do with supply and demand, but stemmed rather from a breakdown of the cosmic worldview that tied them to the game they killed in a spiritual relationship of parity and mutual obligation.

The hunt, according to Martin, was conceived not primarily as a phys- 20 ical activity but as a spiritual quest, in which the spirit of the hunter must overmaster the spirit of the game animal before the kill can take place. The animal, in effect, *allows* itself to be found and killed, once the hunter has mastered its spirit. The hunter prepared himself through rituals of fasting, sweating, or dreaming which revealed the identity of his prey and where he can find it. The physical act of killing is the least important element in the process. Once the animal is killed, eaten, and its parts used for clothing or implements, its remains must be disposed of in ritually prescribed fashion, or the game boss, the "keeper" of that species, will not permit more animals to be killed. The relationship between Indians and animals, then, is contractual; each side must hold up its end of the bargain, or no further transactions can occur.

What happened, according to Martin, was that as a result of diseases introduced into the animal population by Europeans, the game suddenly disappeared, began to act in inexplicable ways, or sickened and died in plain view, and communicated their diseases to the Indians. The Indians, consequently, believed that their compact with the animals had been broken and that the keepers of the game, the tutelary spirits of each animal species whom they had been so careful to propitiate, had betrayed them. And when missionization, wars with the Europeans, and displacement from their tribal lands had further weakened Indian society and its belief structure, the Indians, no longer restrained by religious sanctions, in effect, turned on the animals in a holy war of revenge.

Whether or not Martin's specific claim about the "holy war" was correct, his analysis made it clear to me that, given the Indians' understanding of economic, religious, and physical processes, an Indian account of what transpired when the European settlers arrived here would look nothing like our own. Their (potential, unwritten) history of the conflict could bear only a marginal resemblance to Eurocentric views. I began to think that the key to understanding European-Indian relations was to see them as an encounter between wholly disparate cultures, and that therefore either defending or attacking the colonists was beside the point since, given the cultural disparity between the two groups, conflict was inevitable and in large part a product of mutual misunderstanding.

But three years after Martin's book appeared, Shepard Krech III edited a collection of seven essays called *Indians, Animals, and the Fur Trade*, attacking Martin's entire project. Here the authors argued that we don't need an ideological or religious explanation for the fur trade. As Charles Hudson writes,

> The Southeastern Indians slaughtered deer (and were prompted to enslave and kill each other) because of their position on the outer fringes of an expanding modern world-system. . . . In the modern world-system there is a core region which establishes *economic* relations with its colonial periphery. . . . If the Indians could not produce commodities, they were on the road to cultural extinction. . . . To maximize his chances for survival, an eighteenth-century Southeastern Indian had to . . . live in the interior, out of range of European cattle, forestry, and agriculture. . . . He had to produce a commodity which was valuable enough to earn him some protection from English slavers.[11]

Though we are talking here about Southeastern Indians, rather than the subarctic and Northeastern tribes Martin studied, what really accounts for these divergent explanations of why Indians slaughtered the game are the assumptions that underlie them. Martin believes that the Indians acted on the basis of perceptions made available to them by their own cosmology; that is, he explains their behavior as the Indians themselves would have explained it (insofar as he can), using a logic and a set of values that are not Eurocentric but derived from within Amerindian culture. Hudson, on the other hand, insists that the Indians' own beliefs are irrelevant to an explanation of how they acted, which can only be understood, as far as he is concerned, in the terms of a Western materialist economic and political analysis. Martin and Hudson, in short, don't agree on what counts as an explanation, and this disagreement sheds light on the preceding accounts as well. From this standpoint, we can see that Vaughan, who thought that the Puritans were superior to the Indians, and Jennings, who thought the reverse, are both, like Hudson, using Eurocentric criteria of description and evaluation. While all three critics (Vaughan, Jennings, and Hudson) acknowledge that Indians and Europeans behave differently from one another, the behavior differs, as it were, within the order of the same: all three assume, though only Hudson makes the assumption explicit, that an understanding of relations between the Europeans and the Indians must be elaborated in European terms. In Martin's analysis, however, what we have are not only two different sets of behavior but two incommensurable ways of describing and assigning meaning to events. This difference at the level of explanation calls into question the possibility of obtaining any theory-independent account of interaction between Indians and Europeans.

At this point, dismayed and confused by the wildly divergent views of colonial history the twentieth-century historians had provided, I decided to look at some primary materials. I thought, perhaps, if I looked at some firsthand accounts and at some scholars looking at those accounts, it would be possible to decide which experts were right and which were wrong by comparing their views with the evidence. Captivity narratives seemed a good place to begin, since it was logical to suppose that the records left by whites who had been captured by Indians would furnish the sort of firsthand information I wanted.

I began with two fascinating essays based on these materials written by the ethnohistorian James Axtell, "The White Indians of Colonial America" and "The Scholastic Philosophy of the Wilderness."[12] These essays suggest that it would have been a privilege to be captured by North American Indians and taken off to Canada to dwell in a wigwam for the rest of one's life. Axtell's reconstruction of the process by which Indians taught European captives to feel comfortable in the wilderness, first taking their shoes away and giving them moccasins, carrying the children on their backs, sharing the scanty food supply equally, ceremonially cleansing them of their old identities, giving them Indian clothes and jewelry, assiduously teaching them the Indian language, finally adopting them into their families, and even visiting them after many years if, as sometimes happened, they were restored to white society—all of this creates a compelling portrait of Indian culture and helps to explain the extraordinary attraction that Indian culture apparently exercised over Europeans.

But, as I had by now come to expect, this beguiling portrait of the Indians' superior humanity is called into question by other writings on Indian captivity—for example, Norman Heard's *White into Red*, whose summation of the comparative treatment of captive children east and west of the Mississippi seems to contradict some of Axtell's conclusions:

> The treatment of captive children seems to have been similar in initial stages. . . . Most children were treated brutally at the time of capture.

145

Babies and toddlers usually were killed immediately and other small children would be dispatched during the rapid retreat to the Indian villages if they cried, failed to keep the pace, or otherwise indicated a lack of fortitude needed to become a worthy member of the tribe. Upon reaching the village, the child might face such ordeals as running the gauntlet or dancing in the center of a throng of threatening Indians. The prisoner might be so seriously injured at this time that he would no longer be acceptable for adoption.[13]

One account which Heard reprints is particularly arresting. A young girl captured by the Comanches who had not been adopted into a family but used as a slave had been peculiarly mistreated. When they wanted to wake her up the family she belonged to would take a burning brand from the fire and touch it to her nose. When she was returned to her parents, the flesh of her nose was completely burned away, exposing the bone.[14]

Since the pictures drawn by Heard and Axtell were in certain respects irreconcilable, it made sense to turn to a firsthand account to see how the Indians treated their captives in a particular instance. Mary Rowlandson's "The Soveraignty and Goodness of God," published in Boston around 1680, suggested itself because it was so widely read and had set the pattern for later narratives. Rowlandson interprets her captivity as God's punishment on her for failing to keep the Sabbath properly on several occasions. She sees everything that happens to her as a sign from God. When the Indians are kind to her, she attributes her good fortune to divine Providence; when they are cruel, she blames her captors. But beyond the question of how Rowlandson interprets events is the question of what she saw in the first place and what she considered worth reporting. The following passage, with its abrupt shifts of focus and peculiar emphases, makes it hard to see her testimony as evidence of anything other than the Puritan point of view:

Then my heart began to fail: and I fell weeping, which was the first time to my remembrance, that I wept before them. Although I had met with so much Affliction, and my heart was many times ready to break, yet could I not shed one tear in their sight: but rather had been all this while in a maze, and like one astonished: but not I may say as, Psal. 137.1. *By the Rivers of Babylon, there we sate down; yea, we wept when we remembered Zion.* There one of them asked me, why I wept, I could hardly tell what to say: yet I answered, they would kill me: No, said he, none will hurt you. Then came one of them and gave me two spoon-fulls of Meal to comfort me, and another gave me half a pint of Pease; which was more worth than many Bushels at another time. Then I went to see King Philip, he bade me come in and sit down, and asked me whether I woold smoke it (a usual

Complement nowadayes among Saints and Sinners) but this no way suited me. For though I had formerly used Tobacco, yet I had left it ever since I was first taken. It seems to be a Bait, the Devil layes to make men loose their precious time: I remember with shame, how formerly, when I had taken two or three pipes, I was presently ready for another, such a bewitching thing it is: But I thank God, he has now given me power over it; surely there are many who may be better imployed than to ly sucking a stinking Tobacco-pipe.[15]

Anyone who has ever tried to give up smoking has to sympathize with Rowlandson, but it is nonetheless remarkable, first, that a passage which begins with her weeping openly in front of her captors, and comparing herself to Israel in Babylon, should end with her railing against the vice of tobacco; and, second, that it has not a word to say about King Philip, the leader of the Indians who captured her and mastermind of the campaign that devastated the white population of the English colonies. The fact that Rowlandson has just been introduced to the chief of chiefs makes hardly any impression on her at all. What excites her is a moral issue which was being hotly debated in the seventeenth century: to smoke or not to smoke (Puritans frowned on it, apparently, because it wasted time and presented a fire hazard). What seem to us the peculiar emphases in Rowlandson's relation are not the result of her having *screened out* evidence she couldn't handle, but of her way of constructing the world. She saw what her seventeenth-century English Separatist background made visible. It is when one realizes that the biases of twentieth-century historians like Vaughan or Axtell cannot be corrected for simply by consulting the primary materials, since the primary materials are constructed according to *their* authors' biases, that one begins to envy Miller his vision at Matadi. Not for what he didn't see—the Indian and the black—but for his epistemological confidence.

Since captivity narratives made a poor source of evidence for the nature of European-Indian relations in early New England because they were so relentlessly pietistic, my hope was that a better source of evidence might be writings designed simply to tell Englishmen what the American natives were like. These authors could be presumed to be less severely biased, since they hadn't seen their loved ones killed by Indians or been made to endure the hardships of captivity, and because they weren't writing propaganda calculated to prove that God had delivered his chosen people from the hands of Satan's emissaries.

The problem was that these texts were written with aims no less specific than those of the captivity narratives, though the aims were of a different sort. Here is a passage from William Wood's *New England's Prospect*, published in London in 1634.

To enter into a serious discourse concerning the natural conditions of these Indians might procure admiration from the people of any civilized nations, in regard of their civility and good natures. . . . These Indians are of affable, courteous and well disposed natures, ready to communicate the best of their wealth to the mutual good of one another; . . . so . . . perspicuous is their love . . . that they are as willing to part with a mite in poverty as treasure in plenty. . . . If it were possible to recount the courtesies they have showed the English, since their first arrival in those parts, it would not only steady belief, that they are a loving people, but also win the love of those that never saw them, and wipe off that needless fear that is too deeply rooted in the conceits of many who think them envious and of such rancorous and inhumane dispositions, that they will one day make an end of their English inmates.[16]

However, in a pamphlet published twenty-one years earlier, Alexander Whitaker of Virginia has this to say of the natives:

These naked slaves . . . serve the divell for feare, after a most base manner, sacrificing sometimes (as I have heere heard) their own Children to him. . . . They live naked in bodie, as if their shame of their sinne deserved no covering: Their names are as naked as their bodie: They esteem it a virtue to lie, deceive and steale as their master the divell teacheth to them.[17]

According to Robert Berkhofer in *The White Man's Indian*, these divergent reports can be explained by looking at the authors' motives. A favorable report like Wood's, intended to encourage new emigrants to America, naturally represented Indians as loving and courteous, civilized and generous, in order to allay the fears of prospective colonists. Whitaker, on the other hand, a minister who wishes to convince his readers that the Indians are in need of conversion, paints them as benighted agents of the devil. Berkhofer's commentary constantly implies that white men were to blame for having represented the Indians in the image of their own desires and needs.[18] But the evidence supplied by Rowlandson's narrative, and by the accounts left by early reporters such as Wood and Whitaker, suggests something rather different. Though it is probably true that in certain cases Europeans did consciously tamper with the evidence, in most cases there is no reason to suppose that they did not record faithfully what they saw. And what they saw was not an illusion, was not determined by selfish motives in any narrow sense, but was there by virtue of a *way* of seeing which they could no more consciously manipulate than they could choose not to have been born. At this point, it seemed to me, the ethnocentric bias of the firsthand observers invited an investigation of the cultural situation

148

they spoke from. Karen Kupperman's *Settling with the Indians* (1980) supplied just such an analysis.

Kupperman argues that Englishmen inevitably looked at Indians   35
in exactly the same way that they looked at other Englishmen. For instance, if they looked down on Indians and saw them as people to be exploited, it was not because of racial prejudice or antique notions about savagery, it was because they looked down on ordinary English men and women and saw them as subjects for exploitation as well.[19] According to Kupperman, what concerned these writers most when they described the Indians were the insignia of social class, of rank, and of prestige. Indian faces are virtually never described in the earliest accounts, but clothes and hairstyles, tattoos and jewelry, posture and skin color are. "Early modern Englishmen believed that people can create their own identity, and that therefore one communicates to the world through signals such as dress and other forms of decoration who one is, what group or category one belongs to."[20]

Kupperman's book marks a watershed in writings on European-Indian relations, for it reverses the strategy employed by Martin two years before. Whereas Martin had performed an ethnographic analysis of Indian cosmology in order to explain, from within, the Indians' motives for engaging in the fur trade, Kupperman performs an ethnographic study of seventeenth-century England in order to explain, from within, what motivated Englishmen's behavior. The sympathy and understanding that Martin, Axtell, and others extend to the Indians are extended in Kupperman's work to the English themselves. Rather than giving an account of "what happened" between Indians and Europeans, like Martin, she reconstructs the worldview that gave the experience of one group its content. With her study, scholarship on European-Indian relations comes full circle.

It may well seem to you at this point that, given the tremendous variation among the historical accounts, I had no choice but to end in relativism. If the experience of encountering conflicting versions of the "same" events suggests anything certain it is that the attitude a historian takes up in relation to a given event, the way in which he or she judges and even describes "it"—and the "it" has to go in quotation marks because depending on the perspective, that event either did or did not occur—this stance, these judgments and descriptions are a function of the historian's position in relation to the subject. Miller, standing on the banks of the Congo, couldn't see the black men he was supervising because of his background, his assumptions, values, experiences, goals. Jennings, intent on exposing the distortions introduced into the historical record by Vaughan and his predecessors stretching all the way back to Winthrop, couldn't see that Winthrop and his peers were not racists but only Englishmen who looked at other cultures in the way their own culture had taught them to see one another. The historian can never escape the limitations of his or her own position in history and so inevitably gives an account that is an extension of the circumstances from which it springs. But it seems to me that when one is confronted with this particular succession of stories, cultural and historical relativism is not a position that one can comfortably assume. The phenomena to which these histories testify — conquest, massacre, and genocide, on the one hand; torture, slavery, and murder on the other — cry out for judgment. When faced with claims and counterclaims of this magnitude one feels obligated to reach an understanding of what actually did occur. The dilemma posed by the study of European-Indian relations in early America is that the highly charged nature of the materials demands a moral decisiveness which the succession of conflicting accounts effectively precludes. That is the dilemma I found myself in at the end of this course of reading, and which I eventually came to resolve as follows.

After a while it began to seem to me that there was something wrong with the way I had formulated the problem. The statement that the materials on European-Indian relations were so highly charged that they demanded moral judgment, but that the judgment couldn't be made because all possible descriptions of what happened were biased, seemed to contain an internal contradiction. The statement implied that in order to make a moral judgment about something, you have to know something else first — namely, the facts of the case you're being called upon to judge. My complaint was that their perspectival nature would disqualify any facts I might encounter and that therefore I couldn't judge. But to say as I did that the materials I had read were "highly charged" and therefore demanded judgment suggests both that I was reacting to something real — to some facts — *and* that I had judged them. Perhaps I wasn't so much in the lurch morally or epistemologically as I had thought. If you — or I — react with horror to the story of the girl captured and enslaved by Comanches who touched a firebrand to her nose every time they wanted to wake her up, it's because we read this as a story about cruelty and suffering, and not as a story about the conventions of prisoner exchange or the economics of Comanche life. The *seeing* of the story as a cause for alarm rather than as a droll anecdote or a piece of curious information is evidence of values we already hold, of judgments already made, of facts already perceived as facts.

My problem presupposed that I couldn't judge because I didn't know what the facts were. All I had, or could have, was a series of different perspectives, and so nothing that would count as an authoritative source on which moral judgments could be based. But, as I have just shown, I did judge, and that is because, as I now think, I did have some facts. I seemed to accept as facts that ninety percent of the native American population of New England died after the first hundred years of contact, that tribes in eastern Canada and the northeastern United States had a compact with the game they killed, that Comanches had subjected a captive girl to casual cruelty, that King Philip smoked a pipe, and so on. It was only where different versions of the same event came into conflict that I doubted the text was a record of something real. And even then, there was no question about certain major catastrophes. I believed that four hundred Pequots were killed near Saybrook, that Winthrop was the Governor of the Massachusetts Bay Colony when it happened, and so on. My sense that certain events, such as the Pequot War, did occur in no way reflected the indecisiveness that overtook me when I tried to choose among the various historical versions. In fact, the need I felt to make up my mind was impelled by the conviction that certain things *had* happened that shouldn't have happened. Hence it was never the case that "what happened" was completely unknowable or unavailable. It's rather that in the process of reading so many different approaches to the same phenomenon I became aware of the difference in the attitudes that informed these approaches. This awareness of the interests motivating each version cast suspicion over everything, in retrospect, and I ended by claiming that there was nothing I could know. This, I now see, was never really the case. But how did it happen?   40

Someone else, confronted with the same materials, could have decided that one of these historical accounts was correct. Still another person might have decided that more evidence was needed in order to decide among them. Why did I conclude that none of the accounts was accurate because they were all produced from some particular angle of vision? Presumably there was something in my background that enabled me to see the problem in this way. That something, very likely, was poststructuralist theory. I let my discovery that Vaughan was a product of the fifties, Jennings of the sixties, Rowlandson of a Puritan worldview, and so on lead me to the conclusion that all facts are theory dependent because that conclusion was already a thinkable one for me. My inability to come up with a true account was not the product of being situated nowhere; it was the product of certitude that existed *somewhere else*, namely, in contemporary literary theory. Hence, the level at which my indecision came into play was a function of particular beliefs I held. I was never in a position of epistemological indeterminacy, I was never *en abyme*. The idea that all accounts are perspectival seemed to me a superior standpoint from which to view all the versions of "what happened," and to regard with sympathetic condescension any person so

151

old-fashioned and benighted as to believe that there really was some way of arriving at the truth. But this skeptical standpoint was just as firm as any other. The fact that it was also seriously disabling—it prevented me from coming to any conclusion about what I had read—did not render it any less definite.

At this point something is beginning to show itself that has up to now been hidden. The notion that all facts are only facts within a perspective has the effect of emptying statements of their content. Once I had Miller and Vaughan and Jennings, Martin and Hudson, Axtell and Heard, Rowlandson and Wood and Whitaker, and Kupperman; I had Europeans and Indians, ships and canoes, wigwams and log cabins, bows and arrows and muskets, wigs and tattoos, whiskey and corn, rivers and forts, treaties and battles, fire and blood—and then suddenly all I had was a metastatement about perspectives. The effect of bringing perspectivism to bear on history was to wipe out completely the subject matter of history. And it follows that bringing perspectivism to bear in this way on any subject matter would have a similar effect; everything is wiped out and you are left with nothing but a single idea—perspectivism itself.

But—and it is a crucial but—all this is true only if you believe that there is an alternative. As long as you think that there are or should be facts that exist outside of any perspective, then the notion that facts are perspectival will have this disappearing effect on whatever it touches. But if you are convinced that the alternative does not exist, that there really are no facts except as they are embedded in some particular way of seeing the world, then the argument that a set of facts derives from some particular worldview is no longer an argument against that set of facts. If all facts share this characteristic, to say that any one fact is perspectival doesn't change its factual nature in the slightest. It merely reiterates it.

This doesn't mean that you have to accept just anybody's facts. You can show that what someone else asserts to be a fact is false. But it does mean that you can't argue that someone else's facts are not facts *because they are only the product of a perspective,* since this will be true of the facts that you perceive as well. What this means then is that arguments about "what happened" have to proceed much as they did before post-structuralism broke in with all its talk about language-based reality and culturally produced knowledge. Reasons must be given, evidence adduced, authorities cited, analogies drawn. Being aware that all facts are motivated, believing that people are always operating inside some particular interpretive framework or other is a pertinent argument when what is under discussion is the way beliefs are grounded. But it doesn't give one any leverage on the facts of a particular case.[21]

What this means for the problem I've been addressing is that I must piece together the story of European-Indian relations as best I can, believing this version up to a point, that version not at all, another almost entirely, according to what seems reasonable and plausible, given everything else that I know. And this, as I've shown, is what I was already doing in the back of my mind without realizing it, because there was nothing else I *could* do. If the accounts don't fit together neatly, that is not a reason for rejecting them all in favor of a metadiscourse about epistemology; on the contrary, one encounters contradictory facts and divergent points of view in practically every phase of life, from deciding whom to marry to choosing the right brand of cat food, and one decides as best one can given the evidence available. It is only the nature of the academic situation which makes it appear that one can linger on the threshold of decision in the name of an epistemological principle. What has really happened in such a case is that the subject of debate has changed from the question of what happened in a particular instance to the question of how knowledge is arrived at. The absence of pressure to decide what happened creates the possibility for this change of venue.

The change of venue, however, is itself an action taken. In diverting 45 attention from the original problem and placing it where Miller did, on "the mind of man," it once again ignores what happened and still is happening to American Indians. The moral problem that confronts me now is not that I can never have any facts to go on, but that the work I do is not directed toward solving the kinds of problems that studying the history of European-Indian relations has awakened me to.

Notes

1. See Vine Deloria, Jr., *God Is Red* (New York, 1973), pp. 39–56.

2. Perry Miller, *Errand into the Wilderness* (Cambridge, Mass., 1964), p. vii; all further references will be included in the text.

3. This passage from John Winthrop's *Journal* is excerpted by Perry Miller in his anthology *The American Puritans: Their Prose and Poetry* (Garden City, N.Y., 1956), p. 43. In his headnote to the selections from the *Journal,* Miller speaks of Winthrop's "characteristic objectivity" (p. 37).

4. Alden T. Vaughan, *New England Frontier: Puritans and Indians, 1620–1675* (Boston, 1965), pp. vi–vii; all further references to this work, abbreviated *NEF,* will be included in the text.

5. John Higham, intro. to *New Directions in American Intellectual History,* ed. Higham and Paul K. Conkin (Baltimore, 1979), p. xii.

6. Ibid.

7. See Francis Jennings, *The Invasion of America: Indians, Colonialism, and the Cant of Conquest* (New York, 1975), pp. 3–31. Jennings writes: "The so-called settlement of America was a resettlement, reoccupation of a land made waste by the diseases and demoralization introduced by the newcomers. Although the source data pertaining to populations have never been compiled, one careful scholar, Henry F. Dobyns, has provided a relatively conservative and meticulously

reasoned estimate conforming to the known effects of conquest catastrophe. Dobyns has calculated a total aboriginal population for the western hemisphere within the range of 90 to 112 million, of which 10 to 12 million lived north of the Rio Grande" (p. 30).

8. Jennings, fig. 7, p. 229; and see pp. 186–229.

9. James Axtell, *The European and the Indian: Essays in the Ethnohistory of Colonial North America* (Oxford, 1981), p. viii.

10. See Calvin Martin, *Keepers of the Game: Indian-Animal Relationships and the Fur Trade* (Berkeley and Los Angeles, 1978).

11. See the essay by Charles Hudson in *Indians, Animals, and the Fur Trade: A Critique of "Keepers of the Game,"* ed. Shepard Krech III (Athens, Ga., 1981), pp. 167–69.

12. See Axtell, "The White Indians of Colonial America" and "The Scholastic Philosophy of the Wilderness," *The European and the Indian,* pp. 168–206 and 131–67.

13. J. Norman Heard, *White into Red: A Study of the Assimilation of White Persons Captured by Indians* (Metuchen, N.J., 1973), p. 97.

14. See ibid., p. 98.

15. Mary Rowlandson, "The Soveraignty and Goodness of God, Together with the Faithfulness of His Promises Displayed; Being a Narrative of the Captivity and Restauration of Mrs. Mary Rowlandson (1676)," in *Held Captive by Indians: Selected Narratives, 1642–1836,* ed. Richard VanDerBeets (Knoxville, Tenn., 1973), pp. 57–58.

16. William Wood, *New England's Prospect,* ed. Vaughan (Amherst, Mass., 1977), pp. 88–89.

17. Alexander Whitaker, *Goode Newes from Virginia* (1613), quoted in Robert F. Berkhofer, Jr., *The White Man's Indian: Images of the American Indian from Columbus to the Present* (New York, 1978), p. 19.

18. See, for example, Berkhofer's discussion of the passages he quotes from Whitaker (*The White Man's Indian,* pp. 19, 20).

19. See Karen Ordahl Kupperman, *Settling with the Indians: The Meeting of English and Indian Cultures in America, 1580–1640* (Totowa, N.J., 1980), pp. 3, 4.

20. Ibid., p. 35.

21. The position I've been outlining is a version of neopragmatism. For an exposition, see *Against Theory: Literary Studies and the New Pragmatism,* ed. W. J. T. Mitchell (Chicago, 1985).

SHERMAN ALEXIE   [b. 1966]

What Sacagawea Means to Me

Of Spokane/Coeur d'Alene Native American descent, **Sherman Alexie** was born on an Indian Reservation in Wellpinit, Washington. He earned his B.A. from Washington State University in Pullman. He has published eight books of poetry and several novels and collections of short fiction, including *The Lone Ranger and Tonto Fistfight in Heaven* (1993), which won a PEN/Hemingway award for a best first book of fiction. He based the script for the film *Smoke Signals* on one of his short stories.

In his essay "What Sacagawea Means to Me," Alexie rethinks the Lewis and Clark expedition and examines what it says about American identity. Even as he cringes at the wrongdoing he sees in American culture and history, Alexie manages to find beauty in America's contradictions. He juxtaposes a "tragic and violent" history of colonization with some of the achievements of America's greatest thinkers.

In the future, every U.S. citizen will get to be Sacagawea for fifteen minutes. For the low price of admission, every American, regardless of race, religion, gender, and age, will climb through the portal into Sacagawea's Shoshone Indian brain. In the multicultural theme park called Sacagawea Land, you will be kidnapped as a child by the Hidatsa tribe and sold to Toussaint Charbonneau, the French-Canadian trader who will take you as one of his wives and father two of your children. Your first child, Jean-Baptiste will be only a few months old as you carry him during your long journey with Lewis and Clark. The two captains will lead the adventure, fighting rivers, animals, weather, and diseases for thousands of miles, and you will march right beside them. But you, the aboriginal multitasker, will also breastfeed. And at the end of your Sacagawea journey, you will be shown the exit and given a souvenir T-shirt that reads, IF THE U.S. IS EDEN, THEN SACAGAWEA IS EVE.

Sacagawea is our mother. She is the first gene pair of the American DNA. In the beginning, she was the word, and the word was possibility.

155

I revel in the wondrous possibilities of Sacagawea. It is good to be joyous in the presence of her spirit, because I hope she had moments of joy in what must have been a grueling life. This much is true: Sacagawea died of some mysterious illness when she was only in her twenties. Most illnesses were mysterious in the nineteenth century, but I suspect that Sacagawea's indigenous immune system was defenseless against an immigrant virus. Perhaps Lewis and Clark infected Sacagawea. If that is true, then certain postcolonial historians would argue that she was murdered not by germs but by colonists who carried those germs. I don't know much about the science of disease and immunities, but I know enough poetry to recognize that individual human beings are invaded and colonized by foreign bodies, just as individual civilizations are invaded and colonized by foreign bodies. In that sense, colonization might be a natural process, tragic and violent to be sure, but predictable and ordinary as well, and possibly necessary for the advance, however constructive and destructive, of all civilizations.

After all, Lewis and Clark's story has never been just the triumphant tale of two white men, no matter what the white historians might need to believe. Sacagawea was not the primary hero of this story either, no matter what the Native American historians and I might want to believe. The story of Lewis and Clark is also the story of the approximately forty-five nameless and faceless first- and second-generation European Americans who joined the journey, then left or completed it, often without monetary or historical compensation. Considering the time and place, I imagine those forty-five were illiterate, low-skilled laborers subject to managerial whims and nineteenth-century downsizing. And it is most certainly the story of the black slave York, who also cast votes during this allegedly democratic adventure. It's even the story of Seaman, the domesticated Newfoundland dog who must have been a welcome and friendly presence and who survived the risk of becoming supper during one lean time or another. The Lewis and Clark Expedition was exactly the kind of multicultural, trigenerational, bigendered, animal-friendly, government-supported, partly French-Canadian project that should rightly be celebrated by liberals and castigated by conservatives.

In the end, I wonder if colonization might somehow be magical. After all, Miles Davis is the direct descendant of slaves and slave owners. Hank Williams is the direct descendant of poor whites and poorer Indians. In 1876 Emily Dickinson was writing her poems in an Amherst attic while Crazy Horse was killing Custer on the banks of the Little Big Horn. I remain stunned by these contradictions, by the successive generations of social, political, and artistic mutations that can be so beautiful and painful. How did we get from there to here? This country somehow gave life to Maria Tallchief and Ted Bundy, to Geronimo and Joe McCarthy, to

Nathan Bedford Forrest and Toni Morrison, to the Declaration of Independence and Executive Order No. 1066, to Cesar Chavez and Richard Nixon, to theme parks and national parks, to smallpox and the vaccine for smallpox.

As a Native American, I want to hate this country and its contradictions. 5
I want to believe that Sacagawea hated this country and its contradictions. But this country exists, in whole and in part, because Sacagawea helped Lewis and Clark. In the land that came to be called Idaho, she acted as diplomat between her long-lost brother and the Lewis and Clark party. Why wouldn't she ask her brother and her tribe to take revenge against the men who had enslaved her? Sacagawea is a contradiction. Here in Seattle, I exist, in whole and in part, because a half-white man named James Cox fell in love with a Spokane Indian woman named Etta Adams and gave birth to my mother. I am a contradiction; I am Sacagawea.

[2002]

Tommie Smith and John Carlos, gold and bronze medalists in the 200-meter dash, raise their fists in a black power salute on the victory stand at the 1968 Olympics in Mexico City. (AP Photo.)

CORNEL WEST [b. 1953]

On Black Fathering

Cornel West was born in 1953 and raised in Sacramento, California. He attended Harvard University and graduated *magna cum laude* in three years. He went on to earn his M.A. in 1975 and Ph.D. in 1980 from Princeton University. His teaching career has brought him to the Union Theological Seminary and Yale Divinity School. From 1988 to 1993 West served as a professor of religion and the director of the Program in African-American Studies at Princeton. In 1993 West joined the W.E.B. Du Bois Institute for Afro-American Research at Harvard University, becoming the Alphonse Fletcher Jr. University Professor in 1998. In 2002 West returned to Princeton University as the Class of 1943 University Professor of Religion and African American Studies. Influenced by philosophy, Marxism, and his Baptist faith, West has authored and coauthored over fifteen books; his 1993 collection of essays, *Race Matters*, became a national best seller. Known for and controversial because of his ongoing political activism, West was involved in the Million Man March and Russell Simon's Hip Hop Summit, and has also served in an advisory capacity to such political figures as Louis Farrakhan, Al Sharpton, Bill Bradley, and Ralph Nader. A long-time member of the Democratic Socialists of America, West now serves as an honorary Chair.

In his article "On Black Fathering," originally published in Andre C. Willis's *Faith of Our Fathers*, West opens with a discussion of the monumental efforts required of black American men to be loving and unwaveringly supportive fathers. West's critique of black fatherhood takes a personal turn when he reflects on his own fathering and father. The essay closes with the eulogy West delivered upon the death of his dad, Clifton Lincoln West Jr., a man remembered, emulated, and praised for his "legacy of love."

One of the most difficult tasks to accomplish in American society is to be a solid, caring, and loving black father. To be a good black father, first you have to negotiate all of the absurd attacks and assaults on your humanity and on your capacity and status as a human being. Second, you have to provide materially and economically, as well as nurture psychologically, personally, and existentially. All of this requires a deep level of maturity. By maturity I mean a solid understanding of who one is as a person, and a sense of sacrifice and courage. For black men to reach that level of maturity and understanding is almost miraculous given the dehumanizing context for black men, and yet millions and millions have done it. It is a tribute to fulfill the highest standards of fatherhood. When I think of my own particular case, I think of my father, my grandfather, and his father, because what they were able to do was to sustain some sense of dignity and sacrifice even as they dealt with all the arrows that were coming at them on every level in American society.

Let's consider the economic level. In America, generally speaking, patriarchal definitions of men in relation to the economic front mean you have a job and provide for your family. Many black men did not (and do not) make enough money to provide for their families adequately because of their exclusion from jobs with a living wage. They then oftentimes tended, and tend, to accent certain patriarchal identities (e.g., predatory or abusive behavior) in lieu of the fact that they could not perform the traditional patriarchal roles in American society.

Then on the home front, where black men had and have, oftentimes, wives who were and are subject to such white supremacist abuse, either at the white home where these sisters work(ed) or as a service worker in other parts of white society, most black men had to deal with the kinds of scars and bruises that come from knowing that you were supposed to protect your woman, as it were, which is also part of the patriarchal identity in America—a man ought to be able to protect his woman but could not protect her from the vicious abuse. Many black men also recognized that there was a relation between their not being able to get a job given the discrimination and segregation on the one hand and the tremendous power wielded by those white men who were often condoning the abuse of their own wives.

How children perceive their father is another interesting component of the dynamic that black fathers have to negotiate. How are black fathers able to convey to their children some affirmative sense of self, some sense of reality—given what is happening to these men on the economic front, given what many of them know is happening to their wives outside of the house, and given the perception by their own children that they are unable to fulfill the expected patriarchal role? In the tradition of the black father, the best ones—I think my grandfather and dad are good examples—came up with ways of negotiating a balance so that they would recognize that exclusion from the economic sphere was real, and recognize that possible abuse of their wives was real, and also recognize that they had to sustain a connection with their kids in which their

160

kids could see the best in them despite the limited and dehumanizing circumstances under which they functioned.

My mother happened to be a woman who was not abused in the fashion described above. I remember one incident when a white policeman disrespected my mother. Dad went at him verbally and, in the eyes of the police, ended up violating the law. At that point he just drew a line in the sand that said, "You're going too far." I thank God that a number of incidents like that didn't happen, or he would have ended up in jail forever—like so many other brothers who just do not allow certain levels of disrespect of their mother, wife, sister, or daughter. As a man, what I was able to see in Dad was his ability to transform his own pain with a sense of laughter, and a sense of empathy, and a sense of compassion for others. This was a real act of moral genius Dad accomplished, and I think that it is part of the best of a tradition of moral genius. Unfortunately, large numbers of black men do not reach that level because the rage and the anger are just too deep; they just burn them out and consume their soul. Fortunately, on the other hand, you do have many black men that achieve this level and some that go beyond it.

In my own case as a father, I certainly tried to emulate and imitate Dad's very ingenious ways of negotiating the balances between what was happening on these different fronts, but because of the sacrifices he and Mom made, I had access to opportunities that he did not. When my son Cliff was born, I was convinced that I wanted to try to do for him what Dad had done for me. But it was not to be—there was no way that I could be the father to my son that my dad was to me. Part of it was that my circumstances were very different. Another part was simply that I was not the man that my father was. My brother is actually the shining example of building on the rich legacy of my dad as a father much more than I am, because he gives everything—right across the board. He is there—whatever the circumstance—has spent time with the kids; he is always there in the same way that Dad was there for us. I'll always try to be a rich footnote to my brother, yet as a father I have certainly not been the person that he was. The effort has been there, the endeavor too, but the circumstances (as well as my not being as deep a person as he or my father) have not enabled me to measure up. On the other hand, my son Cliff turned out to be a decent and fascinating person—and he is still in process, of course.

The bottom line for my dad was always love, and he was a deeply Christian man—his favorite song was "I Will Trust in the Lord." He had a profound trust. His trust was much more profound than mine in some ways, even though I work at it. He had a deep love, and that's the thing I've tried to build on with Cliff. My hope and my inclination are that Cliff feels this love, but certainly it takes more than love to nurture and father a son or a daughter.

The most important things for black fathers to try to do are to give of themselves, to try to exemplify in their own behavior what they want to see in their sons and daughters, and, most important, to spend time with and give attention to their children. This is a big challenge, yet it is critical as we move into the twenty-first century.

The most difficult task of my life was to give the eulogy for my father. Everything else pales in the face of this challenge. Hence what Dad means to me—like my family, Cliff and Elleni—constitutes who and what I am and will be.

EULOGY

Clifton Lincoln West, Jr. What a man. What an individual. What a person. What a servant. We gather here this afternoon in this sacred place and this consecrated space to say good-bye. To bid farewell to a good man, a great Christian who lived a grand and loving life. When I think of my father, I cannot but think of what he said to that reporter from the *Sacramento Bee* when they asked him, "What is it about you and what is it about your family—do you have a secret?" Dad said, "No, we live by Grace—in addition to that, me and his mother, we try to *be there.*" I shall never forget that my father was not simply a man of quiet dignity, steadfast integrity, and high intelligence, but fundamentally and quintessentially he was a man of love, and love means being there for others. That's why when I think of Dad I recall that precious moment in the fifteenth chapter of John in the eleventh and twelfth verse: "These things have I given unto you that my joy might remain in you, and that your joy might be full. This is my commandment that ye love one another as I have loved you."

In the midst of Dad's sophistication and refinement he was always for real. He was someone who was down-to-earth because he took this commandment seriously, and it meant he had to cut against the grain in a world in which he was going to endure lovingly and with compassion. Isn't that what the very core of the gospel is about? The thirteenth chapter of I Corinthians—that great litany of love that Dr. King talked about—deals with it. Dad used to read it all the time. I will never forget when he took me to college in Cambridge, the first time I ever flew on an airplane (it cost about ninety-five dollars then). Dad told me, "Corn, we're praying for you, and always remember: 'Though I speak with the tongues of men and of angels and have not love, I become as a sounding brass or a tinkling cymbal. And though I have the gift of prophecy, and understand all mysteries, and all knowledge; and though I have all faith, so that I could remove mountains, and have not love, I am nothing.'"

As we stand here on these stormy banks of Jordan and watch Dad's ship go by, may I remind each and every one of you that we come from a loving family, a courageous people of African descent, and a rich Christian tradition. We have seen situations in which history has pushed our backs against the wall, and life has knocked us to our knees. In the face of despair and degradation sometimes we know that all we can do is sing a song, or crack a smile, or say a prayer. Yet we refuse to allow grief and misery to have the last word.

Dad was a man of love, and if I was to adopt his perspective at this very moment, he would say, "Corn, don't push me in the limelight, keep your mother in mind, don't focus on me, keep the family in mind—I'm just a servant passing through." That's the kind of father I had.

But he didn't come to it by himself, you see. He was part of a family, he was part of a people, he was part of a tradition that went all the way back to gut-bucket Jim Crow Louisiana, September 7, 1928. He was not supposed to make it, you see. Nobody would have believed that Clifton Lincoln West, Jr., the third child of C. L. West and Lovey West, would have been able to aspire to the heights that he did. No one would have predicted or projected that he would make it through the first three months in Louisiana—Cliff was not supposed to make that trip, you know. He was born the year before the stock market crashed. His family stayed three months in Louisiana, and Grandfather and Grandmother, with three young children in a snowstorm, journeyed on a train to Tulsa, Oklahoma. You all know what Tulsa, Oklahoma, was like. It was seven years after the major riot in this country in which over three hundred folks—black folks—were killed and Greenwood, Archer and Pine— that GAP corner—the Wall Street of black America was all burned out. But Grandmama had something else in mind, and the Lord did too.

Dad went on to Paul Laurence Dunbar Elementary School—to give you an idea of what side of town they were living on—and George Washington Carver Junior High School, and Booker T. Washington High School. It was there that he got to choose the idea of pulling from the best of the world but remaining not of the world. I like that about Dad. He wasn't so excessively pious or so excessively rigid that he became naive and got caught up in narrow doctrines and creeds and thought he was better than anybody else. That's not the kind of man he was. No. His faith was grounded in a love because he knew that he had fallen short of the glory of God. He knew he had inadequacies and shortcomings, but he was going to struggle anyhow; he was going to keep keeping on anyway.

After high school he went on to the military for three years. He could have easily given his life for this country. When he returned to Tulsa, Oklahoma,

15

he was refused admission at the University of Tulsa, and then went on to that grand institution, Fisk University, where he met that indescribably wonderful, beautiful, lovable honor student from Orange, Texas—Irene Bias. I'll never forget when we were at Fisk together, he described the place right outside Jubilee Hall where they met. I said, "Dad, that's a special place," and he said, "Yes, that meeting was the beginning of the peak of my life." As their love began to grow and multiply, the army grabbed him back again for eighteen months, but in the years to come they had young Clifton, my brother, to whom I'm just a footnote; myself, of course; and Cynthia and Cheryl. We moved from Oklahoma through Topeka, Kansas, on our way to 8008 48th Avenue, Glen Elder. Yes, how proud we were driving up in that bright orange Mercury. We were at the cutting edge of residential breakdown in Sacramento, but along the way, for almost a decade, Dad, and the men of Glen Elder—Mr. Peters, Mr. Pool, Mr. Powell, Mr. Reed—these were black men who cared and who worked together. These overworked yet noble men built the little league diamond by themselves, and then they organized the league into ten teams—minor and major leagues for the neighborhood. They provided a means by which character and integrity could be shaped among the young brothers. Then every Sunday, onto Shiloh—"can't wait for the next sermon of Reverend Willie P. Cooke, just hope that he didn't go too long"—but we knew that the Lord was working in him. Dad would always tell us, "You know how blessed I am, how blessed we are. Never think that we've come as far as we have on our own."

When we were in trouble, there was Mr. Fields, Mrs. Ray, and Mrs. Harris —there were hundreds of folks who made a difference. You all remember when Dad went to the hospital when he was thirty-one years old and the doctors had given up on him. There was a great sadness on Forty-eighth Avenue because he had left Mom with four little children. Granddad— the Reverend C. L. West, left his church for months to come and be with Mom—Grandmom came as well—and Dad was in the hospital in Oakland. They had given up on him; the medical profession had reached its conclusion and said they could do nothing. And we said, "We know the power. Let Him step in." We knew that Reverend Cook hadn't been preaching that "Jesus is a rock in a weary land, and water in dry places, and food when you are hungry, and a mind regulator and a heart fixer" for nothing. And we came to Calvary in prayer.

Can you imagine how different our lives would have been if we had lost Dad then, in 1961, rather than 1994? Even in the midst of our fear we rejoice. It would have been a different world for each and every one of us, especially the children. Dad kept going after his recovery. He worked at McClellan Air Force Base—steadily missed some of those promotions he should have got, but he stayed convinced that he was going to teach people right no matter what, even given his own situation.

That's another thing I loved about him. People always ask me, "West, why do you still talk about love? It's played out. Why when you talk about blackness is it always linked to white brothers and sisters and yellow brothers and sisters and red brothers and sisters and brown brothers and sisters?" And I tell them about John 15:11–12. I tell them that I dedicated my life a long time ago to the same Jesus that Dad dedicated his life to, to the same Jesus that Reverend C. L. West dedicated his life, to the same Jesus that my grandfather on my mother's side and my grandmother on my mother's side dedicated their lives to, but, more important, I saw in the concrete, with Dad and Mom, a love that transcends skin pigmentation. I saw it on the ground. Dad taught us that even as you keep track of the injustice, you don't lose track of the humanity. That's what love and being there are all about. Dad made it a priority and preference to be there for us. He made a choice. It meant that he would live a life of interruptions because those who are fundamentally committed to being there are going to be continually interrupted—your own agenda, your own project, are going to be interfered with. Dad was always open to that kind of interruption. He was able to translate a kind of unpredictable interruption into a supportive intervention in somebody else's life. More important, Dad realized that a being-there kind of love meant that you had to have follow up and follow through. One could not just show up—one has to follow up and follow through. This is the most difficult aspect of it. Love is inseparable from pain and hurt and sadness and sorrow and disappointment, but Dad knew that you had to have follow up and follow through. He knew that you had to struggle in the midst of that pain and that hurt—you had to have just not simply the high moments of love, but the funk of love, the stink and the stench of love. In all of his relationships Dad embodied precisely that struggle with the high moments of love and the low moments of love. He knew that the cross was not just about smiles and that it was not just about celebration—it was about sadness, stench, and funk. That is what the blood was about, not Kool-aid but blood. That's how inseparable scars, bruises, and wounds are from joy, affirmation, and wholeness. If you were serious about love, if you were serious about being there for people you were going to be there in the midst of any situation, any circumstances, any condition. Dad realized that God being there for us in any situation and circumstances meant that if he was going to be Godlike, he had to be there in any situation for us. I've been alive now for forty years, and on Thursday I'll be forty-one years old, and *not once has my mother or father disappointed me.* They have always been there. That is a blessing, and I do not deserve it. It's a blessing, and I am thankful for it.

So as we bid farewell to Dad, I want you all to know that I am looking forward to a family reunion. I am looking forward to union together on

20

the other side of the Jordan. I am looking forward to seeing Dad in a place where the wicked will cease their troubling and the weary shall be at rest. I tell you when I get there, I'm going down Revelation Boulevard to the corner of John Street, right around the corner from Mark's place. But I want to go to Nahum's place. I don't want to be in Jeremiah's house, it would be too crowded. I don't even want to be down on Peter Street, too many people there—I want some quiet time. I want to sit down with C. L. West, I want to sit down with Nick Bias, and I want to sit down with Aunt Juanita, and I want to sit down with Aunt Tiny. And I want to sit down with Dad! I want to let them know that we did the best that we could to keep alive the best of the legacy of love that they left to us. And when we come together, we will come together in a way in which there will be no more tears, no more heartache, no more heartbreak, no more sadness and sorrow, no more agony and anguish. We shall sit at the feet of the Lord and be blessed, and our souls will look back and wonder how we got over, how we got over.

Rosa Parks sits at the front of a bus on December 21, 1956, the first day
that the transportation system in Montgomery, Alabama, was integrated.
(Bettmann/Corbis.)

MAYA ANGELOU   [b. 1928]

Champion of the World

Born Marguerite Johnson in St. Louis, Missouri, in 1928, **Maya Angelou** has been a successful dancer, actor, poet, playwright, fiction writer, producer, director, newspaper editor, civil rights leader, and academic, among other accomplishments. Her autobiographical book *I Know Why the Caged Bird Sings* (1969) was nominated for a National Book Award. In 1993 she delivered her poem, "On the Pulse of Morning," at the inauguration of President Clinton.

In "Champion of the World," from *I Know Why the Caged Bird Sings*, Angelou describes the camaraderie of her townfolk as they listen, crowded and apprehensive, to a radio broadcast playing a fight between heavyweight boxing champion Joe Louis and a white contender. United in the hope for the Brown Bomber's victory, the spirits among listeners soar and plummet as the fight progresses. Angelou's narration draws the reader into the story, to share in the anxiety of the fight, to burn with anguish at the possibility of defeat, and to burst with pride in the resounding victory, a victory that reaffirms the self-worth and humanity of all black Americans.

The last inch of space was filled, yet people continued to wedge themselves along the walls of the Store. Uncle Willie had turned the radio up to its last notch so that youngsters on the porch wouldn't miss a word. Women sat on kitchen chairs, dining-room chairs, stools and upturned wooden boxes. Small children and babies perched on every lap available and men leaned on the shelves or on each other.

The apprehensive mood was shot through with shafts of gaiety, as a black sky is streaked with lightning.

"I ain't worried 'bout this fight. Joe's gonna whip that cracker like it's open season."

"He gone whip him till that white boy call him Momma."

At last the talking finished and the string-along songs about razor 5 blades were over and the fight began.

"A quick jab to the head." In the Store the crowd grunted. "A left to the head and a right and another left." One of the listeners cackled like a hen and was quieted.

"They're in a clinch, Louis is trying to fight his way out."

Some bitter comedian on the porch said, "That white man don't mind hugging that niggah now, I betcha."

"The referee is moving in to break them up, but Louis finally pushed the contender away and it's an uppercut to the chin. The contender is hanging on, now he's backing away. Louis catches him with a short left to the jaw."

A tide of murmuring assent poured out the door and into the yard.   10

"Another left and another left. Louis is saving that mighty right..." The mutter in the Store had grown into a baby roar and it was pierced by the clang of a bell and the announcer's "That's the bell for round three, ladies and gentlemen."

As I pushed my way into the Store I wondered if the announcer gave any thought to the fact that he was addressing as "ladies and gentlemen" all the Negroes around the world who sat sweating and praying, glued to their "master's voice."

There were only a few calls for R. C. Colas, Dr. Peppers, and Hires root beer. The real festivities would begin after the fight. Then even the old Christian ladies who taught their children and tried themselves to practice turning the other check would buy soft drinks, and if the Brown Bomber's victory was a particularly bloody one they would order peanut patties and Baby Ruths also.

Bailey and I laid the coins on top of the cash register. Uncle Willie didn't allow us to ring up sales during a fight. It was too noisy and might shake up the atmosphere. When the gong rang for the next round we pushed through the near-sacred quiet to the herd of children outside.

"He's got Louis against the ropes and now it's a left to the body and a   15 right to the ribs. Another right to the body, it looks like it was low...Yes, ladies and gentlemen, the referee is signaling but the contender keeps raining the blows on Louis. It's another to the body, and it looks like Louis is going down."

My race groaned. It was our people falling. It was another lynching, yet another Black man hanging on a tree. One more woman ambushed and raped. A Black boy whipped and maimed. It was hounds on the trail of a man running through slimy swamps. It was a white woman slapping her maid for being forgetful.

The men in the Store stood away from the walls and at attention. Women greedily clutched the babes on their laps while on the porch the shufflings and smiles, flirtings and pinching of a few minutes before were gone. This might be the end of the world. If Joe lost we were back in slavery and beyond help. It would all be true, the accusations that we were lower types of human beings. Only a little higher than apes. True that we were stupid and ugly and lazy and dirty and, unlucky and worst of all, that God Himself hated us and ordained us to be hewers of wood and drawers of water, forever and ever, world without end.

We didn't breathe. We didn't hope. We waited.

"He's off the ropes, ladies and gentlemen. He's moving towards the center of the ring." There was no time to be relieved. The worst might still happen.

"And now it looks like Joe is mad. He's caught Carnera with a left hook 20 to the head and a right to the head. It's a left jab to the body and another left to the head. There's a left cross and a right to the head. The contender's right eye is bleeding and he can't seem to keep his block up. Louis is penetrating every block. The referee is moving in, but Louis sends a left to the body and it's an uppercut to the chin and the contender is dropping. He's on the canvas, ladies and gentlemen."

Babies slid to the floor as women stood up and men leaned toward the radio.

"Here's the referee. He's young. One, two, three, four, five, six, seven... Is the contender trying to get up again?"

All the men in the store shouted, "NO."

"—eight, nine, ten." There were a few sounds from the audience, but they seemed to be holding themselves in against tremendous pressure.

"The fight is all over, ladies and gentlemen. Let's get the microphone 25 over to the referee... Here he is. He's got the Brown Bomber's hand, he's holding it up... Here he is..."

Then the voice, husky and familiar, came to wash over us—"The winnah, and still heavyweight champeen of the world...Joe Louis."

Champion of the world. A Black boy. Some Black mother's son. He was the strongest man in the world. People drank Coca-Colas like ambrosia and ate candy bars like Christmas. Some of the men went behind the Store and poured white lightning in their soft-drink bottles, and a few of the bigger boys followed them. Those who were not chased away came back blowing their breath in front of themselves like proud smokers.

It would take an hour or more before the people would leave the Store and head for home. Those who lived too far had made arrangements to stay in town. It wouldn't do for a Black man and his family to be caught on a lonely country road on a night when Joe Louis had proved that we were the strongest people in the world.

ZORA NEALE HURSTON   [1891–1960]

Sweat

Born in rural Alabama and raised in Florida, **Zora Neale Hurston** arrived in New York at the height of the Harlem Renaissance, a flowering of African American literature, art, music, and scholarship in the 1920s and 1930s. She became an active participant, writing stories and coauthoring a play with Langston Hughes. Her interest in the folk culture of the South, influenced by her studies with noted anthropologist Franz Boas, led to her return to Florida to study her native community and, eventually, to the work for which she is best known, the novel *Their Eyes Were Watching God* (1937). Written in 1926 when Hurston was a student at Barnard College, "Sweat" is the story of Delia Jones, a washerwoman, and her cruel husband, Sykes.

I

It was eleven o'clock of a Spring night in Florida. It was Sunday. Any other night, Delia Jones would have been in bed for two hours by this time. But she was a washwoman, and Monday morning meant a great deal to her. So she collected the soiled clothes on Saturday when she returned the clean things. Sunday night after church, she sorted and put the white things to soak. It saved her almost a half-day's start. A great hamper in the bedroom held the clothes that she brought home. It was so much neater than a number of bundles lying around.

She squatted on the kitchen floor beside the great pile of clothes, sorting them into small heaps according to color, and humming a song in a mournful key, but wondering through it all where Sykes, her husband, had gone with her horse and buckboard.

Just then something long, round, limp, and black fell upon her shoulders and slithered to the floor beside her. A great terror took hold of her. It softened her knees and dried her mouth so that it was a full minute before she could cry out or move. Then she saw that it was the big bull whip her husband liked to carry when he drove.

She lifted her eyes to the door and saw him standing there bent over with laughter at her fright. She screamed at him.

"Sykes, what you throw dat whip on me like dat? You know it would   5
skeer me—looks just like a snake, an' you knows how skeered Ah is of
snakes."

"Course Ah knowed it! That's how come Ah done it." He slapped his
leg with his hand and almost rolled on the ground in his mirth. "If you
such a big fool dat you got to have a fit over a earth worm or a string, Ah
don't keer how bad Ah skeer you."

"You ain't got no business doing it. Gawd knows it's a sin. Some day
Ah'm gointuh drop dead from some of yo' foolishness. 'Nother thing,
where you been wid mah rig? Ah feeds dat pony. He ain't fuh you to be
drivin' wid no bull whip."

"You sho' is one aggravatin' nigger woman!" he declared and stepped into
the room. She resumed her work and did not answer him at once. "Ah done
tole you time and again to keep them white folks' clothes outa dis house."

He picked up the whip and glared at her. Delia went on with her work.
She went out into the yard and returned with a galvanized tub and set it
on the washbench. She saw that Sykes had kicked all of the clothes
together again, and now stood in her way truculently, his whole manner
hoping, *praying*, for an argument. But she walked calmly around him
and commenced to re-sort the things.

"Next time, Ah'm gointer kick 'em outdoors," he threatened as he   10
struck a match along the leg of his corduroy breeches.

Delia never looked up from her work, and her thin, stooped shoulders
sagged further.

"Ah ain't for no fuss t'night, Sykes. Ah just come from taking sacrament at the church house."

He snorted scornfully. "Yeah, you just come from de church house on a
Sunday night, but heah you is gone to work on them clothes. You ain't nothing but a hypocrite. One of them amen-corner Christians—sing, whoop,
and shout, then come home and wash white folks' clothes on the Sabbath."

He stepped roughly upon the whitest pile of things, kicking them
helter-skelter as he crossed the room. His wife gave a little scream of
dismay, and quickly gathered them together again.

"Sykes, you quit grindin' dirt into these clothes! How can Ah git   15
through by Sat'day if Ah don't start on Sunday?"

"Ah don't keer if you never git through. Anyhow, Ah done promised
Gawd and a couple of other men, Ah ain't gointer have it in mah house.
Don't gimme no lip neither, else Ah'll throw 'em out and put mah fist up
side yo' head to boot."

Delia's habitual meekness seemed to slip from her shoulders like a
blown scarf. She was on her feet; her poor little body, her bare knuckly
hands bravely defying the strapping hulk before her.

172

"Looka heah, Sykes, you done gone too fur. Ah been married to you fur fifteen years, and Ah been takin' in washin' fur fifteen years. Sweat, sweat, sweat! Work and sweat, cry and sweat, pray and sweat!"

"What's that got to do with me?" he asked brutally.

"What's it got to do with you, Sykes? Mah tub of suds is filled yo' belly 20 with vittles more times than yo' hands is filled it. Mah sweat is done paid for this house and Ah reckon Ah kin keep on sweatin' in it."

She seized the iron skillet from the stove and struck a defensive pose, which act surprised him greatly, coming from her. It cowed him and he did not strike her as he usually did.

"Naw you won't," she panted, "that ole snaggle-toothed black woman you runnin' with ain't comin' heah to pile up on *mah* sweat and blood. You ain't paid for nothin' on this place, and Ah'm gointer stay right heah till Ah'm toted out foot foremost."

"Well, you better quit gittin' me riled up, else they'll be totin' you out sooner than you expect. Ah'm so tired of you Ah don't know whut to do. Gawd! How Ah hates skinny wimmen!"

A little awed by this new Delia, he sidled out of the door and slammed the back gate after him. He did not say where he had gone, but she knew too well. She knew very well that he would not return until nearly day-break also. Her work over, she went on to bed but not to sleep at once. Things had come to a pretty pass!

She lay awake, gazing upon the debris that cluttered their matrimonial 25 trail. Not an image left standing along the way. Anything like flowers had long ago been drowned in the salty stream that had been pressed from her heart. Her tears, her sweat, her blood. She had brought love to the union and he had brought a longing after the flesh. Two months after the wedding, he had given her the first brutal beating. She had the memory of his numerous trips to Orlando with all of his wages when he had returned to her penniless, even before the first year had passed. She was young and soft then, but now she thought of her knotty, muscled limbs, her harsh knuckly hands, and drew herself up into an unhappy little ball in the mid-dle of the big feather bed. Too late now to hope for love, even if it were not Bertha it would be someone else. This case differed from the others only in that she was bolder than the others. Too late for everything except her little home. She had built it for her old days, and planted one by one the trees and flowers there. It was lovely to her, lovely.

Somehow, before sleep came, she found herself saying aloud: "Oh well, whatever goes over the Devil's back, is got to come under his belly. Sometime or ruther, Sykes, like everybody else, is gointer reap his sowing." After that she was able to build a spiritual earthworks against her hus-band. His shells could no longer reach her. AMEN. She went to sleep and slept until he announced his presence in bed by kicking her feet and rudely snatching the covers away.

"Gimme some kivah heah, an' git yo' damn foots over on yo' own side! Ah oughter mash you in yo' mouf fuh drawing dat skillet on me."

Delia went clear to the rail without answering him. A triumphant indifference to all that he was or did.

II

The week was full of work for Delia as all other weeks, and Saturday found her behind her little pony, collecting and delivering clothes.

It was a hot, hot day near the end of July. The village men on Joe 30 Clarke's porch even chewed cane listlessly. They did not hurl the cane-knots as usual. They let them dribble over the edge of the porch. Even conversation had collapsed under the heat.

"Heah come Delia Jones," Jim Merchant said, as the shaggy pony came 'round the bend of the road toward them. The rusty buckboard was heaped with baskets of crisp, clean laundry.

"Yep," Joe Lindsay agreed. "Hot or col', rain or shine, jes'ez reg'lar ez de weeks roll roun' Delia carries 'em an' fetches 'em on Sat'day."

"She better if she wanter eat," said Moss. "Syke Jones ain't wuth de shot an' powder hit would tek tuh kill 'em. Not to *huh* he ain't."

"He sho' ain't," Walter Thomas chimed in. "It's too bad, too, cause she wuz a right pretty li'l trick when he got huh. Ah'd uh mah'ied huh mah-self if he hadnter beat me to it."

Delia nodded briefly at the men as she drove past. 35

"Too much knockin' will ruin *any* 'oman. He done beat huh 'nough tuh kill three women, let 'lone change they looks," said Elijah Moseley. "How Syke kin stommuck dat big black greasy Mogul he's layin' roun' wid, gits me. Ah swear dat eight-rock couldn't kiss a sardine can Ah done thowed out de back do' 'way las' yeah."

"Aw, she's fat, thass how come. He's allus been crazy 'bout fat women," put in Merchant. "He'd a' been tied up wid one long time ago if he could a' found one tuh have him. Did Ah tell yuh 'bout him come sidlin' roun' *mah* wife—bringin' her a basket uh pecans outa his yard fuh a present? Yessir, mah wife! She tol' him tuh take 'em right straight back home, 'cause Delia works so hard ovah dat washtub she reckon everything on de place taste lak sweat an' soapsuds. Ah jus' wisht Ah'd a' caught 'im 'roun' dere! Ah'd a' made his hips ketch on fiah down dat shell road."

174

"Ah know he done it, too. Ah sees 'im grinnin' at every 'oman dat passes," Walter Thomas said. "But even so, he useter eat some mighty big hunks uh humble pie tuh git dat li'l 'oman he got. She wuz ez pretty ez a speckled pup! Dat wuz fifteen years ago. He useter be so skeered uh losin' huh, she could make him do some parts of a husband's duty. Dey never wuz de same in de mind."

"There oughter be a law about him," said Lindsay. "He ain't fit tuh carry guts tuh a bear."

Clarke spoke for the first time. "Tain't no law on earth dat kin make a   40
man be decent if it ain't in 'im. There's plenty men dat takes a wife lak dey do a joint uh sugar-cane. It's round, juicy, an' sweet when dey gits it. But dey squeeze an' grind, squeeze an' grind an' wring tell dey wring every drop uh pleasure dat's in 'em out. When dey's satisfied dat dey is wrung dry, dey treats 'em jes' lak dey do a cane-chew. Dey thows 'em away. Dey knows whut dey is doin' while dey is at it, an' hates theirselves fuh it but they keeps on hangin' after huh tell she's empty. Den dey hates huh fuh bein' a cane-chew an' in de way."

"We oughter take Syke an' dat stray 'oman uh his'n down in Lake Howell swamp an' lay on de rawhide till they cain't say Lawd a' mussy. He allus wuz uh ovahbearin niggah, but since dat white 'oman from up north done teached 'im how to run a automobile, he done got too beggety to live—an' we oughter kill 'im," Old Man Anderson advised.

A grunt of approval went around the porch. But the heat was melting their civic virtue and Elijah Moseley began to bait Joe Clarke.

"Come on, Joe, git a melon outa dere an' slice it up for yo' customers. We'se all sufferin' wid de heat. De bear's done got *me!*"

"Thass right, Joe, a watermelon is jes' whut Ah needs tuh cure de eppizudicks," Walter Thomas joined forces with Moseley. "Come on dere, Joe. We all is steady customers an' you ain't set us up in a long time. Ah chooses dat long, bowlegged Floridy favorite."

"A god, an' be dough. You all gimme twenty cents and slice away,"   45
Clarke retorted. "Ah needs a col' slice m'self. Heah, everybody chip in. Ah'll lend y'all mah meat knife."

The money was all quickly subscribed and the huge melon brought forth. At that moment, Sykes and Bertha arrived. A determined silence fell on the porch and the melon was put away again.

Merchant snapped down the blade of his jacknife and moved toward the store door.

"Come on in, Joe, an' gimme a slab uh sow belly an' uh pound uh coffee—almost fuhgot 'twas Sat'day. Got to git on home." Most of the men left also.

Just then Delia drove past on her way home, as Sykes was ordering magnificently for Bertha. It pleased him for Delia to see.

"Git whutsoever yo' heart desires, Honey. Wait a minute, Joe. Give huh 50 two bottles uh strawberry soda-water, uh quart parched ground-peas, an' a block uh chewin' gum."

With all this they left the store, with Sykes reminding Bertha that this was his town and she could have it if she wanted it.

The men returned soon after they left, and held their watermelon feast.

"Where did Syke Jones git da 'oman from nohow?" Lindsay asked.

"Ovah Apopka. Guess dey musta been cleanin' out de town when she lef'. She don't look lak a thing but a hunk uh liver wid hair on it."

"Well, she sho' kin squall," Dave Carter contributed. "When she gits 55 ready tuh laff, she jes' opens huh mouf an' latches it back tuh de las' notch. No ole granpa alligator down in Lake Bell ain't got nothin' on huh."

III

Bertha had been in town three months now. Sykes was still paying her room-rent at Della Lewis'—the only house in town that would have taken her in. Sykes took her frequently to Winter Park to "stomps." He still assured her that he was the swellest man in the state.

"Sho' you kin have dat li'l ole house soon's Ah git dat 'oman outa dere. Everything b'longs tuh me an' you sho' kin have it. Ah sho' 'bominates uh skinny 'oman. Lawdy, you sho' is got one portly shape on you! You kin git *anything* you wants. Dis is *mah* town an' you sho' kin have it."

Delia's work-worn knees crawled over the earth in Gethsemane and up the rocks of Calvary many, many times during these months. She avoided the villagers and meeting places in her efforts to be blind and deaf. But Bertha nullified this to a degree, by coming to Delia's house to call Sykes out to her at the gate.

Delia and Sykes fought all the time now with no peaceful interludes. They slept and ate in silence. Two or three times Delia had attempted a timid friendliness, but she was repulsed each time. It was plain that the breaches must remain agape.

The sun had burned July to August. The heat streamed down like a 60 million hot arrows, smiting all things living upon the earth. Grass withered, leaves browned, snakes went blind in shedding, and men and dogs went mad. Dog days!

Delia came home one day and found Sykes there before her. She wondered, but started to go on into the house without speaking, even though he was standing in the kitchen door and she must either stoop under his arm or ask him to move. He made no room for her. She noticed a soap box beside the steps, but paid no particular attention to it, knowing that he must have brought it there. As she was stooping to pass under his outstretched arm, he suddenly pushed her backward, laughingly.

"Look in de box dere Delia, Ah done brung yuh somethin'!"

She nearly fell upon the box in her stumbling, and when she saw what it held, she all but fainted outright.

"Syke! Syke, mah Gawd! You take dat rattlesnake 'way from heah! You *gottuh.* Oh, Jesus, have mussy!"

"Ah ain't got tuh do nuthin' uh de kin'—fact is Ah ain't got tuh do 65 nothin' but die. Tain't no use uh you puttin' on airs makin' out lak you skeered uh dat snake—he's gointer stay right heah tell he die. He wouldn't bite me cause Ah knows how tuh handle 'im. Nohow he wouldn't risk breakin' out his fangs 'gin *yo* skinny laigs."

"Naw, now Syke, don't keep dat thing 'round tryin' tuh skeer me tuh death. You knows Ah'm even feared uh earth worms. Thass de biggest snake Ah evah did se. Kill 'im Syke, please."

"Doan ast me tuh do nothin' fuh yuh. Goin' 'round tryin' tuh be so damn asterperious. Naw, Ah ain't gonna kill it. Ah think uh damn sight mo' uh him dan you! Dat's a nice snake an' anybody doan lak 'im kin jes' hit de grit."

The village soon heard that Sykes had the snake, and came to see and ask questions.

"How de hen-fire did you ketch dat six-foot rattler, Syke?" Thomas asked.

"He's full uh frogs so he cain't hardly move, thass how Ah eased up on 70 'm. But Ah'm a snake charmer an' knows how tuh handle 'em. Shux, dat ain't nothin'. Ah could ketch one eve'y day if Ah so wanted tuh."

"Whut he needs is a heavy hick'ry club leaned real heavy on his head. Dat's de bes' way tuh charm a rattlesnake."

"Naw, Walt, y'all jes' don't understand dese diamon' backs lak Ah do," said Sykes in a superior tone of voice.

The village agreed with Walter, but the snake stayed on. His box remained by the kitchen door with its screen wire covering. Two or three days later it had digested its meal of frogs and literally came to life. It rattled at every movement in the kitchen or the yard. One day as Delia came down the kitchen steps she saw his chalky-white fangs curved like scimitars hung in the wire meshes. This time she did not run away with averted eyes as usual. She stood for a long time in the doorway in a red fury that grew bloodier for every second that she regarded the creature that was her torment.

That night she broached the subject as soon as Sykes sat down to the table.

"Syke, Ah wants you tuh take dat snake 'way fum heah. You done 75 starved me an' Ah put up widcher, you done beat me an Ah took dat, but you don kilt all mah insides bringin' dat varmint heah."

Sykes poured out a saucer full of coffee and drank it deliberately before he answered her.

"A whole lot Ah keer 'bout how you feels inside uh out. Dat snake ain't goin' no damn wheah till Ah gits ready fuh 'im tuh go. So fur as beatin' is concerned, yuh ain't took near all dat you gointer take ef yuh stay 'round *me*."

Delia pushed back her plate and got up from the table. "Ah hates you, Sykes," she said calmly. "Ah hates you tuh de same degree dat Ah useter love yuh. Ah done took an' took till mah belly is full up tuh mah neck. Dat's de reason Ah got mah letter fum de church an' moved mah membership tuh Woodbridge—so Ah don't haftuh take no sacrament wid yuh. Ah don't wantuh see yuh 'round me atall. Lay 'round wid dat 'oman all yuh wants tuh, but gwan 'way from me an' mah house. Ah hates yuh lak uh suck-egg dog."

Sykes almost let the huge wad of corn bread and collard greens he was chewing fall out of his mouth in amazement. He had a hard time whipping himself up to the proper fury to try to answer Delia.

"Well, Ah'm glad you does hate me. Ah'm sho' tiahed uh you hangin' 80 ontuh me. Ah don't want yuh. Look at yuh stringey ole neck! Yo' rawbony laigs an' arms is enough tuh cut uh man tuh death. You looks jes' lak de devvul's doll-baby tuh *me*. You cain't hate me no worse dan Ah hates you. Ah been hatin' *you* fuh years."

"Yo' ole black hide don't look lak nothin' tuh me, but uh passle uh wrinkled up rubber, wid yo' big ole yeahs flappin' on each side lak uh paih uh buzzard wings. Don't think Ah'm gointuh be run 'way fum mah house neither. Ah'm goin' tuh de white folks 'bout *you*, mah young man, de very nex' time you lay yo' han's on me. Mah cup is done run ovah." Delia said this with no signs of fear and Sykes departed from the house, threatening her, but made not the slightest move to carry out any of them.

That night he did not return at all, and the next day being Sunday, Delia was glad she did not have to quarrel before she hitched up her pony and drove the four miles to Woodbridge.

She stayed to the night service—"love feast"—which was very warm and full of spirit. In the emotional winds her domestic trials were borne far and wide so that she sang as she drove homeward,

> *Jurden water, black an' col*
> *Chills de body, not de soul*
> *An' Ah wantah cross Jurden in uh calm time.*

She came from the barn to the kitchen door and stopped.

"Whut's de mattah, ol' Satan, you ain't kicken' up yo' racket?" She addressed the snake's box. Complete silence. She went on into the house with a new hope in its birth struggles. Perhaps her threat to go to the white folks had frightened Sykes! Perhaps he was sorry! Fifteen years of misery and suppression had brought Delia to the place where she would hope *anything* that looked towards a way over or through her wall of inhibitions.

She felt in the match-safe behind the stove at once for a match. There 85 was only one there.

"Dat niggah wouldn't fetch nothin' heah tuh save his rotten neck, but he kin run thew whut Ah brings quick enough. Now he done toted off nigh on tuh haff uh box uh matches. He done had dat 'oman heah in mah house, too."

Nobody but a woman could tell how she knew this even before she struck the match. But she did and it put her into a new fury.

Presently she brought in the tubs to put the white things to soak. This time she decided she need not bring the hamper out of the bedroom; she would go in there and do the sorting. She picked up the pot-bellied lamp and went in. The room was small and the hamper stood hard by the foot of the white iron bed. She could sit and reach through the bedposts — resting as she worked.

"Ah wantah cross Jurden in uh calm time." She was singing again. The mood of the "love feast," had returned. She threw back the lid of the basket almost gaily. Then, moved by both horror and terror, she sprang back toward the door. *There lay the snake in the basket!* He moved sluggishly at first, but even as she turned round and round, jumped up and down in an insanity of fear, he began to stir vigorously. She saw him pouring his awful beauty from the basket upon the bed, then she seized the lamp and ran as fast as she could to the kitchen. The wind from the open door blew out the light and the darkness added to her terror. She sped to the darkness of the yard, slamming the door after her before she thought to set down the lamp. She did not feel safe even on the ground, so she climbed up in the hay barn.

There for an hour or more she lay sprawled upon the hay a gibbering 90 wreck.

Finally she grew quiet, and after that came coherent thought. With this stalked through her a cold, bloody rage. Hours of this. A period of introspection, a space of retrospection, then a mixture of both. Out of this an awful calm.

"Well, Ah done de bes' Ah could. If things ain't right, Gawd knows tain't mah fault."

She went to sleep—a twitch sleep—and woke up to a faint gray sky. There was a loud hollow sound below. She peered out. Sykes was at the woodpile, demolishing a wire-covered box.

He hurried to the kitchen door, but hung outside there some minutes before he entered, and stood some minutes more inside before he closed it after him.

The gray in the sky was spreading. Delia descended without fear now, 95 and crouched beneath the low bedroom window. The drawn shade shut out the dawn, shut in the night. But the thin walls held back no sound.

"Dat ol' scratch is woke up now!" She mused at the tremendous whirr inside, which every woodsman knows, is one of the sound illusions. The rattler is a ventriloquist. His whirr sounds to the right, to the left, straight ahead, behind, close under foot—everywhere but where it is. Woe to him who guesses wrong unless he is prepared to hold up his end of the argument! Sometimes he strikes without rattling at all.

Inside, Sykes heard nothing until he knocked a pot lid off the stove while trying to reach the match-safe in the dark. He had emptied his pockets at Bertha's.

The snake seemed to wake up under the stove and Sykes made a quick leap into the bedroom. In spite of the gin he had had, his head was clearing now.

"Mah Gawd!" he chattered, "ef Ah could on'y strack uh light!"

The rattling ceased for a moment as he stood paralyzed. He waited. It 100 seemed that the snake waited also.

"Oh, fuh de light! Ah thought he'd be too sick"—Sykes was muttering to himself when the whirr began again, closer, right underfoot this time. Long before this, Sykes' ability to think had been flattened down to primitive instinct and he leaped—onto the bed.

Outside Delia heard a cry that might have come from a maddened chimpanzee, a stricken gorilla. All the terror, all the horror, all the rage that man possibly could express, without a recognizable human sound.

A tremendous stir inside there, another series of animal screams, the intermittent whirr of the reptile. The shade torn violently down from the window, letting in the red dawn, a huge brown hand seizing the window stick, great dull blows upon the wooden floor punctuating the gibberish of sound long after the rattle of the snake had abruptly subsided. All this Delia could see and hear from her place beneath the window, and it made her ill. She crept over to the four o'clocks and stretched herself on the cool earth to recover.

She lay there. "Delia, Delia!" She could hear Sykes calling in a most despairing tone as one who expected no answer. The sun crept on up, and he called. Delia could not move—her legs had gone flabby. She never moved, he called, and the sun kept rising.

"Mah Gawd!" She heard him moan, "Mah Gawd fum Heben!" She   105
heard him stumbling about and got up from her flower-bed. The sun was
growing warm. As she approached the door she heard him call out hope-
fully, "Delia, is dat you Ah heah?"

She saw him on his hands and knees as soon as she reached the door.
He crept an inch or two toward her—all that he was able, and she saw
his horribly swollen neck and his one open eye shining with hope. A
surge of pity too strong to support bore her away from that eye that
must, could not, fail to see the tubs. He would see the lamp. Orlando
with its doctors was too far. She could scarcely reach the chinaberry
tree, where she waited in the growing heat while inside she knew the
cold river was creeping up and up to extinguish that eye which must
know by now that she knew.

[1926]

LANGSTON HUGHES [1902–1967]

Harlem

Born in Joplin, Missouri, **Langston Hughes** (1902–1967) grew up in Lincoln, Illinois, and Cleveland, Ohio. He began writing poetry during his high school years. After attending Columbia University for one year, he held odd jobs as an assistant cook, a launderer, and a busboy and traveled to Africa and Europe working as a seaman. In 1924 he moved to Harlem. Hughes's first book of poetry, *The Weary Blues*, was published in 1926. He finished his college education at Lincoln University in Pennsylvania three years later. He wrote novels, short stories, plays, songs, children's books, essays, and memoirs as well as poetry, and is also known for his engagement with the world of jazz and the influence it had on his writing. His life and work were enormously important in shaping the artistic contributions of the Harlem Renaissance of the 1920s.

What happens to a dream deferred?

Does it dry up
like a raisin in the sun?
Or fester like a sore —
And then run?   5
Does it stink like rotten meat?
Or crust and sugar over —
like a syrupy sweet?

Maybe it just sags
like a heavy load.   10

Or does it explode?

[1951]

JOHN KESSLER

Sushi USA:
The Japanese Paradigm

Based in Decatur, Illinois, **John Kessler** is a food writer and chief dining critic for the *Atlanta Journal-Constitution*. A graduate of Williams College in Williamstown, Massachusetts, Kessler also attended
L'Academie de Cuisine culinary school in Bethesda, Maryland. Before
his time at the *Atlanta Journal-Constitution*, Kessler worked in several
restaurants and taught English in Japan.

Kessler's article "The Japanese Paradigm" explores the prevalence
and misappropriation of Japanese food in American culture. He
claims that for Americans, in contrast to the Japanese, the focus is on
quantity over quality. Using obesity and life expectancy statistics as
evidence, Kessler argues that the American "translation" of Japanese
cuisine—such as deep-fried sushi—fails to capture Japan's healthy
approach toward food.

Sit down to a Sinatra roll at Shout restaurant, and this is what you get:
a sushi roll stuffed with three kinds of fish and cream cheese, breaded
and deep-fat-fried, and served up with spicy mayonnaise and a syrupy
brown sauce.

My friend, I'll say it clear; I'll state my case of which I'm certain: Sushi
"my way" is just so wrong.

How did it come to this? How did we Americans take an iconic Japanese dish that should be the essence of simplicity and freshness and turn
it into seppuku on a plate?

Sushi is everywhere—so everywhere that it's turned into American
food.

Supermarkets may no longer have butchers or bakers on site, but 5
thousands now have chefs who spend all day pressing California rolls.
There's even one at the Wal-Mart in Plano, Texas. I saw it. Two nice

Burmese men prepare 300 boxes each day next to a wall of Velveeta. The franchiser, AFC Corp., hopes to be in 200 more Wal-Marts soon.

We claim to love Japanese food, but we simply don't get it. Every good thing about the Japanese diet has been lost in translation.

Granted, the Japanese way of eating, unique to the culture that produced it, does not cross cultures easily. We may be in thrall to the small part we know, but we're still blind to the big picture of the Japanese diet — both its untold pleasures and its implications for health and well-being.

Japan today has the thinnest people among 30 industrialized countries, with an obesity rate around 3 percent, as opposed to America's 31 percent. Japan also has the world's longest life expectancy. Yet the Japanese encounter the same lifestyle issues most often implicated in America's rampant obesity problem. They face the same daily stresses, the same disappearing family dinner hour, the same reliance on processed foods, and the same sedentary workplaces.

The Japanese eat more fish and vegetables and less overall fat. But the vital difference, I think, is in how they present flavors, approach meals, respond to hunger and engage all their senses at the table. Simply put, the Japanese know how to eat less and enjoy their food more.

The only way to explain this truth is to tell it.   10

In 1983, after graduating from college, I moved to the Kansai region of western Japan for two years to teach English. When I first arrived, each meal seemed booby-trapped. The yellow spongy tile on the sashimi platter was merely sweetened egg. But the pinkish goo in the small dish? Fermented squid innards that tasted like shark chum mixed with ammonia.

Learning to appreciate this food took patience. Some of my expat friends gave up hope and subsisted on McDonald's and care packages bearing Old El Paso taco kits.

For me, the turnaround came after I had been in the country for about a month and an American colleague who knew the ropes invited me out to dinner. The meal was unlike any Japanese meal I had eaten back home. The restaurant was in the labyrinth of Osaka's uptown entertainment district, in a dark underground bunker of a dining room. It was an *izakaya* — a kind of pub with an extended menu of snacks and other small dishes.

My friend and I knocked back draft beers as he did the ordering — crisp grilled rice balls, dressed boiled spinach, pork dumplings and a few other easy-to-like dishes.

No squid goo.   15

The food arrived helter-skelter, and we shared it all. We ordered more as needed, but after eight or 10 plates, our diminished appetites cut us off.

This one meal encapsulated everything I would come to learn about Japanese food over the next two years.

For starters, it offered a far greater variety of foods than any I had eaten before. Variety, above all, is key to the Japanese diet.

At restaurants, at home, in packed lunches, Japanese meals do not seem complete without constant contrasts. A boneless chicken breast with rice and one vegetable? This kind of "wholesome American meal" would never pass muster in Japan.

Tokyo-based author Elizabeth Andoh attributes this deeply ingrained 20 Japanese impulse to a 1,200-year-old set of dietary guidelines. In her new cookbook, *Washoku* (Ten Speed Press, $35), she notes that washoku, a derivation of Buddhist practice, suggests that each meal should contain five different colors, primary tastes (sweet, salty, etc.), textures and cooking preparations. These principles are not something most modern Japanese think about, but, as Andoh maintains, they are second nature.

"You could follow a girl who's been up all night in a club into a konbini [convenience store], and the assortment of junk food she puts into her kaato [shopping cart] will follow washoku," says Andoh.

The Japanese Health Ministry published a more contemporary set of nutrition guidelines in 1985 with the slogan "ichi nichi sanju hinmoku tabeyo," or "eat 30 different foods each day." (Japan's Martha Stewart, popular cookbook author Harumi Kurihara, still recommends this.) Compare this to the original USDA Food Guide Pyramid from 1992, with its suggested 15 to 26 servings of the various food groups, and the message is telling: Americans quantify what they eat, the Japanese qualify.

With such variety on the table, no one dish can predominate. Granted, my izakaya meal was similar to a tapas spread (albeit with more, smaller dishes), but in Japan this kind of decentralized approach is the norm, whether at a formal dinner, in a quick-service restaurant or sitting around the family dinner table.

"There's no main dish, but many small dishes," says Shinobu Kitayama, a University of Michigan psychologist who studies group dynamics. At a typical home dinner, he says, each member of the family gets a bowl of miso soup and rice, while the group shares a variety of *sozai*, or side dishes.

But these are not really sides in the American sense. They may be sea- 25 soned vegetables, meat or fish. Most often, sozai combine vegetables with small amounts of animal protein; any given meal might feature fish, beef and pork.

"Basically, Japanese are meat-eating vegetarians," says Kitayama. "You'd never see a 500-gram steak like you would in America."

Sozai may be homemade but will just as likely come from the freezer case, a supermarket, a convenience store or from the vast food halls in the basements of department stores. Everything is portioned and individually packaged—hundreds of small dishes for the taking. Compare this deli experience to, say, Whole Foods Market, where the hot bar, salads and cheesy casseroles come by the pound.

Again, it's quality vs. quantity.

With so many small dishes on the table, the vessels themselves matter. Any Japanese meal presents a tableau of artfully mismatched dishware. Home pantries brim with small plates and bowls.

On a formal level, the art of Japanese food arranging is as codified as 30 flower arranging; in daily practice, people cook from a huge repertoire of dishes, each of which has an accepted "look." Embedded in the aesthetic lie constant visual clues to portion size.

Bear in mind this describes the sushi experience in Japan. Diners sit at the bar and order sushi by the piece or pair directly from the chef or, in an inexpensive kaitenzushi shop, taking plates off a conveyor belt. Most small neighborhood restaurants operate in a similar fashion. The moment a bite of food is ready, the cook hands it to you.

The Japanese approach to satiety is a parabolic curve with an infinite endpoint. "Stuffed" is never the desirable conclusion.

Kitayama believes this is why Japanese food favors subtle seasoning. "Strong tastes can stimulate your appetite, like in Chinese food." Japan may have the only national cuisine with no traditional use for garlic.

If an incremental, small-plates meal leaves someone with a big appetite hungry two hours later, there's a time-honored tradition called shime—"closing" the evening at a soup noodle stand. The broth will be dashi—the ubiquitous stock made from dried skipjack tuna and sea kelp—and it will be filled with umami.

This Japanese notion of a fifth primary taste (in addition to sweet, 35 sour, bitter and salty) was proven by researchers at the University of Miami in 2000, who isolated receptors on the tongue for the amino acids naturally abundant in dashi and many other foods.

In the West, we associate the satisfaction of umami with meats, cheeses and other caloric sources of animal protein. Because the Japanese didn't eat meat until the Meiji Restoration of 1868, the cuisine found ways to extract umami from sea vegetables, fish and plants. The food is low in fat but richer in sources of umami. On the most basic neurochemical level, it tastes meatier that actual meat.

That izakaya meal was for me the beginning of a lifelong passion for Japanese food. When I returned home after two years, I remember thinking how unnecessarily large the portions were here and how the food sat in my stomach after meals. Sadly, the feeling didn't last.

Fried anything—even sushi—is easy enough to eat.

[2006]

Jeff Widener, *Tank Man*, 1989. An unidentified man blocks tanks headed toward Tiananmen Square in Beijing, China, on June 5, 1989. An estimated 3,000 people were massacred by the Chinese government during several weeks of protests. (AP Photo/Jeff Widener.)

EDWARD SAID   [1935–2003]

Clashing Civilizations?

Edward Said (1935–2003), was a world-renowned scholar, literary critic, and pro-Palestinian activist. Born in Jerusalem to wealthy Christian Palestinian parents, his father an American citizen, Said spent his formative years in Cairo and, briefly, Jerusalem. As an adolescent he continued his education in the United States, eventually earning his B.A. from Princeton University and his M.A. and Ph.D. from Harvard University. In 1963 he began teaching English and comparative literature at Columbia University, becoming a University Professor, Columbia's most-honored academic rank, in 1992. Said also taught at Harvard, Johns Hopkins, and Yale universities. The recipient of numerous honors and awards, including Columbia's Trilling Award and the Wellek Prize of the American Comparative Literature Association, Said's renown comes mostly from his influential albeit controversial book *Orientalism* (1978), in which he argues that Western scholarship of Eastern history and peoples is unduly permeated by Eurocentric prejudices. While academic circles embroiled themselves in the disputation and endorsement of the validity of his assertions, Said persisted in his outspoken advocacy of the Palestinian cause, stirring controversy until his death from leukemia in 2003.

Excerpted from Said's essay "We All Swim Together," first published in *New Statesman* just after the terrorist attacks of September 11, 2001, "Clashing Civilizations?" is Said's refutation of the argument that Islamic fundamentalists suffer from a sense of cultural inferiority which has led to a clash of so-called "civilizations." Said takes issue with both the pejorative relegation of Islamic peoples to the backwater of history as well as the egotistical and reductive assumption that there exists a clear line of demarcation separating the "the West" from "Islam."

Samuel Huntington's article "The Clash of Civilizations?" appeared in the summer 1993 issue of *Foreign Affairs*, where it immediately attracted a surprising amount of attention and reaction. Because the article was intended to supply Americans with an original thesis about "a new phase" in world politics after the end of the Cold War, Huntington's terms of argument seemed compellingly large, bold, even visionary. "It is my hypothesis," he wrote,

> that . . . the great divisions among humankind and the dominating source of conflict will be cultural. Nation-states will remain the most powerful actors in world affairs, but the principal conflicts of global politics will occur between nations and groups of different civilizations. The clash of civilizations will dominate global politics. The fault lines between civilizations will be the battle lines of the future.

Most of the argument in the pages that followed relied on a vague notion of something Huntington called "civilization identity" and "the interactions among seven or eight [sic] major civilizations," of which the conflict between two of them, Islam and the West, gets the lion's share of his attention. In this belligerent kind of thought, he relies heavily on a 1990 article by the veteran orientalist Bernard Lewis, whose ideological colors are manifest in its title, "The Roots of Muslim Rage." In both articles, the personification of enormous entities called "the West" and "Islam" is recklessly affirmed, as if hugely complicated matters such as identity and culture existed in a cartoonlike world where Popeye and Bluto bash each other mercilessly, with one always more virtuous pugilist getting the upper hand over his adversary. Certainly neither Huntington nor Lewis has much time to spare for the internal dynamics and plurality of every civilization; or for considering that the major contest in most modern cultures concerns the definition or interpretation of each culture; or for the unattractive possibility that a great deal of demagogy and downright ignorance is involved in presuming to speak for a whole religion or civilization. No, the West is the West, and Islam is Islam.

The basic model of west versus the rest (the Cold War opposition reformulated) is what has persisted, often insidiously and implicitly, in discussion since the terrible events of September 11. The carefully planned and horrendous, pathologically motivated suicide attack and mass slaughter by a small group of deranged militants has been turned into proof of Huntington's thesis. Instead of seeing it for what it is—the capture of big ideas (I use the word loosely) by a tiny band of crazed fanatics for criminal purposes—international luminaries from the former Pakistani prime minister Benazir Bhutto to the Italian prime minister, Silvio Berlusconi, have pontificated about Islam's troubles and, in the latter's case, have used Huntington's ideas to rant on about the West's superiority, how "we" have Mozart and Michelangelo and they don't.

But why not instead see parallels, admittedly less spectacular in their destructiveness, to Osama Bin Laden and his followers in such cults as the Branch Davidians, or the disciples of the Reverend Jim Jones in Guyana, or the Japanese Aum Shinrikyo? Even *The Economist*, in its issue of September 22–28, 2001, couldn't resist reaching for the vast generalization, praising Huntington extravagantly for his "cruel and sweeping, but nonetheless acute" observations about Islam. "Today," the journal says, Huntington writes that "the world's billion or so Muslims are 'convinced of the superiority of their culture, and obsessed with the inferiority of their power.'" Did he canvass one hundred Indonesians, two hundred Moroccans, five hundred Egyptians and fifty Bosnians? Even if he did, what sort of sample is that?

Uncountable are the editorials in every American and European news-   5
paper and magazine of note adding to this vocabulary of gigantism and apocalypse, each use of which is plainly designed to inflame the reader's indignant passion as a member of the "West," and what we need to do. Churchillian rhetoric° is used inappropriately by self-appointed combatants in the West's, and especially America's, war against its haters, despoilers, destroyers, with scant attention to complex histories that defy such reductiveness and have seeped from one territory into another, overriding the boundaries that are supposed to separate us all into divided armed camps.

This is the problem with unedifying labels such as *Islam* and *the West:* They mislead and confuse the mind, which is trying to make sense of a disorderly reality that won't be pigeonholed. I remember interrupting a man who, after a lecture I had given at a West Bank° university in 1994, rose from the audience and started to attack my ideas as "Western," as opposed to the strict Islamic ones he espoused. "Why are you wearing a suit and tie?" was the first retort that came to mind. "They're Western, too." He sat down with an embarrassed smile on his face, but I recalled the incident when information on the September 11 terrorists started to come in: how they had mastered all the technical details required to inflict their homicidal evil on the World Trade Center, the Pentagon and the aircraft they had commandeered. Where does one draw the line between "Western" technology and, as Berlusconi declared, "Islam's" inability to be a part of "modernity"?

One cannot easily do so. How finally inadequate are the labels, generalizations and cultural assertions. At some level, for instance, primitive passions and sophisticated know-how converge in ways that give

Churchillian rhetoric: A statesman and gifted orator, Winston Churchill (1874–1965) was British prime minister during World War II, when his stirring speeches fortified his embattled nation's resolve to fight the Germans.   **West Bank:** Disputed territory adjacent to Israel, controlled partly by Israel and partly by the Palestinian Authority.

the lie to a fortified boundary not only between "West" and "Islam," but also between past and present, us and them, to say nothing of the very concepts of identity and nationality about which there is unending debate. A unilateral decision made to undertake crusades, to oppose their evil with our good, to extirpate terrorism and, in Paul Wolfowitz's° nihilistic vocabulary, to end nations entirely, doesn't make the supposed entities any easier to see; rather, it speaks to how much simpler it is to make bellicose statements for the purpose of mobilizing collective passions than to reflect, examine, sort out what it is we are dealing with in reality, the interconnectedness of innumerable lives, "ours" as well as "theirs."

Paul Wolfowitz: Deputy secretary of defense under President George W. Bush.

J. Howard Miller, *We Can Do It!*, 1942. During World War II, many women filled the positions left vacant when men went off to war. J. Howard Miller's poster was commissioned by a labor management committee during World War II in support of the war effort. (Corbis.)

AARON DEVOR   [b. 1951]

Becoming Members
of Society: Learning the
Social Meanings of Gender

Professor of Sociology and Dean of Graduate Studies at the University
of Victoria in British Columbia, Canada, **Aaron Devor** focuses on the
study of gender and sexuality, particularly in regard to lesbians, transgen-
dered females, and female-to-male transsexuals. Devor coined the term
"gender-blending" in his first book, *Gender Blending: Confronting the Limits of Duality* (1989), in which he examines gender as a social construct
and how it affects women who don't necessarily conform to cultural
expectations of femininity. Devor's second book, *FTM: Female-to-Male
Transsexuals in Society* (1997), narrates the life experiences of forty-five
female-to-male transsexuals in an effort to better understand the relationships among sex, gender, and sexuality. Currently his research spot-
lights transgender and gay rights activist Reed Erickson, a transsexed
man and founder of the Erickson Educational Foundation. One of ten
recipients of the coveted 3M Teaching Fellowship Awards for Teaching
and Learning in Higher Education in 2000, Devor is highly rated for his
challenging and innovative course material, his teaching style, his rap-
port with students, and his dedication to their academic success. It was
in 2003 that Devor—born Holly Devor in 1951—adopted the name
Aaron and made public his decision to live as a man.

   This essay from Devor's pivotal *Gender Blending: Confronting the
Limits of Duality* looks at how children react to social indicators and
identify themselves as gendered beings as toddlers. Devor asserts that,
over time, gender definitions become so ingrained that they appear
natural rather than socially prescribed.

THE GENDERED SELF

   The task of learning to be properly gendered members of society only
begins with the establishment of gender identity. Gender identities act as

cognitive filtering devices guiding people to attend to and learn gender role behaviors appropriate to their statuses. Learning to behave in accordance with one's gender identity is a lifelong process. As we move through our lives, society demands different gender performances from us and rewards, tolerates, or punishes us differently for conformity to, or digression from, social norms. As children, and later adults, learn the rules of membership in society, they come to see themselves in terms they have learned from the people around them.

Children begin to settle into a gender identity between the age of eighteen months and two years.[1] By the age of two, children usually understand that they are members of a gender grouping and can correctly identify other members of their gender.[2] By age three they have a fairly firm and consistent concept of gender. Generally, it is not until children are five to seven years old that they become convinced that they are permanent members of their gender grouping.[3]

Researchers test the establishment, depth, and tenacity of gender identity through the use of language and the concepts mediated by language. The language systems used in populations studied by most researchers in this field conceptualize gender as binary and permanent. All persons are either male or female. All males are first boys and then men; all females are first girls and then women. People are believed to be unable to change genders without sex change surgery, and those who do change sex are considered to be both disturbed and exceedingly rare.

This is by no means the only way that gender is conceived in all cultures. Many aboriginal cultures have more than two gender categories and accept the idea that, under certain circumstances, gender may be changed without changes being made to biological sex characteristics. Many North and South American native peoples had a legitimate social category for persons who wished to live according to the gender role of another sex. Such people were sometimes revered, sometimes ignored, and occasionally scorned. Each culture had its own word to describe such persons, most commonly translated into English as "berdache." Similar institutions and linguistic concepts have also been recorded in early Siberian, Madagascan, and Polynesian societies, as well as in medieval Europe.[4]

Very young children learn their culture's social definitions of gender 5 and gender identity at the same time that they learn what gender behaviors are appropriate for them. But they only gradually come to understand the meaning of gender in the same way as the adults of their society do. Very young children may learn the words which describe their gender and be able to apply them to themselves appropriately, but their comprehension of their meaning is often different from that used by adults. Five-year-olds, for example, may be able to accurately recognize their own gender and the genders of the people around them, but they will often make such ascriptions on the basis of role information, such as hair style, rather than physical attributes, such as genitals, even when physical cues are clearly known to them. One result of this level of understanding of gender is that children in this age group often believe that people may change their gender with a change in clothing, hair style, or activity.[5]

The characteristics most salient to young minds are the more culturally specific qualities which grow out of gender role prescriptions. In one study, young school age children, who were given dolls and asked to identify their gender, overwhelmingly identified the gender of the dolls on the basis of attributes such as hair length or clothing style, in spite of the fact that the dolls were anatomically correct. Only 17 percent of the children identified the dolls on the basis of their primary or secondary sex characteristics.[6] Children five to seven years old understand gender as a function of role rather than as a function of anatomy. Their understanding is that gender (role) is supposed to be stable but that it is possible to alter it at will. This demonstrates that although the standard social definition of gender is based on genitalia, this is not the way that young children first learn to distinguish gender. The process of learning to think about gender in an adult fashion is one prerequisite to becoming a full member of society. Thus, as children grow older, they learn to think of themselves and others in terms more like those used by adults.

Children's developing concepts of themselves as individuals are necessarily bound up in their need to understand the expectations of the society of which they are a part. As they develop concepts of themselves as individuals, they do so while observing themselves as reflected in the eyes of others. Children start to understand themselves as individuals separate from others during the years that they first acquire gender identities and gender roles. As they do so, they begin to understand that others see them and respond to them as particular people. In this way they develop concepts of themselves as individuals, as an "I" (a proactive subject) simultaneously with self-images of themselves as individuals, as a "me" (a member of society, a subjective object). Children learn that they are both as they see themselves and as others see them.[7]

To some extent, children initially acquire the values of the society around them almost indiscriminately. To the degree that children absorb the generalized standards of society into their personal concept of what is correct behavior, they can be said to hold within themselves the attitude of the "generalized other."[8] This "generalized other" functions as a sort of monitoring or measuring device with which individuals may judge their own actions against those of their generalized conceptions of how members of society are expected to act. In this way members of society have available to them a guide, or an internalized observer, to turn the more private "I" into the object of public scrutiny, the "me." In this way, people can monitor their own behavioral impulses and censor actions which might earn them social disapproval or scorn. The tension created by the constant interplay of the personal "I" and the social "me" is the creature known as the "self."

But not all others are of equal significance in our lives, and therefore not all others are of equal impact on the development of the self. Any person is available to become part of one's "generalized other," but certain individuals, by virtue of the sheer volume of time spent in interaction with someone, or by virtue of the nature of particular interactions, become more significant in the shaping of people's values. These "significant others" become prominent in the formation of one's self-image and one's ideals and goals. As such they carry disproportionate weight in one's personal "generalized other."[9] Thus, children's individualistic impulses are shaped into a socially acceptable form both by particular individuals and by a more generalized pressure to conformity exerted by innumerable faceless members of society. Gender identity is one of the most central portions of that developing sense of self. . . .

GENDER ROLE BEHAVIORS AND ATTITUDES

The clusters of social definitions used to identify persons by gender 10 are collectively known as femininity and masculinity. Masculine characteristics are used to identify persons as males, while feminine ones are used as signifiers for femaleness. People use femininity or masculinity to claim and communicate their membership in their assigned, or chosen, sex or gender. Others recognize our sex or gender more on the basis of these characteristics than on the basis of sex characteristics, which are usually largely covered by clothing in daily life.

These two clusters of attributes are most commonly seen as mirror images of one another with masculinity usually characterized by dominance and aggression, and femininity by passivity and submission. A more even-handed description of the social qualities subsumed by femininity and masculinity might be to label masculinity as generally concerned with egoistic dominance and femininity as striving for cooperation or communion.[10] Characterizing femininity and masculinity in such a way does not portray the two clusters of characteristics as being in a hierarchical relationship to one another but rather as being two different approaches to the same question, that question being centrally concerned with the goals, means, and use of power. Such an alternative conception of gender roles captures the hierarchical and competitive masculine thirst for power, which can, but need not, lead to aggression, and the feminine quest for harmony and communal well-being, which can, but need not, result in passivity and dependence.

Many activities and modes of expression are recognized by most members of society as feminine. Any of these can be, and often are, displayed by persons of either gender. In some cases, cross gender behaviors are ignored by observers, and therefore do not compromise the integrity of a person's gender display. In other cases, they are labeled as inappropriate gender role behaviors. Although these behaviors are closely linked to sexual status in the minds and experiences of most people, research shows that dominant persons of either gender tend to use influence tactics and verbal styles usually associated with men and masculinity, while subordinate persons, of either gender, tend to use those considered to be the province of women.[11] Thus it seems likely that many aspects of masculinity and femininity are the result, rather than the cause, of status inequalities.

Popular conceptions of femininity and masculinity instead revolve around hierarchical appraisals of the "natural" roles of males and females. Members of both genders are believed to share many of the same human characteristics, although in different relative proportions; both males and females are popularly thought to be able to do many of the same things, but most activities are divided into suitable and unsuitable categories for each gender class. Persons who perform the activities considered appropriate for another gender will be expected to perform them poorly; if they succeed adequately, or even well, at their endeavors, they may be rewarded with ridicule or scorn for blurring the gender dividing line.

The patriarchal gender schema° currently in use in mainstream North American society reserves highly valued attributes for males and actively supports the high evaluation of any characteristics which might inadvertently become associated with maleness. The ideology which the schema grows out of postulates that the cultural superiority of males is a natural outgrowth of the innate predisposition of males toward aggression and dominance, which is assumed to flow inevitably from evolutionary and biological sources. Female attributes are likewise postulated to find their source in innate predispositions acquired in the evolution of the species. Feminine characteristics are thought to be intrinsic to the female facility for childbirth and breastfeeding. Hence, it is popularly believed that the social position of females is biologically mandated to be intertwined with the care of children and a "natural" dependency on men for the

schema: A mental framework, scheme, or pattern that helps us make sense of experience.

maintenance of mother-child units. Thus the goals of femininity and, by implication, of all biological females are presumed to revolve around heterosexuality and maternity.[12]

Femininity, according to this traditional formulation, "would result in 15 warm and continued relationships with men, a sense of maternity, interest in caring for children, and the capacity to work productively and continuously in female occupations."[13] This recipe translates into a vast number of proscriptions and prescriptions. Warm and continued relations with men and an interest in maternity require that females be heterosexually oriented. A heterosexual orientation requires women to dress, move, speak, and act in ways that men will find attractive. As patriarchy has reserved active expressions of power as a masculine attribute, femininity must be expressed through modes of dress, movement, speech, and action which communicate weakness, dependency, ineffectualness, availability for sexual or emotional service, and sensitivity to the needs of others.

Some, but not all, of these modes of interrelation also serve the demands of maternity and many female job ghettos. In many cases, though, femininity is not particularly useful in maternity or employment. Both mothers and workers often need to be strong, independent, and effectual in order to do their jobs well. Thus femininity, as a role, is best suited to satisfying a masculine vision of heterosexual attractiveness.

Body postures and demeanors which communicate subordinate status and vulnerability to trespass through a message of "no threat" make people appear to be feminine. They demonstrate subordination through a minimizing of spatial use: people appear feminine when they keep their arms closer to their bodies, their legs closer together, and their torsos and heads less vertical then do masculine-looking individuals. People also look feminine when they point their toes inward and use their hands in small or childlike gestures. Other people also tend to stand closer to people they see as feminine, often invading their personal space, while people who make frequent appeasement gestures, such as smiling, also give the appearance of femininity. Perhaps as an outgrowth of a subordinate status and the need to avoid conflict with more socially powerful people, women tend to excel over men at the ability to correctly interpret, and effectively display, nonverbal communication cues.[14]

Speech characterized by inflections, intonations, and phrases that convey nonaggression and subordinate status also make a speaker appear more feminine. Subordinate speakers who use more polite expressions and ask more questions in conversation seem more feminine. Speech characterized by sounds of higher frequencies are often interpreted by listeners as feminine, childlike, and ineffectual.[15] Feminine styles of dress likewise display subordinate status through greater restriction of the free movement of the body, greater exposure of the bare skin, and an emphasis on sexual characteristics. The more gender distinct the dress, the more this is the case.

Masculinity, like femininity, can be demonstrated through a wide variety of cues. Pleck has argued that it is commonly expressed in North American society through the attainment of some level of proficiency at some, or all, of the following four main attitudes of masculinity. Persons who display success and high status in their social group, who exhibit "a manly air of toughness, confidence, and self-reliance" and "the aura of aggression, violence, and daring," and who conscientiously avoid anything associated with femininity are seen as exuding masculinity.[16] These requirements reflect the patriarchal ideology that masculinity results from an excess of testosterone, the assumption being that androgens supply a natural impetus toward aggression, which in turn impels males toward achievement and success. This vision of masculinity also reflects the ideological stance that ideal maleness (masculinity) must remain untainted by female (feminine) pollutants.

Masculinity, then, requires of its actors that they organize themselves and their society in a hierarchical manner so as to be able to explicitly quantify the achievement of success. The achievement of high status in one's social group requires competitive and aggressive behavior from those who wish to obtain it. Competition which is motivated by a goal of individual achievement, or egoistic dominance, also requires of its participants a degree of emotional insensitivity to feelings of hurt and loss in defeated others, and a measure of emotional insularity to protect oneself from becoming vulnerable to manipulation by others. Such values lead those who subscribe to them to view feminine persons as "born losers" and to strive to eliminate any similarities to feminine people from their own personalities. In patriarchally organized societies, masculine values become the ideological structure of the society as a whole. Masculinity thus becomes "innately" valuable and femininity serves a contrapuntal function to delineate and magnify the hierarchical dominance of masculinity.

Body postures, speech patterns, and styles of dress which demonstrate and support the assumption of dominance and authority convey an impression of masculinity. Typical masculine body postures tend to be expansive and aggressive. People who hold their arms and hands in positions away from their bodies, and who stand, sit, or lie with their legs apart—thus maximizing the amount of space that they physically occupy—appear most physically masculine. Persons who communicate an air of authority or a readiness for aggression by standing erect and moving forcefully also tend to appear more masculine. Movements that are abrupt and stiff, communicating force and threat rather than flexibility and cooperation, make an actor look masculine. Masculinity can also be conveyed by stern or serious facial expressions that suggest minimal receptivity to

20

the influence of others, a characteristic which is an important element in the attainment and maintenance of egoistic dominance.[17]

Speech and dress which likewise demonstrate or claim superior status are also seen as characteristically masculine behavior patterns. Masculine speech patterns display a tendency toward expansiveness similar to that found in masculine body postures. People who attempt to control the direction of conversations seem more masculine.[18] Those who tend to speak more loudly, use less polite and more assertive forms, and tend to interrupt the conversations of others more often also communicate masculinity to others. Styles of dress which emphasize the size of upper body musculature, allow freedom of movement, and encourage an illusion of physical power and a look of easy physicality all suggest masculinity. Such appearances of strength and readiness to action serve to create or enhance an aura of aggressiveness and intimidation central to an appearance of masculinity. Expansive postures and gestures combine with these qualities to insinuate that a position of secure dominance is a masculine one.

Gender role characteristics reflect the ideological contentions underlying the dominant gender schema in North American society. That schema leads us to believe that female and male behaviors are the result of socially directed hormonal instructions which specify that females will want to have children and will therefore find themselves relatively helpless and dependent on males for support and protection. The schema claims that males are innately aggressive and competitive and therefore will dominate over females. The social hegemony° of this ideology ensures that we are all raised to practice gender roles which will confirm this vision of the nature of the sexes. Fortunately, our training to gender roles is neither complete nor uniform. As a result, it is possible to point to multitudinous exceptions to, and variations on, these themes. Biological evidence is equivocal about the source of gender roles; psychological androgyny° is a widely accepted concept. It seems most likely that gender roles are the result of systematic power imbalances based on gender discrimination.[19]

Notes

1. Much research has been devoted to determining when gender identity becomes solidified in the sense that a child knows itself to be unequivocally either male or female. John Money and his colleagues have proposed eighteen months of age because it is difficult or impossible to change a child's gender identity once

hegemony: System of preponderant influence, authority, or dominance.
androgyny: The state of having both male and female characteristics.

it has been established around the age of eighteen months. Money and Ehrhardt, p. 243.

2. Mary Driver Leinbach and Beverly I. Fagot, "Acquisition of Gender Labels: A Test for Toddlers," *Sex Roles* 15 (1986), pp. 655–66.

3. Maccoby, pp. 225–29; Kohlberg and Ullian, p. 211.

4. See Susan Baker, "Biological Influences on Human Sex and Gender," in *Women: Sex and Sexuality*, ed. Catherine R. Stimpson and Ethel S. Person (Chicago: University of Chicago Press, 1980), p. 186; Evelyn Blackwood, "Sexuality and Gender in Certain Native American Tribes: The Case of Cross-Gender Females," *Signs* 10 (1984), pp. 27–42; Vern L. Bullough, "Transvestites in the Middle Ages," *American Journal of Sociology* 79 (1974), 1381–89; J. Cl. DuBois, "Transsexualisme et Anthropologie Culturelle," *Gynecologie Practique* 6 (1969), pp. 431–40; Donald C. Forgey, "The Institution of Berdache among the North American Plains Indians," *Journal of Sex Research* 11 (Feb. 1975), pp. 1–15; Walter L. Williams, *The Spirit and the Flesh: Sexual Diversity in American Indian Culture* (Boston: Beacon, 1986).

5. Maccoby, p. 255.

6. Ibid., p. 227.

7. George Herbert Mead, "Self," in *The Social Psychology of George Herbert Mead*, ed. Anselm Strauss (Chicago: Phoenix Books, 1962, 1934), pp. 212–60.

8. G. H. Mead.

9. Hans Gerth and C. Wright Mills, *Character and Social Structure: The Psychology of Social Institutions* (New York: Harcourt, Brace and World, 1953), p. 96.

10. Egoistic dominance is a striving for superior rewards for oneself or a competitive striving to reduce the rewards for one's competitors even if such action will not increase one's own rewards. Persons who are motivated by desires for egoistic dominance not only wish the best for themselves but also wish to diminish the advantages of others whom they may perceive as competing with them. See Maccoby, p. 217.

11. Judith Howard, Philip Blumstein, and Pepper Schwartz, "Sex, Power, and Influence Tactics in Intimate Relationships," *Journal of Personality and Social Psychology* 51 (1986), pp. 102–09; Peter Kollock, Philip Blumstein, and Pepper Schwartz, "Sex and Power in Interaction: Conversational Privileges and Duties," *American Sociological Review* 50 (1985), pp. 34–46.

12. Chodorow, p. 134.

13. Jon K. Meyer and John E. Hoopes, "The Gender Dysphoria Syndromes: A Position Statement on So-Called 'Transsexualism'," *Plastic and Reconstructive Surgery* 54 (Oct. 1974), pp. 444–51.

14. Erving Goffman, *Gender Advertisements* (New York: Harper Colophon Books, 1976); Judith A. Hall, *Non-Verbal Sex Differences: Communication Accuracy and Expressive Style* (Baltimore: Johns Hopkins University Press, 1984); Nancy M. Henley, *Body Politics: Power, Sex and Non-Verbal Communication* (Englewood Cliffs, New Jersey: Prentice Hall, 1979); Marianne Wex, *"Let's Take Back Our Space": "Female" and "Male" Body Language as a Result of Patriarchal Structures* (Berlin: Frauenliteraturverlag Hermine Fees, 1979).

15. Karen L. Adams, "Sexism and the English Language: The Linguistic Implications of Being a Woman," in *Women: A Feminist Perspective*, 3rd edition, ed. Jo Freeman (Palo Alto, Calif.: Mayfield, 1984), pp. 478–91; Hall, pp. 37, 130–37.

16. Elizabeth Hafkin Pleck, *Domestic Tyranny: The Making of Social Policy Against Family Violence from Colonial Times to the Present* (Cambridge: Oxford University Press, 1989), p. 139.

17. Goffman, *Gender Advertisements;* Hall; Henley; Wex.

18. Adams; Hall, pp. 37, 130–37.

19. Howard, Blumstein, and Schwartz; Kollock, Blumstein, and Schwartz.

Lewis W. Hine, *Powerhouse Mechanic*, **1920.** A mechanic works on a steam pump in an electric powerhouse in one of Lewis Hine's best-known photographs. (Courtesy George Eastman House.)

Why Boys Don't Play
With Dolls

Katha Pollitt is an American feminist author. Educated at Harvard and the Columbia School for the Arts, Pollitt has achieved a national reputation for her poetry and essays. Though she has written nonfiction for a variety of publications, she is best known for her "Subject to Debate" column, which appears regularly in *The Nation* and the *Washington Post*. A suberb stylist, Pollitt is known for her sharp, provocative analyses of popular culture and politics. In 1992, her essay on the culture wars, "Why We Read," won the National Magazine Award for essays and criticism. Pollitt has received a National Endowment for the Arts grant for her poetry, as well as a Guggenheim Fellowship. Pollitt's 1998 book, *The Antarctic Traveller*, received the National Book Critics Circle Award. Pollitt's poems have appeared in the *New Yorker, Atlantic Monthly, New Republic, Yale Review*, and other publications. She has been a guest on National Public Radio's *Fresh Air* and *All Things Considered*, and on several television shows, including *The McLaughlin Group* and *Dateline NBC*.

It's twenty-eight years since the founding of NOW, and boys still like trucks and girls still like dolls. Increasingly, we are told that the source of these robust preferences must lie outside society—in prenatal hormonal influences, brain chemistry, genes—and that feminism has reached its natural limits. What else could possibly explain the love of preschool girls for party dresses or the desire of toddler boys to own more guns than Mark from Michigan.°

True, recent studies claim to show small cognitive differences between the sexes: he gets around by orienting himself in space, she does it by remembering landmarks. Time will tell if any deserve the hoopla with

Mark from Michigan: Mark Koernke, a former right-wing talk-show host who supports the militia movement's resistance to federal government.

Katha Pollitt, "Why Boys Don't Play with Dolls" from *The New York Times Magazine*, October 8, 1995. Copyright © 1995 by Katha Pollitt. Reprinted by permission of The New York Times.

which each is invariably greeted, over the protests of the researchers themselves. But even if the results hold up (and the history of such research is not encouraging), we don't need studies of sex-differentiated brain activity in reading, say, to understand why boys and girls still seem so unalike.

The feminist movement has done much for some women, and something for every woman, but it has hardly turned America into a playground free of sex roles. It hasn't even got women to stop dieting or men to stop interrupting them.

Instead of looking at kids to "prove" that differences in behavior by sex are innate, we can look at the ways we raise kids as an index to how unfinished the feminist revolution really is, and how tentatively it is embraced even by adults who fully expect their daughters to enter previously male-dominated professions and their sons to change diapers.

I'm at a children's birthday party. "I'm sorry," one mom silently mouths   5
to the mother of the birthday girl, who has just torn open her present—
Tropical Splash Barbie. Now, you can love Barbie or you can hate Barbie, and there are feminists in both camps. But *apologize* for Barbie? Inflict Barbie, against your own convictions, on the child of a friend you know will be none too pleased?

Every mother in that room had spent years becoming a person who had to be taken seriously, not least by herself. Even the most attractive, I'm willing to bet, had suffered over her body's failure to fit the impossible American ideal. Given all that, it seems crazy to transmit Barbie to the next generation. Yet to reject her is to say that what Barbie represents— being sexy, thin, stylish—is unimportant, which is obviously not true, and children know it's not true.

Women's looks matter terribly in this society, and so Barbie, however ambivalently, must be passed along. After all, there are worse toys. The Cut and Style Barbie styling head, for example, a grotesque object intended to encourage "hair play." The grown-ups who give that probably apologize, too.

How happy would most parents be to have a child who flouted sex conventions? I know a lot of women, feminists, who complain in a comical, eyeball-rolling way about their sons' passion for sports: the ruined weekends, obnoxious coaches, macho values. But they would not think of discouraging their sons from participating in this activity they find so foolish. Or do they? Their husbands are sports fans, too, and they like their husbands a lot.

Could it be that even sports-resistant moms see athletics as part of manliness? That if their sons wanted to spend the weekend writing up their diaries, or reading, or baking, they'd find it disturbing? Too antisocial? Too lonely? Too gay?

Theories of innate differences in behavior are appealing. They let parents 10
off the hook—no small recommendation in a culture that holds moms, and
sometimes even dads, responsible for their children's every misstep on the
road to bliss and success.

They allow grown-ups to take the path of least resistance to the dominant culture, which always requires less psychic effort, even if it means
more actual work: just ask the working mother who comes home
exhausted and nonetheless finds it easier to pick up her son's socks than
make him do it himself. They let families buy for their children, without
too much guilt, the unbelievably sexist junk that the kids, who have been
watching commercials since birth, understandably crave.

But the thing that theories do most of all is tell adults that the *adult*
world—in which moms and dads still play by many of the old rules even
as they question and fidget and chafe against them—is the way it's supposed to be. A girl with a doll and a boy with a truck "explain" why men
are from Mars and women are from Venus, why wives do housework
and husbands just don't understand.

The paradox is that the world of rigid and hierarchical sex roles evoked
by determinist theories is already passing away. Three-year-olds may
indeed insist that doctors are male and nurses female, even if their own
mother is a physician. Six-year-olds know better. These days, something
like half of all medical students are female, and male applications to
nursing school are inching upward. When tomorrow's three-year-olds
play doctor, who's to say how they'll assign the roles?

With sex roles, as in every area of life, people aspire to what is possible,
and conform to what is necessary. But these are not fixed, especially
today. Biological determinism may reassure some adults about their
present, but it is feminism, the ideology of flexible and converging
sex roles, that fits our children's future. And the kids, somehow,
know this.

That's why, if you look carefully, you'll find that for every kid who fits 15
a stereotype, there's another who's breaking one down. Sometimes it's the
same kid—the boy who skateboards *and* takes cooking in his afterschool
program; the girl who collects stuffed animals *and* A-pluses in science.

Feminists are often accused of imposing their "agenda" on children.
Isn't that what adults always do, consciously and unconsciously? Kids
aren't born religious, or polite, or kind, or able to remember where they
put their sneakers. Inculcating these behaviors, and the values behind
them, is a tremendous amount of work, involving many adults. We don't
have a choice, really, about *whether* we should give our children messages about what it means to be male and female—they're bombarded
with them from morning till night.

The question, as always, is what do we want those messages to be?

JULIA ALVAREZ   [b. 1950]

I Want to Be Miss America

Julia Alvarez was born in New York City but spent much of her childhood in the Dominican Republic. After learning of the brutal murder of
a family involved in the "underground" movement—an episode that
Alvarez refers to in her novel *In the Time of the Butterflies* (1994)—she
returned with her family to New York. In explaining the forces which
have shaped her as a writer and individual, Alvarez refers to the difficult
cultural transition she experienced in adapting to the New York City
public schools. These early conflicts, in combination with a natural affin-
ity for storytelling, influenced Alvarez to write. After earning degrees at
Middlebury College, Syracuse, and the Bread Loaf School of English,
Alvarez began teaching creative writing, traveling among cities with the
Poetry-in-the Schools program. Her success led to college positions and
eventually a tenured job at Middlebury College. Presently, Alvarez divides
her time between teaching and writing and lives with her husband on a
farm in the Champlain Valley of Vermont. Her major works of fiction
include *How the García Girls Lost Their Accent* (1991), *Yo!* (1996), and *In
the Name of Salomé: A Novel* (2000). She has also published poetry in a
variety of magazines and journals.

As young teenagers in our new country, my three sisters and I searched
for clues on how to look as if we belonged here. We collected magazines,
studied our classmates and our new TV, which was where we discovered
the Miss America contest.

Watching the pageant became an annual event in our family. Once a
year, we all plopped down in our parents' bedroom, with Mami and Papi
presiding from their bed. In our nightgowns, we watched the fifty young
women who had the American look we longed for.

The beginning was always the best part—all fifty contestants came on
for one and only one appearance. In alphabetical order, they stepped forward and enthusiastically introduced themselves by name and state. "Hi!
I'm! Susie! Martin! Miss! Alaska!" Their voices rang with false cheer. You

could hear, not far off, years of high-school cheerleading, pom-poms, bleachers full of moon-eyed boys, and moms on phones, signing them up for all manner of lessons and making dentist appointments.

There they stood, fifty puzzle pieces forming the pretty face of America, so we thought, though most of the color had been left out, except for one, or possibly two, light-skinned black girls. If there was a "Hispanic," she usually looked all-American, and only the last name, López or Rodríguez, often mispronounced, showed a trace of a great-great-grandfather with a dark, curled mustache and a sombrero charging the Alamo. During the initial roll-call, what most amazed us was that some contestants were ever picked in the first place. There were homely girls with cross-eyed smiles or chipmunk cheeks. My mother would inevitably shake her head and say, "The truth is, these Americans believe in democracy—even in looks."

We were beginning to feel at home. Our acute homesickness had   5 passed, and now we were like people recovered from a shipwreck, looking around at our new country, glad to be here. "I want to be in America," my mother hummed after we'd gone to see *West Side Story*, and her four daughters chorused, "OK by me in America." We bought a house in Queens, New York, in a neighborhood that was mostly German and Irish, where we were the only "Hispanics." Actually, no one ever called us that. Our teachers and classmates at the local Catholic schools referred to us as "Porto Ricans" or "Spanish." No one knew where the Dominican Republic was on the map. "South of Florida," I explained, "in the same general vicinity as Bermuda and Jamaica." I could just as well have said west of Puerto Rico or east of Cuba or right next to Haiti, but I wanted us to sound like a vacation spot, not a Third World country, a place they would look down on.

Although we wanted to look like we belonged here, the four sisters, our looks didn't seem to fit in. We complained about how short we were, about how our hair frizzed, how our figures didn't curve like those of the bathing beauties we'd seen on TV.

"The grass always grows on the other side of the fence," my mother scolded. Her daughters looked fine just the way they were.

But how could we trust her opinion about what looked good when she couldn't even get the sayings of our new country right? No, we knew better. We would have to translate our looks into English, iron and tweeze them out, straighten them, mold them into Made-in-the-U.S.A. beauty.

So we painstakingly rolled our long, curly hair round and round, using our heads as giant rollers, ironing it until we had long, shining shanks, like our classmates and the contestants, only darker. Our skin was diagnosed by beauty consultants in department stores as sallow; we definitely needed a strong foundation to tone down that olive. We wore tights even in the summer to hide the legs Mami would not let us shave. We begged for permission, dreaming of the contestants' long, silky limbs. We were ten, fourteen, fifteen, and sixteen—merely children, Mami explained. We had long lives ahead of us in which to shave.

We defied her. Giggly and red-faced, we all pitched in to buy a big tube   10 of Nair at the local drugstore. We acted as if we were purchasing contraceptives. That night we crowded into the bathroom, and I, the most courageous along these lines, offered one of my legs as a guinea pig. When it didn't become gangrenous or fall off as Mami had predicted, we creamed the other seven legs. We beamed at each other; we were one step closer to that runway, those flashing cameras, those oohs and ahhs from the audience.

Mami didn't even notice our Naired legs; she was too busy disapproving of the other changes. Our clothes, for one. "You're going to wear that in public!" She'd gawk, as if to say, What will the Americans think of us?

"This is what the Americans wear," we would argue back.

But the dresses we had picked out made us look cheap, she said, like bad, fast girls—gringas without vergüenza, without shame. She preferred her choices: fuchsia skirts with matching vests, flowered dresses with bows at the neck or gathers where you wanted to look slim, everything bright and busy, like something someone might wear in a foreign country.

Our father didn't really notice our new look at all but, if called upon to comment, would say absently that we looked beautiful. "Like Marilina Monroe." Still, during the pageant, he would offer insights into what he thought made a winner. "Personality, Mami," my father would say from his post at the head of the bed, "Personality is the key," though his favorite contestants, whom he always championed in the name of personality, tended to be the fuller girls with big breasts who gushed shamelessly at Bert Parks. "Ay, Papi," we would groan, rolling our eyes at each other. Sometimes, as the girl sashayed back down the aisle, Papi would break out in a little Dominican song that he sang whenever a girl had a lot of swing in her walk:

Yo no tumbo caña,
Que la tumba el viento,
Que la tumba Dora
Con su movimiento!

("I don't have to cut the cane,
The wind knocks it down,
The wind of Dora's movement
As she walks downtown.")

My father would stop on a New York City street when a young woman 15
swung by and sing this song out loud to the great embarrassment of his
daughters. We were sure that one day when we weren't around to make
him look like the respectable father of four girls, he would be arrested.

My mother never seemed to have a favorite contestant. She was an
ex-beauty herself, and no one seemed to measure up to her high standards. She liked the good girls who had common sense and talked about
their education and about how they owed everything to their mothers.
"Tell that to my daughters," my mother would address the screen, as if
none of us were there to hear her. If we challenged her—how exactly did
we not appreciate her?—she'd maintain a wounded silence for the rest
of the evening. Until the very end of the show, that is, when all our dis-
agreements were forgotten and we waited anxiously to see which of the
two finalists holding hands on that near-empty stage would be the next
reigning queen of beauty. How can they hold hands? I always wondered.
Don't they secretly wish the other person would, well, die?

My sisters and I always had plenty of commentary on all the contestants. We were hardly strangers to this ritual of picking the beauty. In our
own family, we had a running competition as to who was the prettiest of
the four girls. We coveted one another's best feature: the oldest's dark,
almond-shaped eyes, the youngest's great mane of hair, the third oldest's
height and figure. I didn't have a preferred feature, but I was often voted
the cutest, though my oldest sister liked to remind me that I had the kind
of looks that wouldn't age well. Although she was only eleven months
older than I was, she seemed years older, ages wiser. She bragged about
the new kind of math she was learning in high school, called algebra,
which she said I would never be able to figure out. I believed her. Dumb
and ex-cute, that's what I would grow up to be.

As for the prettiest Miss America, we sisters kept our choices secret
until the very end. The range was limited—pretty white women who all
really wanted to be wives and mothers. But even the small and inane set
of options these girls represented seemed boundless compared with
what we were used to. We were being groomed to go from being dutiful
daughters to being dutiful wives with hymens intact. No stops along the
way that might endanger the latter; no careers, no colleges, no shared
apartments with girlfriends, no boyfriends, no social lives. But the
young women on-screen, who were being held up as models in this new
country, were in college, or at least headed there. They wanted to do this,
they were going to do that with their lives. Everything in our native culture had instructed us otherwise: girls were to have no aspirations
beyond being good wives and mothers.

Sometimes there would even be a contestant headed for law school or
medical school. "I wouldn't mind having an office visit with her," my

father would say, smirking. The women who caught my attention were the prodigies who bounded onstage and danced to tapes of themselves playing original compositions on the piano, always dressed in costumes they had sewn, with a backdrop of easels holding paintings they'd painted. "Overkill," my older sister insisted. But if one good thing came out of our watching this yearly parade of American beauties, it was that subtle permission we all felt as a family: a girl could excel outside the home and still be a winner.

Every year, the queen came down the runway in her long gown with a 20 sash like an old-world general's belt of ammunition. Down the walkway she paraded, smiling and waving while Bert sang his sappy song that made our eyes fill with tears. When she stopped at the very end of the stage and the camera zoomed in on her misty-eyed beauty and the credits began to appear on the screen, I always felt let down. I knew I would never be one of those girls, ever. It wasn't just the blond, blue-eyed looks or the beautiful, leggy figure. It was who she was—an American— and we were not. We were foreigners, dark-haired and dark-eyed with olive skin that could never, no matter the sun blocks or foundation makeup, be made into peaches and cream.

Had we been able to see into the future, beyond our noses, which we thought weren't the right shape; beyond our curly hair, which we wanted to be straight; and beyond the screen, which inspired us with a limited vision of what was considered beautiful in America, we would have been able to see the late sixties coming. Soon, ethnic looks would be in. Even Barbie, that quintessential white girl, would suddenly be available in different shades of skin color with bright, colorful outfits that looked like the ones Mami had picked out for us. Our classmates in college wore long braids like Native Americans and embroidered shawls and peasant blouses from South America, and long, diaphanous skirts and dangly earrings from India. They wanted to look exotic—they wanted to look like us.

We felt then a gratifying sense of inclusion, but it had unfortunately come too late. We had already acquired the habit of doubting ourselves as well as the place we came from. To this day, after three decades of living in America, I feel like a stranger in what I now consider my own country. I am still that young teenager sitting in front of the black-and-white TV in my parents' bedroom, knowing in my bones I will never be the beauty queen. There she is, Miss America, but even in my up-to-date, enlightened dreams, she never wears my face.

211

SANDRA CISNEROS [b. 1954]

The House on Mango Street

Born in a Hispanic neighborhood in Chicago, **Sandra Cisneros** (b. 1954) spoke Spanish at home with her Mexican father, Chicana mother, and six brothers. At ten she began writing poetry, and soon experimented with other forms. In 1977, when she was studying in the M.F.A. program at the University of Iowa Writers' Workshop, she came to see herself as a Chicana writer. Cisneros has published three books of poems; a book of interrelated narratives, *The House on Mango Street* (1983); and a fiction collection, *Woman Hollering Creek and Other Stories* (1991).

We didn't always live on Mango Street. Before that we lived on Loomis on the third floor, and before that we lived on Keeler. Before Keeler it was Paulina, and before that I can't remember. But what I remember most is moving a lot. Each time it seemed there'd be one more of us. By the time we got to Mango Street we were six—Mama, Papa, Carlos, Kiki, my sister Nenny, and me.

The house on Mango Street is ours, and we don't have to pay rent to anybody, or share the yard with the people downstairs, or be careful not to make too much noise, and there isn't a landlord banging on the ceiling with a broom. But even so, it's not the house we'd thought we'd get.

We had to leave the flat on Loomis quick. The water pipes broke and the landlord wouldn't fix them because the house was too old. We had to leave fast. We were using the washroom next door and carrying water over in empty milk gallons. That's why Mama and Papa looked for a house, and that's why we moved into the house on Mango Street, far away, on the other side of town.

They always told us that one day we would move into a house, a real house that would be ours for always so we wouldn't have to move each year. And our house would have running water and pipes that worked. And inside it would have real stairs, not hallway stairs, but stairs inside like the houses on T.V. And we'd have a basement and at least three washrooms so when we took a bath we wouldn't have to tell everybody. Our house would be white with trees around it, a great big yard and grass growing without a fence. This was the house Papa talked about when he held a lottery ticket and this was the house Mama dreamed up in the stories she told us before we went to bed.

But the house on Mango Street is not the way they told it at all. It's small and red with tight steps in front and windows so small you'd think they were holding their breath. Bricks are crumbling in places, and the front door is so swollen you have to push hard to get in. There is no front yard, only four little elms the city planted by the curb. Out back is a small garage for the car we don't own yet and a small yard that looks smaller between the two buildings on either side. There are stairs in our house, but they're ordinary hallway stairs, and the house has only one washroom. Everybody has to share a bedroom — Mama and Papa, Carlos and Kiki, me and Nenny.

Once when we were living on Loomis, a nun from my school passed by and saw me playing out front. The laundromat downstairs had been boarded up because it had been robbed two days before and the owner had painted on the wood YES WE'RE OPEN so as not to lose business.

Where do you live? she asked.

There, I said pointing up to the third floor.

You live *there?*

There. I had to look to where she pointed — the third floor, the paint peeling, wooden bars Papa had nailed on the windows so we wouldn't fall out. You live *there?* The way she said it made me feel like nothing. *There.* I lived *there.* I nodded.

I knew then I had to have a house. A real house. One I could point to. But this isn't it. The house on Mango Street isn't it. For the time being, Mama says. Temporary, says Papa. But I know how those things go.

[1983]

JUDITH ORTIZ COFER   [b. 1952]

Latin Women Pray

Judith Ortiz Cofer was born and raised in Puerto Rico, but moved to
New Jersey in her childhood. She is a poet, fiction writer, and auto-
biographer, and teaches literature and writing at the University of
Georgia. Much of her work, such as her novel *The Line of the Sun*
(1989) and *The Latin Deli: Prose and Poetry* (1993), explores her experi-
ences as a Puerto Rican émigré and a Latina. Her most recent book is
Woman in Front of the Sun: Becoming a Writer (2000). "Latin Women
Pray" was the title poem of Cofer's original poetry collection.

Latin women pray
in incense-sweet churches;
they pray in Spanish to an Anglo God
with a Jewish heritage.

And this Great White Father, 5
imperturbable in His marble pedestal
looks down upon His brown daughters,
votive candles shining like lust
in His all-seeing eyes,
unmoved by their persistent prayers. 10

Yet year after year,
before his image they kneel,
Margarita, Josefina, María and Isabel,
all fervently hoping
that if not omnipotent, 15
at least He be bilingual.

[1981]

VIRGINIA WOOLF   [1882–1941]

Shakespeare's Sister

Born Adeline Virginia Stephen in London in 1882, **Virginia Woolf** is
one of the most important writers not just of her time but of all literary
history. A modernist, Woolf, along with contemporaries such as James
Joyce, T. S. Eliot, Ezra Pound, and Gertrude Stein, revolutionized literature by inventing new forms that explored the rich inner lives of their
subjects. She is known especially for the novels *Mrs. Dalloway* (1925)
and *To the Lighthouse* (1927), but also for the nonfiction and feminist *A
Room of One's Own* (1929).

The essay "Shakespeare's Sister" is excerpted from *A Room of One's
Own*. Reflecting on the Elizabethan period, Woolf wonders why, when
so many powerful women were depicted in the literature, works written by women do not also appear on her shelves.

It was disappointing not to have brought back in the evening some
important statement, some authentic fact. Women are poorer than men
because—this or that. Perhaps now it would be better to give up seeking
for the truth, and receiving on one's head an avalanche of opinion hot as
lava, discoloured as dish-water. It would be better to draw the curtains;
to shut out distractions; to light the lamp; to narrow the enquiry and to
ask the historian, who records not opinions but facts, to describe under
what conditions women lived, not throughout the ages, but in England,
say in the time of Elizabeth.

For it is a perennial puzzle why no woman wrote a word of that
extraordinary literature when every other man, it seemed, was capable
of song or sonnet. What were the conditions in which women lived, I
asked myself; for fiction, imaginative work that is, is not dropped like a
pebble upon the ground, as science may be; fiction is like a spider's web,
attached ever so lightly perhaps, but still attached to life at all four corners. Often the attachment is scarcely perceptible; Shakespeare's plays,
for instance, seem to hang there complete by themselves. But when the
web is pulled askew, hooked up at the edge, torn in the middle, one

remembers that these webs are not spun in midair by incorporeal creatures, but are the work of suffering human beings, and are attached to grossly material things, like health and money and the houses we live in.

I went, therefore, to the shelf where the histories stand and took down one of the latest, Professor Trevelyan's *History of England*. Once more I looked up Women, found "position of," and turned to the pages indicated. "Wife-beating," I read, "was a recognised right of man, and was practised without shame by high as well as low.... Similarly," the historian goes on, "the daughter who refused to marry the gentleman of her parents' choice was liable to be locked up, beaten and flung about the room, without any shock being inflicted on public opinion. Marriage was not an affair of personal affection, but of family avarice, particularly in the 'chivalrous' upper classes.... Betrothal often took place while one or both of the parties was in the cradle, and marriage when they were scarcely out of the nurses' charge." That was about 1470, soon after Chaucer's time. The next reference to the position of women is some two hundred years later, in the time of the Stuarts. "It was still the exception for women of the upper and middle class to choose their own husbands, and when the husband had been assigned, he was lord and master, so far at least as law and custom could make him. Yet even so," Professor Trevelyan concludes, "neither Shakespeare's women nor those of authentic seventeenth-century memoirs, like the Verneys and the Hutchinsons, seem wanting in personality and character." Certainly, if we consider it, Cleopatra must have had a way with her; Lady Macbeth, one would suppose, had a will of her own; Rosalind, one might conclude, was an attractive girl. Professor Trevelyan is speaking no more than the truth when he remarks that Shakespeare's women do not seem wanting in personality and character. Not being a historian, one might go even further and say that women have burnt like beacons in all the works of all the poets from the beginning of time—Clytemnestra, Antigone, Cleopatra, Lady Macbeth, Phèdre, Cressida, Rosalind, Desdemona, the Duchess of Malfi, among the dramatists; then among the prose writers: Millamant, Clarissa, Becky Sharp, Anna Karenina, Emma Bovary, Madame de Guermantes—the names flock to mind, nor do they recall women "lacking in personality and character." Indeed, if woman had no existence save in the fiction written by men, one would imagine her a person of the utmost importance; very various; heroic and mean; splendid and sordid; infinitely beautiful and hideous in the extreme; as great as a man, some think even greater.[1] But this is woman in fiction. In fact, as Professor Trevelyan points out, she was locked up, beaten, and flung about the room.

A very queer, composite being thus emerges. Imaginatively she is of the highest importance; practically she is completely insignificant. She pervades poetry from cover to cover; she is all but absent from history. She dominates the lives of kings and conquerors in fiction; in fact she was the slave of any boy whose parents forced a ring upon her finger. Some of the most inspired words, some of the most profound thoughts in literature fall from her lips; in real life she could hardly read, could scarcely spell, and was the property of her husband.

It was certainly an odd monster that one made up by reading the his- 5
torians first and the poets afterwards—a worm winged like an eagle; the spirit of life and beauty in a kitchen chopping up suet. But these monsters, however amusing to the imagination, have no existence in fact. What one must do to bring her to life was to think poetically and prosaically at one and the same moment, thus keeping in touch with fact— that she is Mrs. Martin, aged thirty-six, dressed in blue, wearing a black hat and brown shoes; but not losing sight of fiction either—that she is a vessel in which all sorts of spirits and forces are coursing and flashing perpetually. The moment, however, that one tries this method with the Elizabethan woman, one branch of illumination fails; one is held up by the scarcity of facts. One knows nothing detailed, nothing perfectly true and substantial about her. History scarcely mentions her. And I turned to Professor Trevelyan again to see what history meant to him. I found by looking at his chapter headings that it meant—

"The Manor Court and the Methods of Open-field Agriculture...The Cistercians and Sheep-farming...The Crusades...The University... The House of Commons...The Hundred Years' War...The Wars of the Roses...The Renaissance Scholars...The Dissolution of the Monasteries...Agrarian and Religious Strife...The Origin of English Sea-power...The Armada..." and so on. Occasionally an individual woman is mentioned, an Elizabeth, or a Mary; a queen or a great lady. But by no possible means could middle-class women with nothing but brains and character at their command have taken part in any one of the great movements which, brought together, constitute the historian's view of the past. Nor shall we find her in any collection of anecdotes. Aubrey hardly mentions her. She never writes her own life and scarcely keeps a diary; there are only a handful of her letters in existence. She left no plays or poems by which we can judge her. What one wants, I thought— and why does not some brilliant student at Newnham or Girton supply it?—is a mass of information; at what age did she marry; how many children had she as a rule; what was her house like; had she a room to herself; did she do the cooking; would she be likely to have a servant? All these facts lie somewhere, presumably, in parish registers and account books; the life of the average Elizabethan woman must be scattered about somewhere, could one collect it and make a book of it. It would be ambitious beyond my daring, I thought, looking about the shelves for books that were not there, to suggest to the students of those famous colleges that they should re-write history, though I own that it often seems a little queer as it is, unreal, lopsided; but why should they not add a supplement to history? calling it, of course, by some inconspicuous name so that women might figure there without impropriety? For one often catches a glimpse of them in the lives of the great, whisking away into the background, concealing, I sometimes think, a wink, a laugh, perhaps a tear. And, after all, we have lives enough of Jane Austen; it scarcely seems necessary to consider again the influence of the tragedies of Joanna Baillie upon the poetry of Edgar Allan Poe; as for myself, I should not mind if the homes and haunts of Mary Russell Mitford were closed to the public for a century at least. But what I find deplorable, I continued, looking about the bookshelves again, is that nothing is known about women before the eighteenth century. I have no model in my mind to turn about this way and that. Here I am asking why women did not write poetry in the Elizabethan age, and I am not sure how they were educated; whether they were taught to write; whether they had sitting-rooms to themselves; how many women had children before they were twenty-one; what, in short, they did from eight in the morning till eight at night. They had no money evidently; according to Professor Trevelyan they were married whether they liked it or not before they were out of the nursery, at fifteen or sixteen very likely. It would have been extremely odd, even upon this showing, had one of them suddenly written the plays of Shakespeare, I concluded, and I thought of that old gentleman, who is dead now, but was a bishop, I think, who declared that it was impossible for any woman, past, present, or to come, to have the genius of Shakespeare. He wrote to the papers about it. He also told a lady who applied to him for information that cats do not as a matter of fact go to heaven, though they have, he added, souls of a sort. How much thinking those old gentlemen used to save one! How the borders of ignorance shrank back at their approach! Cats do not go to heaven. Women cannot write the plays of Shakespeare.

Be that as it may, I could not help thinking, as I looked at the works of Shakespeare on the shelf, that the bishop was right at least in this; it would have been impossible, completely and entirely, for any woman to have written the plays of Shakespeare in the age of Shakespeare. Let me imagine, since facts are so hard to come by, what would have happened had Shakespeare had a wonderfully gifted sister, called Judith, let us say. Shakespeare himself went, very probably—his mother was an heiress—to the grammar school, where he may have learnt Latin—Ovid, Virgil, and Horace—and the elements of grammar and logic. He was, it is well known, a wild boy who poached rabbits, perhaps shot a deer, and had, rather sooner than he should have done, to marry a woman in the neighbourhood, who bore him a child rather quicker than was right. That escapade sent him to seek his fortune in London. He had, it seemed, a taste for the theatre; he began by holding horses at the stage door. Very soon he got work in the theatre, became a successful actor, and lived at the hub of the universe, meeting everybody, knowing everybody, practising his art on the boards, exercising his wits in the streets, and even getting access to the palace of the queen. Meanwhile his extraordinarily gifted sister, let us suppose, remained at home. She was as adventurous, as imaginative, as agog to see the world as he was. But she was not sent to school. She had no chance of learning grammar and logic, let alone of reading Horace and Virgil. She picked up a book now and then, one of her brother's perhaps, and read a few pages. But then her parents came in and told her to mend the stockings or mind the stew and not moon about with books and papers. They would have spoken sharply but kindly, for they were substantial people who knew the conditions of life for a woman and loved their daughter—indeed, more likely than not she was the apple of her father's eye. Perhaps she scribbled some pages up in an apple loft on the sly, but was careful to hide them or set fire to them. Soon, however, before she was out of her teens, she was to be betrothed to the son of a neighbouring wool-stapler. She cried out that marriage was hateful to her, and for that she was severely beaten by her father. Then he ceased to scold her. He begged her instead not to hurt him, not to shame him in this matter of her marriage. He would give her a chain of beads or a fine petticoat, he said; and there were tears in his eyes. How could she disobey him? How could she break his heart? The force of her own gift alone drove her to it. She made up a small parcel of her belongings, let herself down by a rope one summer's night and took the road to London. She was not seventeen. The birds that sang in the hedge were not more musical than she was. She had the quickest fancy, a gift like her brother's, for the tune of words. Like him, she had a taste for the theatre. She stood at the stage door; she wanted to act, she said. Men laughed in her face. The manager—a fat, loose-lipped man—guffawed. He bellowed something about poodles dancing and women acting—no woman, he said, could possibly be an actress. He hinted—you can imagine what. She could get no training in her craft. Could she even seek her dinner in a tavern or roam the streets at midnight? Yet her genius was for fiction and lusted to feed abundantly upon the lives of men and women and the study of their ways. At last—for she was very young, oddly like Shakespeare the poet in her face, with the same grey eyes and rounded brows—at last Nick Greene the actor-manager took pity on her; she found herself with child by that gentleman and so—who shall measure the heat and violence of the poet's heart when caught and tangled in a woman's body?—killed herself one winter's night and lies buried at some cross-roads where the omnibuses now stop outside the Elephant and Castle.

That, more or less, is how the story would run, I think, if a woman in Shakespeare's day had had Shakespeare's genius. But for my part, I agree with the deceased bishop, if such he was—it is unthinkable that any woman in Shakespeare's day should have had Shakespeare's genius. For genius like Shakespeare's is not born among labouring, uneducated, servile people. It was not born in England among the Saxons and the Britons. It is not born today among the working classes. How, then, could it have been born among women whose work began, according to Professor Trevelyan, almost before they were out of the nursery, who were forced to it by their parents and held to it by all the power of law and custom? Yet genius of a sort must have existed among women as it must have existed among the working classes. Now and again an Emily Brontë or a Robert Burns blazes out and proves its presence. But certainly it never got itself on to paper. When, however, one reads of a witch being ducked, of a woman possessed by devils, of a wise woman selling herbs, or even of a very remarkable man who had a mother, then I think we are on the track of a lost novelist, a suppressed poet, of some mute and inglorious Jane Austen, some Emily Brontë who dashed her brains out on the moor or mopped and mowed about the highways crazed with the torture that her gift had put her to. Indeed, I would venture to guess that Anon, who wrote so many poems without signing them, was often a woman. It was a woman Edward Fitzgerald, I think, suggested who made the ballads and the folksongs, crooning them to her children, beguiling her spinning with them, or the length of the winter's night.

This may be true or it may be false—who can say?—but what is true in it, so it seemed to me, reviewing the story of Shakespeare's sister as I had made it, is that any woman born with a great gift in the sixteenth century would certainly have gone crazed, shot herself, or ended her days in some lonely cottage outside the village, half witch, half wizard, feared and mocked at. For it needs little skill in psychology to be sure that a highly gifted girl who had tried to use her gift for poetry would have been so thwarted and hindered by other people, so tortured and pulled asunder by her own contrary instincts, that she must have lost her health and sanity to a certainty. No girl could have walked to London and stood at a stage door and forced her way into the presence of actor-managers without doing herself a violence and suffering an anguish which may have been irrational—for chastity may be a fetish invented by certain societies for unknown reasons—but were none the less inevitable. Chastity had then, it has even now, a religious importance in a woman's life, and has so wrapped itself round with nerves and instincts that to cut it free and bring it to the light of day demands courage of the rarest. To have lived a free life in London in the sixteenth century would have meant for a woman who was poet and playwright a nervous stress and dilemma which might well have killed her. Had she survived, whatever she had written would have been twisted and deformed, issuing from a strained and morbid imagination. And undoubtedly, I thought, looking at the shelf where there are no plays by women, her work would have gone unsigned. That refuge she would have sought certainly. It was the relic of the sense of chastity that dictated anonymity to women even so late as the nineteenth century. Currer Bell, George Eliot, George Sand, all the victims of inner strife as their writings prove, sought ineffectively to veil themselves by using the name of a man. Thus they did homage to the convention, which if not implanted by the other sex was liberally encouraged by them (the chief glory of a woman is not to be talked of, said Pericles, himself a much-talked-of man), that publicity in women is detestable. Anonymity runs in their blood. The desire to be veiled still possesses them. They are not even now as concerned about the health of their fame as men are, and, speaking generally, will pass a tombstone or a signpost without feeling an irresistible desire to cut their names on it, as Alf, Bert, or Chas. must do in obedience to their instinct, which murmurs if it sees a fine woman go by, or even a dog, Ce chien est à moi. And, of course, it may not be a dog, I thought, remembering Parliament Square, the Sieges Allee and other avenues; it may be a piece of land or a man with curly black hair. It is one of the great advantages of being a woman that one can pass even a very fine negress without wishing to make an Englishwoman of her.

That woman, then, who was born with a gift of poetry in the sixteenth 10
century, was an unhappy woman, a woman at strife against herself. All the conditions of her life, all her own instincts, were hostile to the state of mind which is needed to set free whatever is in the brain. But what is the state of mind that is most propitious to the act of creation, I asked. Can one come by any notion of the state that furthers and makes possible that strange activity? Here I opened the volume containing the Tragedies of Shakespeare. What was Shakespeare's state of mind, for instance, when he wrote *Lear* and *Antony and Cleopatra*? It was certainly the state of mind most favourable to poetry that there has ever existed. But Shakespeare himself said nothing about it. We only know casually and by chance that he "never blotted a line." Nothing indeed was ever said by the artist himself about his state of mind until the eighteenth century perhaps. Rousseau perhaps began it. At any rate, by the nineteenth century self-consciousness had developed so far that it was the habit for men of letters to describe their minds in confessions and autobiographies. Their lives also were written, and their letters were printed after their deaths. Thus, though we do not know what Shakespeare went

through when he wrote *Lear*, we do know what Carlyle went through when he wrote the *French Revolution*; what Flaubert went through when he wrote *Madame Bovary*; what Keats was going through when he tried to write poetry against the coming of death and the indifference of the world.

And one gathers from this enormous modern literature of confession and self-analysis that to write a work of genius is almost always a feat of prodigious difficulty. Everything is against the likelihood that it will come from the writer's mind whole and entire. Generally material circumstances are against it. Dogs will bark; people will interrupt; money must be made; health will break down. Further, accentuating all these difficulties and making them harder to bear is the world's notorious indifference. It does not ask people to write poems and novels and histories; it does not need them. It does not care whether Flaubert finds the right word or whether Carlyle scrupulously verifies this or that fact. Naturally, it will not pay for what it does not want. And so the writer, Keats, Flaubert, Carlyle, suffers, especially in the creative years of youth, every form of distraction and discouragement. A curse, a cry of agony, rises from those books of analysis and confession. "Mighty poets in their misery dead" — that is the burden of their song. If anything comes through in spite of all this, it is a miracle, and probably no book is born entire and uncrippled as it was conceived.

But for women, I thought, looking at the empty shelves, these difficulties were infinitely more formidable. In the first place, to have a room of her own, let alone a quiet room or a sound-proof room, was out of the question, unless her parents were exceptionally rich or very noble, even up to the beginning of the nineteenth century. Since her pin money, which depended on the good will of her father, was only enough to keep her clothed, she was debarred from such alleviations as came even to Keats or Tennyson or Carlyle, all poor men, from a walking tour, a little journey to France, from the separate lodging which, even if it were miserable enough, sheltered them from the claims and tyrannies of their families. Such material difficulties were formidable; but much worse were the immaterial. The indifference of the world which Keats and Flaubert and other men of genius have found so hard to bear was in her case not indifference but hostility. The world did not say to her as it said to them, Write if you choose; it makes no difference to me. The world said with a guffaw, Write? What's the good of your writing? Here the psychologists of Newnham and Girton might come to our help, I thought, looking again at the blank spaces on the shelves. For surely it is time that the effect of discouragement upon the mind of the artist should be measured, as I have seen a dairy company measure the effect of ordinary milk and Grade A milk upon the body of the rat. They set two rats in cages side by side, and of the two one was furtive, timid, and small, and the other was glossy, bold, and big. Now what food do we feed women as artists upon? I asked, remembering, I suppose, that dinner of prunes and custard. To answer that question I had only to open the evening paper and to read that Lord Birkenhead is of opinion—but really I am not going to trouble to copy out Lord Birkenhead's opinion upon the writing of women. What Dean Inge says I will leave in peace. The Harley Street specialist may be allowed to rouse the echoes of Harley Street with his vociferations without raising a hair on my head. I will quote, however, Mr. Oscar Browning, because Mr. Oscar Browning was a great figure in Cambridge at one time, and used to examine the students at Girton and Newnham. Mr. Oscar Browning was wont to declare "that the impression left on his mind, after looking over any set of examination papers, was that, irrespective of the marks he might give, the best woman was intellectually the inferior of the worst man." After saying that Mr. Browning went back to his rooms—and it is this sequel that endears him and makes him a human figure of some bulk and majesty— he went back to his rooms and found a stable-boy lying on the sofa—"a mere skeleton, his cheeks were cavernous and sallow, his teeth were black, and he did not appear to have the full use of his limbs.... 'That's Arthur' [said Mr. Browning]. 'He's a dear boy really and most high-minded.'" The two pictures always seem to me to complete each other. And happily in this age of biography the two pictures often do complete each other, so that we are able to interpret the opinions of great men not only by what they say, but by what they do.

But though this is possible now, such opinions coming from the lips of important people must have been formidable enough even fifty years ago. Let us suppose that a father from the highest motives did not wish his daughter to leave home and become a writer, painter or scholar. "See what Mr. Oscar Browning says," he would say; and there was not only Mr. Oscar Browning; there was the *Saturday Review*; there was Mr. Greg—the "essentials of a woman's being," said Mr. Greg emphatically, "are that *they are supported by, and they minister to, men*"—there was an enormous body of masculine opinion to the effect that nothing could be expected of women intellectually. Even if her father did not read out loud these opinions, any girl could read them for herself; and the reading, even in the nineteenth century, must have lowered her vitality, and told profoundly upon her work. There would always have been that assertion—you cannot do this, you are incapable of doing that—to protest against, to overcome. Probably for a novelist this germ is no longer of much effect; for there have been women novelists of merit. But for painters it must still have some sting in it; and for musicians, I imagine, is even now active and poisonous in the extreme. The woman composer stands where the actress stood in the time of Shakespeare. Nick Greene, I thought, remembering the story I had made about Shakespeare's sister, said that a woman acting put him in mind of a dog dancing. Johnson repeated the phrase two hundred years later of women preaching. And here, I said, opening a book about music, we have the very words used again in this year of grace, 1928, of women who try to write music. "Of Mlle. Germaine Tailleferre one can only repeat Dr. Johnson's dictum concerning a woman preacher, transposed into terms of music. 'Sir, a woman's composing is like a dog's walking on his hind legs. It is not done well, but you are surprised to find it done at all.'"[2] So accurately does history repeat itself.

Thus, I concluded, shutting Mr. Oscar Browning's life and pushing away the rest, it is fairly evident that even in the nineteenth century a woman was not encouraged to be an artist. On the contrary, she was snubbed, slapped, lectured, and exhorted. Her mind must have been strained and her vitality lowered by the need of opposing this, of disproving that. For here again we come within range of that very interesting and obscure masculine complex which has had so much influence upon the woman's movement; that deep-seated desire, not so much that *she* shall be inferior as that *he* shall be superior, which plants him wherever one looks, not only in front of the arts, but barring the way to politics too, even when the risk to himself seems infinitesimal and the suppliant humble and devoted. Even Lady Bessborough, I remembered, with all her passion for politics, must humbly bow herself and write to Lord Granville Leveson-Gower: "...notwithstanding all my violence in politics and talking so much on that subject, I perfectly agree with you that no woman has any business to meddle with that or any other serious business, farther than giving her opinion (if she is ask'd)." And so she goes on to spend her enthusiasm where it meets with no obstacle whatsoever upon that immensely important subject, Lord Granville's maiden speech in the House of Commons. The spectacle is certainly a strange one, I thought. The history of men's opposition to women's emancipation is more interesting perhaps than the story of that emancipation itself. An amusing book might be made of it if some young student at Girton or Newnham would collect examples and deduce a theory—but she would need thick gloves on her hands, and bars to protect her of solid gold.

But what is amusing now, I recollected, shutting Lady Bessborough, 15 had to be taken in desperate earnest once. Opinions that one now pastes in a book labelled cock-a-doodle-dum and keeps for reading to select audiences on summer nights once drew tears, I can assure you. Among your grandmothers and great-grandmothers there were many that wept their eyes out. Florence Nightingale shrieked aloud in her agony.[3]

Moreover, it is all very well for you, who have got yourselves to college and enjoy sitting-rooms—or is it only bed-sitting-rooms?—of your own to say that genius should disregard such opinions; that genius should be above caring what is said of it. Unfortunately, it is precisely the men or women of genius who mind most what is said of them. Remember Keats. Remember the words he had cut on his tombstone. Think of Tennyson; think—but I need hardly multiply instances of the undeniable, if very unfortunate, fact that it is the nature of the artist to mind excessively what is said about him. Literature is strewn with the wreckage of men who have minded beyond reason the opinions of others.

And this susceptibility of theirs is doubly unfortunate, I thought, returning again to my original enquiry into what state of mind is most propitious for creative work, because the mind of an artist, in order to achieve the prodigious effort of freeing whole and entire the work that is in him, must be incandescent, like Shakespeare's mind, I conjectured, looking at the book which lay open at *Antony and Cleopatra*. There must be no obstacle in it, no foreign matter unconsumed.

For though we say that we know nothing about Shakespeare's state of mind, even as we say that, we are saying something about Shakespeare's state of mind. The reason perhaps why we know so little of Shakespeare—compared with Donne or Ben Jonson or Milton—is that his grudges and spites and antipathies are hidden from us. We are not held up by some "revelation" which reminds us of the writer. All desire to protest, to preach, to proclaim an injury, to pay off a score, to make the world the witness of some hardship or grievance was fired out of him and consumed. Therefore his poetry flows from him free and unimpeded. If ever a human being got his work expressed completely, it was Shakespeare. If ever a mind was incandescent, unimpeded, I thought, turning again to the bookcase, it was Shakespeare's mind.

Notes

1. "It remains a strange and almost inexplicable fact that in Athena's city, where women were kept in almost Oriental suppression as odalisques or drudges, the stage should yet have produced figures like Clytemnestra and Cassandra, Atossa and Antigone, Phèdre and Medea, and all the other heroines who dominate play after play of the 'misogynist' Euripides. But the paradox of this world where in real life a respectable woman could hardly show her face alone in the street, and yet on the stage woman equals or surpasses man, has never been satisfactorily explained. In modern tragedy the same predominance exists. At all events, a very cursory survey of Shakespeare's work (similarly with Webster, though not with Marlowe or Jonson) suffices to reveal how this dominance, this initiative of women, persists from Rosalind to Lady Macbeth. So too in Racine; six of his tragedies bear their heroines' names; and what male characters of his

shall we set against Hermione and Andromaque, Bérénice and Roxane, Phèdre and Athalie? So again with Ibsen; what men shall we match with Solveig and Nora, Hedda and Hilda Wangel and Rebecca West?" –F. L. Lucas, Tragedy, pp. 114–15.

   2. *A Survey of Contemporary Music,* Cecil Gray, p. 246.

   3. See *Cassandra,* by Florence Nightingale, printed in *The Cause,* by R. Strachey.

Hillary and Julie Goodridge, lead plaintiffs in the lawsuit legalizing gay marriage in Massachusetts, wed in Boston on the first day of state-sanctioned gay marriage, May 17, 2004. (AP Photo/Elise Amendola.)

ANDREW SULLIVAN   [b. 1963]

Here Comes the Groom:
A (Conservative) Case
for Gay Marriage

Born in 1963 in England, **Andrew Sullivan** is a writer and lecturer on politics and culture. His work appears in a wide range of publications and forums. He was editor-in-chief of the *New Republic* and has written widely on homosexuality. His best-known work on that subject is *Virtually Normal: An Argument about Homosexuality* (1995); its argument is largely against the discrimination faced by homosexuals in American society.

In "Here Comes the Groom: A (Conservative) Case for Gay Marriage," originally appearing in the *New Republic* (1989), Sullivan argues for gay marriage as a means to avoid ugly legal disputes over which kinds of living arrangements actually constitute "domestic partnerships." With conservatives so concerned about maintaining traditional American values, Sullivan's thought-provoking essay asks, since gays are an undeniable, legally protected, no longer invisible reality in modern society, "why not coax gays into traditional values rather than rail incoherently against them?"

Last month in New York, a court ruled that a gay lover had the right to stay in his deceased partner's rent-control apartment because the lover qualified as a member of the deceased's family. The ruling deftly annoyed almost everybody. Conservatives saw judicial activism in favor of gay rent control: three reasons to be appalled. Chastened liberals (such as the *New York Times* editorial page), while endorsing the recognition of gay relationship, also worried about the abuse of already stretched entitlements that the ruling threatened. What neither side quite contemplated is that they both might be right, and that the way to tackle the issue of unconventional relationships in conventional society is to try something both more radical and more conservative than putting courts in the business of deciding what is and is not a family. That alternative is the legalization of civil gay marriage.

The New York rent-control case did not go anywhere near that far, which is the problem. The rent-control regulations merely stipulated that a "family" member had the right to remain in the apartment. The judge ruled that to all intents and purposes a gay lover is part of his lover's family, inasmuch as a "family" merely means an interwoven social life, emotional commitment, and some level of financial interdependence.

It's a principle now well established around the country. Several cities have "domestic partnership" laws, which allow relationships that do not fit into the category of heterosexual marriage to be registered with the city and qualify for benefits that up till now have been reserved for straight married couples. San Francisco, Berkeley, Madison, and Los Angeles all have legislation, as does the politically correct Washington, D.C., suburb, Takoma Park. In these cities, a variety of interpersonal arrangements qualify for health insurance, bereavement leave, insurance, annuity and pension rights, housing rights (such as rent-control apartments), adoption and inheritance rights. Eventually, according to gay lobby groups, the aim is to include federal income tax and veterans' benefits as well. A recent case even involved the right to use a family member's accumulated frequent-flier points. Gays are not the only beneficiaries; heterosexual "live-togethers" also qualify.

There's an argument, of course, that the current legal advantages extended to married people unfairly discriminate against people who've shaped their lives in less conventional arrangements. But it doesn't take a genius to see that enshrining in the law a vague principle like "domestic partnership" is an invitation to qualify at little personal cost for a vast array of entitlements otherwise kept crudely under control.

To be sure, potential DPs have to prove financial interdependence, shared living arrangements, and a commitment to mutual caring. But they don't need to have a sexual relationship or even closely mirror old-style marriage. In principle, an elderly woman and her live-in nurse could qualify. A couple of uneuphemistically confirmed bachelors could be DPs. So could two close college students, a pair of seminarians, or a couple of frat buddies. Left as it is, the concept of domestic partnership could open a Pandora's box of litigation and subjective judicial decision-making about who qualifies. You either are or are not married; it's not a complex question. Whether you are in a "domestic partnership" is not so clear.

More important, the concept of domestic partnership chips away at the prestige of traditional relationships and undermines the priority we give them. This priority is not necessarily a product of heterosexism.

229

Consider heterosexual couples. Society has good reason to extend legal advantages to heterosexuals who choose the formal sanction of marriage over simply living together. They make a deeper commitment to one another and to society; in exchange, society extends certain benefits to them. Marriage provides an anchor, if an arbitrary and weak one, in the chaos of sex and relationships to which we are all prone. It provides a mechanism for emotional stability, economic security, and the healthy rearing of the next generation. We rig the law in its favor not because we disparage all forms of relationship other than the nuclear family, but because we recognize that not to promote marriage would be to ask too much of human virtue. In the context of the weakened family's effect upon the poor, it might also invite social disintegration. One of the worst products of the New Right's "family values" campaign is that its extremism and hatred of diversity has disguised this more measured and more convincing case for the importance of the marital bond.

The concept of domestic partnership ignores these concerns, indeed directly attacks them. This is a pity, since one of its most important objectives—providing some civil recognition for gay relationships—is a noble cause and one completely compatible with the defense of the family. But the decision to go about it is not to undermine straight marriage; it is to legalize old-style marriage for gays.

The gay movement has ducked this issue primarily out of fear of division. Much of the gay leadership clings to notions of gay life as essentially outsider, anti-bourgeois, radical. Marriage, for them, is co-optation into straight society. For the Stonewall generation, it is hard to see how this vision of conflict will ever fundamentally change. But for many other gays—my guess, a majority—while they don't deny the importance of rebellion 20 years ago and are grateful for what was done, there's now the sense of a new opportunity. A need to rebel quietly ceded to a desire to belong. To be gay and to be bourgeois no longer seems such an absurd proposition. Certainly, since AIDS, to be gay and to be responsible has become a necessity.

Gay marriage squares several circles at the heart of the domestic partnership debate. Unlike domestic partnership, it allows for recognition of gay relationships, while casting no aspersions on traditional marriage. It merely asks that gays be allowed to join in. Unlike domestic partnership, it doesn't open up avenues for heterosexuals to get benefits without the responsibilities of marriage, or a nightmare of definitional litigation. And unlike domestic partnership, it harnesses to an already established social convention the yearnings for stability and acceptance among a fast-maturing gay community.

Gay marriage also places more responsibilities upon gays: it says for 10 the first time that gay relationships are not better or worse than straight relationships, and that the same is expected of them. And it's clear and dignified. There's a legal benefit to a clear, common symbol of commitment. There's also a personal benefit. One of the ironies of domestic partnership is that it's not only more complicated than marriage, it's more demanding, requiring an elaborate statement of intent to qualify. It amounts to a substantial invasion of privacy. Why, after all, should gays be required to prove commitment before they get married in a way we would never dream of asking of straights?

Legalizing gay marriage would offer homosexuals the same deal society now offers heterosexuals: general social approval and specific legal advantages in exchange for a deeper and harder-to-extract-yourself-from commitment to another human being. Like straight marriage, it would foster social cohesion, emotional security, and economic prudence. Since there's no reason gays should not be allowed to adopt or be foster parents, it could also help nurture children. And its introduction would not be some sort of radical break with social custom. As it has become more acceptable for gay people to acknowledge their loves publicly more and more have committed themselves to one another for life in full view of their families and their friends. A law institutionalizing gay marriage would merely reinforce a healthy social trend. It would also, in the wake of AIDS, qualify as a genuine public health measure. Those conservatives who deplore promiscuity among some homosexuals should be among the first to support it. Burke could have written a powerful case for it.

The argument that gay marriage would subtly undermine the unique legitimacy of straight marriage is based upon a fallacy. For heterosexuals, straight marriage would remain the most significant—and only legal—social bond. Gay marriage could only delegitimize straight marriage if it were a real alternative to it, and this is clearly not true. To put it bluntly, there's precious little evidence that straights could be persuaded by any law to have sex with—let alone marry—someone of their own sex. The only possible effect of this sort would be to persuade gay men and women who force themselves into heterosexual marriage (often at appalling cost to themselves and their families) to find a focus for their family instincts in a more personally positive environment. But this is clearly a plus, not a minus: gay marriage could both avoid a lot of tortured families and create the possibility for many happier ones. It is not, in short, a denial of family values. It's an extension of them.

Of course, some would claim that any legal recognition of homosexuality is a de facto attack upon heterosexuality. But even the most hardened conservatives recognize that gays are a permanent minority and aren't likely to go away. Since persecution is not an option in a civilized society, why not coax gays into traditional values rather than rail incoherently against them?

231

There's a less elaborate argument for gay marriage: it's good for gays. It provides role models for young gay people who, after the exhilaration of coming out, can easily lapse into short-term relationships and insecurity with no tangible goal in sight. My own guess is that most gays would embrace such a goal with as much (if not more) commitment as straights. Even in our society as it is, many lesbian relationships are virtual textbook cases of monogamous commitment. Legal gay marriage could also help bridge the gulf often found between gays and their parents. It could bring the essence of gay life—a gay couple—into the heart of the traditional straight family in a way the family can most understand and the gay offspring can most easily acknowledge. It could do as much to heal the gay-straight rift as any amount of gay rights legislation.

If these arguments sound socially conservative, that's no accident. It's 15 one of the richest ironies of our society's blind spot toward gays that essentially conservative social goals should have the appearance of being so radical. But gay marriage is not a radical step. It avoids the mess of domestic partnership; it is humane; it is conservative in the best sense of the word. It's also practical. Given the fact that we already allow legal gay relationships, what possible social goal is advanced by framing the law to encourage those relationships to be unfaithful, undeveloped, and insecure?

GLORIA ANZALDÚA [b. 1942]

How to Tame a Wild Tongue

Gloria Anzaldúa was born in 1942 in the Rio Grande Valley of South
Texas. At age eleven she began working in the fields as a migrant worker
and later worked on her family's land after the death of her father.
Working her way through school, she eventually became a schoolteacher and then an academic, speaking and writing about feminist, lesbian, and Chicana issues and about autobiography. She is best
known for *This Bridge Called My Back: Writings by Radical Women of
Color* (1981), which she edited with Cherríe Moraga, and *Borderlands/
La Frontera: The New Mestiza* (1987).

"How to Tame a Wild Tongue" is from *Borderlands/La Frontera.*
In it, Anzaldúa is concerned with many kinds of borders—between
nations, cultures, classes, genders, languages. When she writes, "So, if
you want to really hurt me, talk badly about my language" (par. 27),
Anzaldúa is arguing for the ways in which identity is intertwined with
the way we speak and for the ways in which people can be made to feel
ashamed of their own tongues. Keeping hers wild—ignoring the closing of linguistic borders—is Anzaldúa's way of asserting her identity.

"We're going to have to control your
tongue," the dentist says, pulling out all the metal from my mouth. Silver
bits plop and tinkle into the basin. My mouth is a motherlode.

The dentist is cleaning out my roots. I
get a whiff of the stench when I gasp. "I can't cap that tooth yet, you're
still draining," he says.

"We're going to have to do something
about your tongue," I hear the anger rising in his voice. My tongue keeps
pushing out the wads of cotton, pushing back the drills, the long thin
needles. "I've never seen anything as strong or as stubborn," he says. And
I think, how do you tame a wild tongue, train it to be quiet, how do you
bridle and saddle it? How do you make it lie down?

*"Who is to say that robbing a people of its language is less
violent than war?"* —RAY GWYN SMITH[1]

I remember being caught speaking Spanish at recess—that was good for three licks on the knuckles with a sharp ruler. I remember being sent to the corner of the classroom for "talking back" to the Anglo teacher when all I was trying to do was tell her how to pronounce my name. "If you want to be American, speak 'American.' If you don't like it, go back to Mexico where you belong."

"I want you to speak English. *Pa' hallar buen trabajo tienes que saber hablar el inglés bien. Qué vale toda tu educación si todavía hablas inglés con un* 'accent,'" my mother would say, mortified that I spoke English like a Mexican. At Pan American University, I and all Chicano students were required to take two speech classes. Their purpose: to get rid of our accents.

Attacks on one's form of expression with the intent to censor are a violation of the First Amendment. *El Anglo con cara de inocente nos arrancó la lengua.* Wild tongues can't be tamed, they can only be cut out.

OVERCOMING THE TRADITION OF SILENCE

> *Ahogadas, escupimos el oscuro.*
> *Peleando con nuestra propia sombra*
> *el silencio nos sepulta.*

En boca cerrada no entran moscas. "Flies don't enter a closed mouth" is a saying I kept hearing when I was a child. *Ser habladora* was to be a gossip and a liar, to talk too much. *Muchachitas bien criadas*, well-bred girls don't answer back. *Es una falta de respeto* to talk back to one's mother or father. I remember one of the sins I'd recite to the priest in the confession box the few times I went to confession: talking back to my mother, *hablar pa' 'tras, repelar. Hocicona, repelona, chismosa*, having a big mouth, questioning, carrying tales are all signs of being *mal criada*. In my culture they are all words that are derogatory if applied to women—I've never heard them applied to men.

The first time I heard two women, a Puerto Rican and a Cuban, say the word *"nosotras,"* I was shocked. I had not known the word existed. Chicanas use *nosotros* whether we're male or female. We are robbed of our female being by the masculine plural. Language is a male discourse.

> *And our tongues have become*
> *dry   the wilderness has*
> *dried out our tongues   and*
> *we have forgotten speech.*
> *—IRENA KLEPFISZ[2]*

234

Even our own people, other Spanish speakers *nos quieren poner candados en la boca.* They would hold us back with their bag of *reglas de academia.*

Oyé como ladra: el lenguaje de la frontera

Quien tiene boca se equivoca.
— MEXICAN SAYING

"*Pocho,* cultural traitor, you're speaking the oppressor's language by 10 speaking English, you're ruining the Spanish language," I have been accused by various Latinos and Latinas. Chicano Spanish is considered by the purist and by most Latinos deficient, a mutilation of Spanish.

But Chicano Spanish is a border tongue which developed naturally. Change, *evolución, enriquecimiento de palabras nuevas por invención o adopción* have created variants of Chicano Spanish, *un nuevo lenguaje. Un lenguaje que corresponde a un modo de vivir.* Chicano Spanish is not incorrect, it is a living language.

For a people who are neither Spanish nor live in a country in which Spanish is the first language; for a people who live in a country in which English is the reigning tongue but who are not Anglo; for a people who cannot entirely identify with either standard (formal, Castillian) Spanish nor standard English, what recourse is left to them but to create their own language? A language which they can connect their identity to, one capable of communicating the realities and values true to themselves — a language with terms that are neither *español ni inglés,* but both. We speak a patois, a forked tongue, a variation of two languages.

Chicano Spanish sprang out of the Chicanos' need to identify ourselves as a distinct people. We needed a language with which we could communicate with ourselves, a secret language. For some of us, language is a homeland closer than the Southwest — for many Chicanos today live in the Midwest and the East. And because we are a complex, heterogeneous people, we speak many languages. Some of the languages we speak are:

1. Standard English
2. Working class and slang English
3. Standard Spanish
4. Standard Mexican Spanish
5. North Mexican Spanish dialect
6. Chicano Spanish (Texas, New Mexico, Arizona, and California have regional variations)
7. Tex-Mex
8. *Pachuco* (called *caló*)

My "home" tongues are the languages I speak with my sister and brothers, with my friends. They are the last five listed, with 6 and 7 being closest to my heart. From school, the media, and job situations, I've picked up standard and working class English. From Mamagrande Locha and from reading Spanish and Mexican literature, I've picked up Standard Spanish and Standard Mexican Spanish. From *los recién llegados*, Mexican immigrants, and *braceros*, I learned the North Mexican dialect. With Mexicans I'll try to speak either Standard Mexican Spanish or the North Mexican dialect. From my parents and Chicanos living in the Valley, I picked up Chicano Texas Spanish, and I speak it with my mom, younger brother (who married a Mexican and who rarely mixes Spanish with English), aunts, and older relatives.

With Chicanas from *Nuevo México* or *Arizona* I will speak Chicano   15
Spanish a little, but often they don't understand what I'm saying. With most California Chicanas I speak entirely in English (unless I forget). When I first moved to San Francisco, I'd rattle off something in Spanish, unintentionally embarrassing them. Often it is only with another Chicana *tejana* that I can talk freely.

Words distorted by English are known as anglicisms or *pochismos*. The *pocho* is an anglicized Mexican or American of Mexican origin who speaks Spanish with an accent characteristic of North Americans and who distorts and reconstructs the language according to the influence of English.[3] Tex-Mex, or Spanglish, comes most naturally to me. I may switch back and forth from English to Spanish in the same sentence or in the same word. With my sister and my brother Nune and with Chicano *tejano* contemporaries I speak in Tex-Mex.

From kids and people my own age I picked up *Pachuco*. *Pachuco* (the language of the zoot suiters) is a language of rebellion, both against Standard Spanish and Standard English. It is a secret language. Adults of the culture and outsiders cannot understand it. It is made up of slang words from both English and Spanish. *Ruca* means girl or woman, *vato* means guy or dude, *chale* means no, *simón* means yes, *churro* is sure, talk is *periquiar*, *pigionear* means petting, *que gacho* means how nerdy, *ponte águila* means watch out, death is called *la pelona*. Through lack of practice and not having others who can speak it, I've lost most of the *Pachuco* tongue.

CHICANO SPANISH

Chicanos, after 250 years of Spanish/Anglo colonization, have developed significant differences in the Spanish we speak. We collapse two adjacent vowels into a single syllable and sometimes shift the stress in certain words such as *maíz/maiz, cohete/cuete*. We leave out certain consonants when they appear between vowels: *lado/lao, mojado/mojao*. Chicanos from South Texas pronounce *f* as *j* as in *jue (fue)*. Chicanos use "archaisms," words that are no longer in the Spanish language, words that have been evolved out. We say *semos, truje, haiga, ansina*, and *naiden*. We retain the "archaic" *j*, as in *jalar*, that derives from an earlier *h*, (the French *halar* or the Germanic *halon* which was lost to standard Spanish in the 16th century), but which is still found in several regional dialects such as the one spoken in South Texas. (Due to geography, Chicanos from the Valley of South Texas were cut off linguistically from other Spanish speakers. We tend to use words that the Spaniards brought over from Medieval Spain. The majority of the Spanish colonizers in Mexico and the Southwest came from Extremadura—Hernán Cortés was one of them—and Andalucía. Andalucians pronounce *ll* like a *y*, and their *d*'s tend to be absorbed by adjacent vowels: *tirado* becomes *tirao*. They brought *el lenguaje popular, dialectos y regionalismos*.[4])

Chicanos and other Spanish speakers also shift *ll* to *y* and *z* to *s*.[5] We leave out initial syllables, saying *tar* for *estar, toy* for *estoy, hora* for *ahora* (*cubanos* and *puertorriqueños* also leave out initial letters of some words). We also leave out the final syllable such as *pa* for *para*. The intervocalic *y*, the *ll* as in *tortilla, ella, botella*, gets replaced by *tortia* or *tortiya, ea, botea*. We add an additional syllable at the beginning of certain words: *atocar* for *tocar, agastar* for *gastar*. Sometimes we'll say *lavaste las vacijas*, other times *lavates* (substituting the *ates* verb endings for the *aste*).

We use anglicisms, words borrowed from English: *bola* from ball, *car-*   20
peta from carpet, *máchina de lavar* (instead of *lavadora*) from washing machine. Tex-Mex argot, created by adding a Spanish sound at the beginning or end of an English word such as *cookiar* for cook, *watchar* for watch, *parkiar* for park, and *rapiar* for rape, is the result of the pressures on Spanish speakers to adapt to English.

We don't use the word *vosotros/as* or its accompanying verb form. We don't say *claro* (to mean yes), *imagínate*, or *me emociona*, unless we picked up Spanish from Latinas, out of a book, or in a classroom. Other Spanish-speaking groups are going through the same, or similar, development in their Spanish.

LINGUISTIC TERRORISM

Deslenguadas. Somos los del español deficiente. We are your linguistic nightmare, your linguistic aberration, your linguistic *mestisaje*, the subject of your *burla*. Because we speak with tongues of fire we are culturally crucified. Racially, culturally, and linguistically *somos huérfanos* — we speak an orphan tongue.

Chicanas who grew up speaking Chicano Spanish have internalized the belief that we speak poor Spanish. It is illegitimate, a bastard language. And because we internalize how our language has been used against us by the dominant culture, we use our language differences against each other.

Chicana feminists often skirt around each other with suspicion and hesitation. For the longest time I couldn't figure it out. Then it dawned on me. To be close to another Chicana is like looking into the mirror. We are afraid of what we'll see there. *Pena.* Shame. Low estimation of self. In childhood we are told that our language is wrong. Repeated attacks on our native tongue diminish our sense of self. The attacks continue throughout our lives.

Chicanas feel uncomfortable talking in Spanish to Latinas, afraid of their censure. Their language was not outlawed in their countries. They had a whole lifetime of being immersed in their native tongue; generations, centuries in which Spanish was a first language, taught in school, heard on radio and TV, and read in the newspaper.

If a person, Chicana or Latina, has a low estimation of my native 25 tongue, she also has a low estimation of me. Often with *mexicanas y latinas* we'll speak English as a neutral language. Even among Chicanas we tend to speak English at parties or conferences. Yet, at the same time, we're afraid the other will think we're *agringadas* because we don't speak Chicano Spanish. We oppress each other trying to out-Chicano each other, vying to be the "real" Chicanas, to speak like Chicanos. There is no one Chicano language just as there is no one Chicano experience. A monolingual Chicana whose first language is English or Spanish is just as much a Chicana as one who speaks several variants of Spanish. A Chicana from Michigan or Chicago or Detroit is just as much a Chicana as one from the Southwest. Chicano Spanish is as diverse linguistically as it is regionally.

By the end of this century, Spanish speakers will comprise the biggest minority group in the U.S., a country where students in high schools and colleges are encouraged to take French classes because French is considered more "cultured." But for a language to remain alive it must be used.[6] By the end of this century English, and not Spanish, will be the mother tongue of most Chicanos and Latinos.

So, if you want to really hurt me, talk badly about my language. Ethnic identity is twin skin to linguistic identity — I am my language. Until I can take pride in my language, I cannot take pride in myself.

Until I can accept as legitimate Chicano Texas Spanish, Tex-Mex, and all the other languages I speak, I cannot accept the legitimacy of myself. Until I am free to write bilingually and to switch codes without having always to translate, while I still have to speak English or Spanish when I would rather speak Spanglish, and as long as I have to accommodate the English speakers rather than having them accommodate me, my tongue will be illegitimate.

I will no longer be made to feel ashamed of existing. I will have my voice: Indian, Spanish, white. I will have my serpent's tongue — my woman's voice, my sexual voice, my poet's voice. I will overcome the tradition of silence.

> *My fingers*
> *move sly against your palm*
> *Like women everywhere, we speak in code.* . . .
> — MELANIE KAYE/KANTROWITZ[7]

"Vistas," corridos, y comida: My Native Tongue

In the 1960s, I read my first Chicano novel. It was *City of Night* by John Rechy, a gay Texan, son of a Scottish father and a Mexican mother. For days I walked around in stunned amazement that a Chicano could write and could get published. When I read *I Am Joaquín*[8] I was surprised to see a bilingual book by a Chicano in print. When I saw poetry written in Tex-Mex for the first time, a feeling of pure joy flashed through me. I felt like we really existed as a people. In 1971, when I started teaching High School English to Chicano students, I tried to supplement the required texts with works by Chicanos, only to be reprimanded and forbidden to do so by the principal. He claimed that I was supposed to teach "American" and English literature. At the risk of being fired, I swore my students to secrecy and slipped in Chicano short stories, poems, a play. In graduate school, while working toward a Ph.D., I had to "argue" with one advisor after the other, semester after semester, before I was allowed to make Chicano literature an area of focus.

Even before I read books by Chicanos or Mexicans, it was the Mexican   30 movies I saw at the drive-in — the Thursday night special of $1.00 a carload — that gave me a sense of belonging. *"Vámonos a las vistas,"* my mother would call out and we'd all — grandmother, brothers, sister, and cousins — squeeze into the car. We'd wolf down cheese and bologna white bread sandwiches while watching Pedro Infante in melodramatic tearjerkers like *Nosotros los pobres,* the first "real" Mexican movie (that was not an imitation of European movies). I remember seeing *Cuando los hijos se van* and surmising that all Mexican movies played up the love a mother has for her children and what ungrateful sons and daughters suffer when they are not devoted to their mothers. I remember the singing-type "westerns" of Jorge Negrete and Miguel Aceves Mejía. When watching Mexican movies, I felt a sense of homecoming as well as alienation. People who were to amount to something didn't go to Mexican movies, or *bailes*, or tune their radios to *bolero*, *rancherita*, and *corrido* music.

The whole time I was growing up, there was *norteño* music sometimes called North Mexican border music, or Tex-Mex music, or Chicano music, or *cantina* (bar) music. I grew up listening to *conjuntos*, three- or four-piece bands made up of folk musicians playing guitar, *bajo sexto*, drums, and button accordion, which Chicanos had borrowed from the German immigrants who had come to Central Texas and Mexico to farm and build breweries. In the Rio Grande Valley, Steve Jordan and Little Joe Hernández were popular, and Flaco Jiménez was the accordion king. The rhythms of Tex-Mex music are those of the polka, also adapted from the Germans, who in turn had borrowed the polka from the Czechs and Bohemians.

I remember the hot, sultry evenings when *corridos* — songs of love and death on the Texas-Mexican borderlands — reverberated out of cheap amplifiers from the local *cantinas* and wafted in through my bedroom window.

Corridos first became widely used along the South Texas/Mexican border during the early conflict between Chicanos and Anglos. The *corridos* are usually about Mexican heroes who do valiant deeds against the Anglo oppressors. Pancho Villa's song, *"La cucaracha,"* is the most famous one. *Corridos* of John F. Kennedy and his death are still very popular in the Valley. Older Chicanos remember Lydia Mendoza, one of the great border *corrido* singers who was called *la Gloria de Tejas*. Her *"El tango negro,"* sung during the Great Depression, made her a singer of the people. The everpresent *corridos* narrated one hundred years of border history, bringing news of events as well as entertaining. These folk musicians and folk songs are our chief cultural mythmakers, and they made our hard lives seem bearable.

I grew up feeling ambivalent about our music. Country-western and rock-and-roll had more status. In the 50s and 60s, for the slightly educated and *agringado* Chicanos, there existed a sense of shame at being caught listening to our music. Yet I couldn't stop my feet from thumping to the music, could not stop humming the words, nor hide from myself the exhilaration I felt when I heard it.

There are more subtle ways that we internalize identification, espe- 35 cially in the forms of images and emotions. For me food and certain smells are tied to my identity, to my homeland. Woodsmoke curling up to an immense blue sky; woodsmoke perfuming my grandmother's clothes, her skin. The stench of cow manure and the yellow patches on the ground; the crack of a .22 rifle and the reek of cordite. Homemade white cheese sizzling in a pan, melting inside a folded *tortilla.* My sister Hilda's hot, spicy *menudo, chile colorado* making it deep red, pieces of *panza* and hominy floating on top. My brother Carito barbequing *fajitas* in the backyard. Even now and 3,000 miles away, I can see my mother spicing the ground beef, pork, and venison with *chile.* My mouth salivates at the thought of the hot steaming *tamales* I would be eating if I were home.

Si le preguntas a mi mamá, "¿Qué eres?"

"Identity is the essential core of who we are as individuals, the conscious experience of the self inside."
— GERSHEN KAUFMAN[9]

Nosotros los Chicanos straddle the borderlands. On one side of us, we are constantly exposed to the Spanish of the Mexicans, on the other side we hear the Anglos' incessant clamoring so that we forget our language. Among ourselves we don't say *nosotros los americanos, o nosotros los españoles, o nosotros los hispanos.* We say *nosotros los mexicanos* (by *mexicanos* we do not mean citizens of Mexico; we do not mean a national identity, but a racial one). We distinguish between *mexicanos del otro lado* and *mexicanos de este lado.* Deep in our hearts we believe that being Mexican has nothing to do with which country one lives in. Being Mexican is a state of soul — not one of mind, not one of citizenship. Neither eagle nor serpent, but both. And like the ocean, neither animal respects borders.

Dime con quien andas y te diré quien eres.
(Tell me who your friends are and I'll tell you who you are.)
— MEXICAN SAYING

Si le preguntas a mi mamá, "¿Qué eres?" te dirá, "Soy mexicana." My brothers and sister say the same. I sometimes will answer *"soy mexicana"* and at others will say *"soy Chicana" o "soy tejana."* But I identified as *"Raza"* before I ever identified as *"mexicana"* or "Chicana."

As a culture, we call ourselves Spanish when referring to ourselves as a linguistic group and when copping out. It is then that we forget our predominant Indian genes. We are 70–80 percent Indian.[10] We call ourselves Hispanic[11] or Spanish-American or Latin American or Latin when linking ourselves to other Spanish-speaking peoples of the Western hemisphere and when copping out. We call ourselves Mexican-American[12] to signify we are neither Mexican nor American, but more the noun "American" than the adjective "Mexican" (and when copping out).

Chicanos and other people of color suffer economically for not acculturating. This voluntary (yet forced) alienation makes for psychological conflict, a kind of dual identity—we don't identify with the Anglo-American cultural values and we don't totally identify with the Mexican cultural values. We are a synergy of two cultures with various degrees of Mexicanness or Angloness. I have so internalized the borderland conflict that sometimes I feel like one cancels out the other and we are zero, nothing, no one. *A veces no soy nada ni nadie. Pero hasta cuando no lo soy, lo soy.*

When not copping out, when we know we are more than nothing, we call ourselves Mexican, referring to race and ancestry; *mestizo* when affirming both our Indian and Spanish (but we hardly ever own our Black ancestry); Chicano when referring to a politically aware people born and/or raised in the U.S.; *Raza* when referring to Chicanos; *tejanos* when we are Chicanos from Texas. 40

Chicanos did not know we were a people until 1965 when Ceasar Chavez and the farmworkers united and *I Am Joaquín* was published and *la Raza Unida* party was formed in Texas. With that recognition, we became a distinct people. Something momentous happened to the Chicano soul—we became aware of our reality and acquired a name and a language (Chicano Spanish) that reflected that reality. Now that we had a name, some of the fragmented pieces began to fall together—who we were, what we were, how we had evolved. We began to get glimpses of what we might eventually become.

Yet the struggle of identities continues, the struggle of borders is our reality still. One day the inner struggle will cease and a true integration take place. In the meantime, *tenémos que hacer la lucha. ¿Quién está protegiendo los ranchos de mi gente? ¿Quién está tratando de cerrar la fisura entre la india y el blanco en nuestra sangre? El Chicano, si, el Chicano que anda como un ladrón en su propia casa.*

Los Chicanos, how patient we seem, how very patient. There is the quiet of the Indian about us.[13] We know how to survive. When other races have given up their tongue, we've kept ours. We know what it is to live under the hammer blow of the dominant *norteamericano* culture. But more than we count the blows, we count the days the weeks the years the centuries the eons until the white laws and commerce and customs will rot in the deserts they've created, lie bleached. *Humildes* yet proud, *quietos* yet wild, *nosotros los mexicanos-Chicanos* will walk by the crumbling ashes as we go about our business. Stubborn, persevering, impenetrable as stone, yet possessing a malleability that renders us unbreakable, we, the *mestizas* and *mestizos*, will remain.

Notes

1. Ray Gwyn Smith, *Moorland Is Cold Country*, unpublished book.

2. Irena Klepfisz, "*Di rayze aheym*/The Journey Home," in *The Tribe of Dina: A Jewish Women's Anthology*, Melanie Kaye/Kantrowitz and Irena Klepfisz, eds. (Montpelier, VT: Sinister Wisdom Books, 1986), 49.

3. R. C. Ortega, *Dialectología Del Barrio*, trans. Hortencia S. Alwan (Los Angeles, CA: R. C. Ortega Publisher & Bookseller, 1977), 132.

4. Eduardo Hernandéz-Chávez, Andrew D. Cohen, and Anthony F. Beltramo, *El Lenguaje de los Chicanos: Regional and Social Characteristics of Language Used by Mexican Americans* (Arlington, VA: Center for Applied Linguistics, 1975), 39.

5. Hernandéz-Chávez, xvii.

6. Irena Klepfisz, "Secular Jewish Identity: Yidishkayt in America," in *The Tribe of Dina*, Kaye/Kantrowitz and Klepfisz, eds., 43.

7. Melanie Kaye/Kantrowitz, "Sign," in *We Speak in Code: Poems and Other Writings* (Pittsburgh, PA: Motheroot Publications, Inc., 1980), 85.

8. Rodolfo Gonzales, *I Am Joaquín/Yo Soy Joaquín* (New York, NY: Bantam Books, 1972). It was first published in 1967.

9. Gershen Kaufman, *Shame: The Power of Caring* (Cambridge, MA: Schenkman Books, Inc., 1980), 68.

10. John R. Chávez, *The Lost Land: The Chicano Images of the Southwest* (Albuquerque, NM: University of New Mexico Press, 1984), 88–90.

11. "Hispanic" is derived from *Hispanis* (*España*, a name given to the Iberian Peninsula in ancient times when it was a part of the Roman Empire) and is a term designated by the U.S. government to make it easier to handle us on paper.

12. The Treaty of Guadalupe Hidalgo created the Mexican-American in 1848.

13. Anglos, in order to alleviate their guilt for dispossessing the Chicano, stressed the Spanish part of us and perpetrated the myth of the Spanish Southwest. We have accepted the fiction that we are Hispanic, that is Spanish, in order to accommodate ourselves to the dominant culture and its abhorrence of Indians. Chávez, 88–91.

[1987]

ALLISON JOSEPH   [b. 1967]

On Being Told I Don't Speak
Like a Black Person

Born in London to Caribbean parents, **Allison Joseph** (b. 1967) grew up in Toronto and the Bronx. She earned her B.A. from Kenyon College and her M.F.A. from Indiana University. She is the author of three collections of poetry: *What Keeps Us Here* (winner of Ampersand Press's 1992 Women Poets Series Competition and the John C. Zacharis First Book Award), *Soul Train* (1997), and *In Every Seam* (1997). Her poems are often attuned to the experiences of women and minorities. She formerly taught at the University of Arkansas and currently is an associate professor at Southern Illinois University, Carbondale, where she is editor of the *Crab Orchard Review*.

Emphasize the "h," you hignorant ass,
was what my mother was told
when colonial-minded teachers
slapped her open palm with a ruler
in that Jamaican schoolroom.   5
Trained in England, they tried
to force their pupils to speak
like Eliza Doolittle after
her transformation, fancying themselves
British as Henry Higgins,   10
despite dark, sun-ripened skin.
Mother never lost her accent,
though, the music of her voice
charming everyone, an infectious lilt
I can imitate, not duplicate.   15
No one in the States told her
to eliminate the accent,
my high school friends adoring
the way her voice would lift

when she called me to the phone,   20
A-ll-i-son, it's friend Cathy.
Why don't you sound like her?,
they'd ask. I didn't sound
like anyone or anything,
no grating New Yorker nasality,   25
no fastidious British mannerisms
like the ones my father affected
when he wanted to sell someone
something. And I didn't sound
like a Black American,   30
college acquaintances observed,
sure they knew what a black person
was supposed to sound like.
Was I supposed to sound lazy,
dropping syllables here, there,   35
not finishing words but
slurring the final letter so that
each sentence joined the next,
sliding past the listener?
Were certain words off limits,   40
too erudite, too scholarly
for someone with a natural tan?
I asked what they meant,
and they stuttered, blushed,
said you know, Black English,   45
applying what they'd learned
from that semester's text.
Does everyone in your family
speak alike?, I'd question,
and they'd say don't take this the   50
wrong way, nothing personal.

Now I realize there's nothing
more personal than speech,
that I don't have to defend
how I speak, how any person,   55
black, white, chooses to speak.
Let us speak. Let us talk
with the sounds of our mothers
and fathers still reverberating
in our minds, wherever our mothers   60
or fathers come from:

245

Arkansas, Belize, Alabama,
Brazil, Aruba, Arizona.
Let us simply speak
to one another,   65
listen and prize the inflections,
differences, never assuming
how any person will sound
until her mouth opens,
until his mouth opens,   70
greetings familiar
in any language.

[1999]

TONY EARLEY [b. 1961]

The Quare Gene

Author **Tony Earley** was born in Texas and raised in North Carolina, where many of his short stories are set. Earley, who strongly identifies with Appalachian culture, studied English at Warren Wilson College before beginning his career first as a reporter, and later as a sports editor and feature writer, for the *Thermal Belt News Journal*. After three and a half years, Earley moved on to the University of Alabama at Tuscaloosa where he received his MFA in creative writing. He has published short stories in a number of small literary magazines, as well as the *New Yorker* and *Harper's*. In 1996, Earley, among whose influences are Ernest Hemingway and Willa Cather, was recognized by the *New Yorker* and *Granta* as one of the best new American novelists. His books include *Jim the Boy* (2000) and its sequel *The Blue Star* (2008). Since 1997, Earley has been a professor in the English department at Vanderbilt University, where he teaches creative writing workshops and seminars in American fiction.

In "The Quare Gene," first published in the *New Yorker* in 1998 and later collected in *Somehow Form a Family: Stories That Are Mostly True* (2001), Earley considers his family's Appalachian dialect, seeking to define a relationship between language and identity. According to Earley, the dialect reveals his family's history; etymologies of words such as "quare"—which originated in Middle English and was preserved in Appalachia as a result of geographic isolation—are akin to the genes that map family identity.

I do not like, have never liked, nor expect to like, watermelon. For the record, I consider this a private, dietary preference, not a political choice, neither sign of failing character, nor renunciation of Southern citizenship. I simply do not like watermelon. Nor, for that matter, grits, blackberries, cantaloupe, buttermilk, okra, baked sweet potatoes, rhubarb, or collard greens. Particularly collard greens. I don't even like to look at collard greens. But, because I am a Southerner, a North Carolinian of

Appalachian, Scots-Irish descent, offspring of farming families on both sides, my family finds my failure to like the foods they like somehow distressing. Whenever I eat at my grandmother Ledbetter's table, my relatives earnestly strive to convince me that I am making a mistake by not sampling this or that, that I do not know what I am saying when I say no, that I should just *try* the greens, have just a little *slice* of watermelon, a small *bite* of cantaloupe, that I would eventually get used to the seeds in blackberries, the mealiness of grits, the swampy odor of greens boiled too long in a big pot. And, when I refuse, as I have been refusing with passion and steadfastness for as long as I could talk, they stare at me for a few seconds as if they do not know me, their mouths set sadly, then look down at their plates as if preparing to offer up a second grace. Then my grandmother says, "Tony Earley. You're just quare."

According to my edition of the *Shorter Oxford English Dictionary, quare* is an Anglo-Irish adjective from the early nineteenth century, meaning "Queer, strange, eccentric." Most dictionaries, if they list the word at all, will tell you that it is dialectical, archaic, or obsolete, an anachronism, only a marginal, aging participant in the clamoring riot of the English language. But when spoken around my grandmother's table, by my parents and aunts and uncles and cousins, *quare* isn't archaic at all, but as current as the breath that produces it, its meaning as pointed as a sharpened stick. For us, *quare* packs a specificity of meaning that *queer, strange, eccentric, odd, unusual, unconventional,* or *suspicious* do not. In our lexicon, the only adjective of synonymous texture would be *squirrelly,* but we are a close bunch and would find the act of calling each other squirrelly impolite. No, in my grandmother's house, when quare is the word we need, quare is the word we use.

Nor is *quare* the only word still hiding out in my grandmother's dining room that dictionaries assure us lost currency years ago. Suppose I brought a quare person to Sunday dinner at Granny's house, and he ate something that disagreed with him. We would say he looked a little peaked (pronounced *peak-éd*). Of course, we might decide he is peaked not because he ate something that disagreed with him, but because he ate a bait of something he liked. We would say, why, he was just too trifling to leave the table, and ate almost the whole mess by himself. And now we have this quare, peaked, trifling person on our hands. How do we get him to leave? Do we job him in the stomach? Do we hit him with a stob? No, we are kinder than that. We would say, "Brother, you liked to have stayed too long." We would put his dessert in a poke and send him on his way.

When I was a child I took these words for granted. They were simply part of the language I heard in the air around me, and I breathed them

248

in. I knew that if I ran with a sharp object I might fall and job my eye out; the idea of jabbing my eye out would have sounded as foreign to me as French. My grandmother's table was the center of the universe. Only when I began to venture away from that center did I come to realize that the language of my family was not the language of the greater world. I was embarrassed and ashamed when my classmates at Rutherfordton Elementary School corrected my speech, but, by the time I entered college, I wasn't surprised to learn in an Appalachian studies class that my family spoke in a *dialect*. I had begun to suspect as much, and was, by that time, bilingual. I spoke in the Appalachian vernacular when I was with my family and standard English when I wasn't. This tailoring of speech to audience, which still feels to me a shade ignoble, is not uncommon among young people from this part of the world. In less generous regions of the greater American culture, the sound of Appalachian dialect has come to signify ignorance, backwardness, intransigence, and, in the most extreme examples, toothlessness, rank stupidity, and an alarming propensity for planting flowers in painted tractor tires.

This is not some sort of misguided, Caucasian appeal for ethnicity, nor is it a battle cry from the radical left against the patriarchal oppression of grammar, but the fact is that, for me, standard English has always been something of a second language. I have intuitively written it correctly from the time I started school, but speaking it still feels slightly unnatural, demands just enough conscious thought on my part to make me question my fluency. When I am introduced to a stranger, when I meet a more showily educated colleague in the English department at Vanderbilt, when I go to parties at which I feel unsure of my place in that evening's social pecking order, I catch myself proofing sentences before I speak them—adding g's to the ends of participles, scanning clauses to make sure they ain't got no double negatives, clipping long vowels to affectless, midwestern dimensions, making sure I use *lay* and *lie* in a manner that would not embarrass my father-in-law, who is a schoolteacher from California. I try, both consciously and unconsciously, with varying degrees of success, to remove words of Appalachian idiom from my public vocabulary before the person I'm talking to decides that I'm stupid. Occasionally even my wife, whose Southern accent is significantly more patrician than my own, will smile and ask, "What did you just say?" I realize then that I have committed a linguistic faux pas, that I have unwittingly slipped into the language of my people, that I have inadvertently become "colorful." I'll rewind my previous sentence inside my head so I can save it as an example of how not to speak to strangers. I say, "What do you think I said?" Only inside the sanctity of Granny's house do I speak my mother tongue with anything resembling peace of mind.

I began thinking about the language I learned as a child, compared to the language I speak today, after reading Horace Kephart's book, *Our Southern Highlanders*. Kephart was a librarian and writer who, following a nervous breakdown, left his wife and children and moved to the mountains around Bryson City, North Carolina, in 1904. Although he traveled there initially to distance himself from human contact, he soon recovered enough to take an active interest in the world in which he found himself. An avid gatherer of information and a compulsive list-maker, Kephart spent the rest of his life compiling exhaustive journals and records detailing the geography, history, culture, and language of the southern Appalachians, a pursuit that resulted in innumerable magazine articles and two editions of *Our Southern Highlanders*.

Although Kephart had chosen the Appalachians over the deserts of the Southwest simply because it was the wilderness area closest to home, he arrived in western North Carolina at a particularly fortuitous time for a man of his particular talents. In the roadless hollows of the Blue Ridge and the Smokies Kephart found a people living largely as their ancestors had lived in the latter half of the eighteenth century, when the great Scots-Irish migration out of Pennsylvania first peopled the region with settlers of European descent. The hostile geography of the mountains had simply walled off the early settlers from the outside world and precluded, for almost a century and a half, extensive contact between their descendants and the greater civilization. "No one can understand the attitude of our highlanders toward the rest of the earth," Kephart writes,

> until he realizes their amazing isolation from all that lies beyond the blue, hazy skyline of their mountains. Conceive a shipload of emigrants cast away on some unknown island, far from the regular track of vessels, and left there for five or six generations, unaided and untroubled by the growth of civilization. Among the descendants of such a company we would expect to find customs and ideas unaltered from the time of their fore-fathers . . . The mountain folk still live in the eighteenth century. The progress of mankind from that age to this is no heritage of theirs.

Kephart was particularly interested in the English dialect he encountered in North Carolina, which he believed was closer to the Elizabethan English of Shakespeare or the Middle English of Chaucer, than anything that had been spoken in England for centuries. Because the Scots-Irish had spoken to, and been influenced by, so few outsiders, the language they brought with them from Scotland and Ireland, by way of Pennsylvania, had been preserved remarkably intact. Coincidentally, had Kephart come to the mountains a generation later, his research would have been by default less definitive. Within a few years of his death in 1931, road-building initiatives, radio, and the Sears-Roebuck catalog began to open even the darkest hollows of the Appalachians to twentieth-century America. In just a very few years, the resulting cultural homogenization turned the southern highlands into a world vastly different than the one he discovered in 1904.

I have since learned that Kephart's research methods were primitive by contemporary standards, and he was one of the first purveyors of what have since become suspect Appalachian generalities, but *Our Southern Highlanders* held for me the power of revelation. Before reading the book, I knew only that I had always been quare, and occasionally peaked. I just never knew why. Kephart's work told me who I was, or at least where I came from, in a way I had never fully understood. All of the words I thought specific to my family had entries in the dictionary compiled from Kephart's research of southern Appalachian idiom. And all of them—with the exception of quare, which is a mere two hundred years old—are words of Middle English origin, which is to say anywhere from five to eight hundred years old. Although most of the people I meet today wouldn't have any idea what it's like to eat a bait, Chaucer would have.

Of course, a word of Middle English origin is a mere babe when compared to the words of Latin, Hebrew, or Greek etymology that constitute much of our language. The Latin and Greek roots of the words *agriculture* and *barbarian* were old long before the primitive tribes of the British Isles painted their faces blue and grunted in a dialect resembling English. And, of course, no language is a static property; the life cycle of words mirrors the life cycles of the individuals who speak them. For specific words to fall out of favor and be replaced by new ones is the natural order of things; every language, given enough time, will replace each of its words, just as every population replaces the old with the young, just as every seven years the human body replaces each of its cells. The self-appointed guardians of English who protest that the word *celibate* means "unmarried" and not "abstinence from sexual intercourse" are wasting their time. "Sounds are too volatile and subtle for legal restraints," Samuel Johnson writes in the 1755 preface to his *Dictionary of the English Language*. "To enchain syllables, and to lash the wind, are equally the undertakings of pride." Understanding this, I am not advocating a return to eighteenth-century Scots-Irish dialect for the residents of western North Carolina. I am less taken by the age of the words of the Appalachian vernacular that found their way into my grandmother's dining room that I am by the specific history they hold.

The word *quare*, for me, contains sea voyages and migrations. It 10
speaks of families stopping after long journeys and saying, for any one of
a thousand reasons, "This is far enough." It speaks to me of generations
of farmers watching red dirt turn below plow blades, of young men step-
ping into furrows when old men step out. It speaks to me of girls fresh
from their mother's houses, crawling into marriage beds and becoming
mothers themselves. It bears witness to a chromosomal line of history,
most of it now unmappable, that led to my human waking beneath these
particular mountains. If language is the mechanism through which we
inherit history and culture, then individual words function as a type of
gene, each bearing with it a small piece of the specific information that
makes us who we are and tells us where we have been. My cousin Greg
and I came down with the same obscure bone disease in the same knee
at the same age. For us the word *quare* is no less a genetic signifier of the
past than the odd, bone-eating chromosome carried down through history by one wonders how many limping Scots-Irish.

The last time I remember talking to my maternal great-grandfather
Womack, he was well into his nineties and our whole family had gathered at the house he had built as a young man along Walnut Creek in the
Sunny View community of Polk County. When I tell this story, I choose
to remember it as a spring day, though it may not have been, simply
because I like to think that the daffodils in his yard were blooming. My
grandmother had helped him plant them when she was a little girl. At
some point, everyone got up and went inside, leaving Paw Womack and
me alone on the porch. I was in high school, a freshman or sophomore,
and was made self-conscious by his legendary age. He had been born in
another century. His father had been wounded at Gettysburg. He was
historical. He had farmed with a mule until well into his eighties. He
never brought another car after the one he bought in 1926 wore out. A
preacher's son, he had never uttered a swear word or tasted alcohol. He
had voted for Woodrow Wilson. I felt somehow chosen by the family to
sit with him; I felt like I needed to say something. I got out of my chair
and approached him as one would a sacred totem. I sat down on the
porch rail facing him, but I had no idea where to start. I remember his
immense, knotted farmer's hands spread out on the arms of his rocker.
We stared at each other for what seemed like a long time. Eventually
I blushed. I smiled at him and nodded. He smiled back and said, "Who
are you?"

I said, "I'm Reba's boy. Clara Mae's grandson."

"Oh," he said. "Reba's boy." If we ever spoke again, I don't remember it.

It seems significant to me now that when I told Paw Womack who I
was, I didn't give him my name. My position as individual was secondary

to my place in the lineage as individual was secondary to my place in the lineage, his lineage, that led to my sitting on his porch. I identified myself as a small part of a greater whole. *Who are you?* I'm Reba's boy, Clara Mae's grandson, Tom Womack's great-grandson. *Where are you from?* Over yonder. *Why don't you like watermelon?* I don't know. I guess I'm just quare.

Ironically, just as I learned, from Horace Kephart, to fully appreciate the 15
history contained in the word *quare*, I also have to accept the fact that it is passing out of my family with my generation. Neither I nor my cousins use it outside of Granny's house unless we temper it first with irony—a sure sign of a word's practical death within a changing language. I tell myself that the passing of Appalachian vernacular out of my family's vocabulary is not a tragedy or a sign of our being assimilated into a dominant culture, but simply the expected arrival of an inevitable end. "Life may be lengthened by care," Dr. Johnson says, "though death cannot be ultimately defeated: tongues, like governments, have a natural tendency to degeneration." I tell myself that it is a natural progression for my children to speak a language significantly different from that of my parents, but the fact that it happened so suddenly, within the course of a single generation, my generation, makes me wonder if I have done something wrong, if I have failed all the people who passed those words down. Sometimes the truest answer to the question "Who are you?" is "I don't know."

A few years ago an ice storm splintered a large stand of pine trees on my grandmother Ledbetter's farm. When the broken timber was logged and removed, our whole family was shocked by how close the mountains were behind the ridge where the trees had stood. We all walked out the road past the barn to have a closer look, almost as if we had never seen them before. "These very mountains of Carolina," Kephart writes in *Our Southern Highlanders*, "are among the ancients of the earth. They were old, very old, before the Alps and the Andes, the Rockies and Himalayas were molded into their primal shapes." Young's Mountain, Rumbling Bald, Chimney Rock, Shumont, World's Edge, White Oak: my family has apparently always lived in their shadow. They preserved in their hollows and laurel hells the words that tell us better than any others who we are. Words and blood are the double helix that connect us to our past.

As the member of a transitional generation, however, I am losing those words and the connection they make. And by losing language, I am losing the small comfort of shared history. I compensate, in the stories I write, by sending people up mountains to look, as Horace Kephart did, for the answers to their questions, to look down from a high place and see what they can see. My characters, at least, can still say the words that bind them to the past without sounding queer, strange, eccentric, odd, unusual, unconventional or suspicious. "Stories," says the writer Tim O'Brien, "can save us." I have put my faith in the idea that words, even new ones, possess that kind of redemptive power. Writers do not write about a place *because* they belong there, but because they want to. It's a quare feeling.

[1998]

DAVID SEDARIS [b. 1956]

Me Talk Pretty One Day

Born in 1956 in Johnson City, New York, **David Sedaris** grew up in
Raleigh, North Carolina. He is a playwright (in collaboration with
his sister Amy) and an essayist whose work has been featured regularly
on National Public Radio and in collections such as *Naked* (1997) and
Me Talk Pretty One Day (2000). Sedaris's work tends toward the satiric,
but even the most wickedly pointed of his pieces are marked by an
ironic stance that includes the author among those humans whose
folly must be satirized. This insistence on turning his satiric eye on
himself is evident in "Me Talk Pretty One Day," taken from the collection of the same name, in which he recounts his efforts to learn French,
to the chagrin of his teacher and to his own evident amusement.

At the age of forty-one, I am returning to school and have to think of myself as what my French textbook calls "a true debutant." After paying my
tuition, I was issued a student ID, which allows me a discounted entry
fee at movie theaters, puppet shows, and Festyland, a far-flung amusement park that advertises with billboards picturing a cartoon stego-
saurus sitting in a canoe and eating what appears to be a ham sandwich.

I've moved to Paris with hopes of learning the language. My school is
an easy ten-minute walk from my apartment, and on the first day of
class I arrived early, watching as the returning students greeted one another in the school lobby. Vacations were recounted, and questions were
raised concerning mutual friends with names like Kang and Vlatnya.
Regardless of their nationalities, everyone spoke in what sounded to me
like excellent French. Some accents were better than others, but the students exhibited an ease and confidence I found intimidating. As an
added discomfort, they were all young, attractive, and well dressed,
causing me to feel not unlike Pa Kettle trapped backstage after a fashion show.

The first day of class was nerve-racking because I knew I'd be expected
to perform. That's the way they do it here — it's everybody into the language pool, sink or swim. The teacher marched in, deeply tanned from
a recent vacation, and proceeded to rattle off a series of administrative

announcements. I've spent quite a few summers in Normandy, and I took a monthlong French class before leaving New York. I'm not completely in the dark, yet I understood only half of what this woman was saying.

"If you have not *meimslsxp* or *lgpdmurct* by this time, then you should not be in this room. Has everyone *apzkiubjxow*? Everyone? Good, we shall begin." She spread out her lesson plan and sighed, saying, "All right, then, who knows the alphabet?"

It was startling because (a) I hadn't been asked that question in a while and (b) I realized, while laughing, that I myself did *not* know the alphabet. They're the same letters, but in France they're pronounced differently. I know the shape of the alphabet but had no idea what it actually sounded like.

"Ahh." The teacher went to the board and sketched the letter *a*. "Do we have anyone in the room whose first name commences with an *ahh*?"

Two Polish Annas raised their hands, and the teacher instructed them to present themselves by stating their names, nationalities, occupations, and a brief list of things they liked and disliked in this world. The first Anna hailed from an industrial town outside of Warsaw and had front teeth the size of tombstones. She worked as a seamstress, enjoyed quiet times with friends, and hated the mosquito.

"Oh, really," the teacher said. "How very interesting. I thought that everyone loved the mosquito, but here, in front of all the world, you claim to detest him. How is it that we've been blessed with someone as unique and original as you? Tell us, please."

The seamstress did not understand what was being said but knew that this was an occasion for shame. Her rabbity mouth huffed for breath, and she stared down at her lap as though the appropriate comeback were stitched somewhere alongside the zipper of her slacks.

The second Anna learned from the first and claimed to love sunshine and detest lies. It sounded like a translation of one of those Playmate of the Month data sheets, the answers always written in the same loopy handwriting: "Turn-ons: Mom's famous five-alarm chili! Turnoffs: insecurity and guys who come on too strong!!!!"

The two Polish Annas surely had clear notions of what they loved and hated, but like the rest of us, they were limited in terms of vocabulary, and this made them appear less than sophisticated. The teacher forged on, and we learned that Carlos, the Argentine bandonion player, loved wine, music, and, in his words, "making sex with the womens of the world." Next came a beautiful young Yugoslav who identified herself as an optimist, saying that she loved everything that life had to offer.

The teacher licked her lips, revealing a hint of the sauce-box we would later come to know. She crouched low for her attack, placed her hands on the young woman's desk, and leaned close, saying, "Oh yeah? And do you love your little war?"

While the optimist struggled to defend herself, I scrambled to think of an answer to what had obviously become a trick question. How often is one asked what he loves in this world? More to the point, how often is one asked and then publicly ridiculed for his answer? I recalled my mother, flushed with wine, pounding the tabletop late one night, saying, "Love? I love a good steak cooked rare. I love my cat, and I love . . ." My sisters and I leaned forward, waiting to hear our names. "Tums," our mother said. "I love Tums."

The teacher killed some time accusing the Yugoslavian girl of masterminding a program of genocide, and I jotted frantic notes in the margins of my pad. While I can honestly say that I love leafing through medical textbooks devoted to severe dermatological conditions, the hobby is beyond the reach of my French vocabulary, and acting it out would only have invited controversy.

When called upon, I delivered an effortless list of things that I detest: 15
blood sausage, intestinal pâtés, brain pudding. I'd learned these words the hard way. Having given it some thought, I then declared my love for IBM typewriters, the French word for *bruise,* and my electric floor waxer. It was a short list, but still I managed to mispronounce *IBM* and assign the wrong gender to both the floor waxer and the typewriter. The teacher's reaction led me to believe that these mistakes were capital crimes in the country of France.

"Were you always this *palicmkrexis?*" she asked. "Even a *fiuscrzsa ticiwelmun* knows that a typewriter is feminine."

I absorbed as much of her abuse as I could understand, thinking—but not saying—that I find it ridiculous to assign a gender to an inanimate object incapable of disrobing and making an occasional fool of itself. Why refer to crack pipe or Good Sir Dishrag when these things could never live up to all that their sex implied?

The teacher proceeded to belittle everyone from German Eva, who hated laziness, to Japanese Yukari, who loved paintbrushes and soap. Italian, Thai, Dutch, Korean, and Chinese—we all left class foolishly believing that the worst was over. She'd shaken us up a little, but surely that was just an act designed to weed out the deadweight. We didn't know it then, but the coming months would teach us what it was like to spend time in the presence of a wild animal, something completely unpredictable. Her temperament was not based on a series of good and bad days but, rather, good and bad moments. We soon learned to dodge chalk and protect our heads and stomachs whenever she approached us with a question. She hadn't yet punched anyone, but it seemed wise to protect ourselves against the inevitable.

Though we were forbidden to speak anything but French, the teacher would occasionally use us to practice any of her five fluent languages.

"I hate you," she said to me one afternoon. Her English was flawless. 20 "I really, really hate you." Call me sensitive, but I couldn't help but take it personally.

After being singled out as a lazy *kfdtinvfm*, I took to spending four hours a night on my homework, putting in even more time whenever we were assigned an essay. I suppose I could have gotten by with less, but I was determined to create some sort of identity for myself: David the hard worker, David the cut-up. We'd have one of those "complete this sentence" exercises, and I'd fool with the thing for hours, invariably settling on something like "A quick run around the lake? I'd love to! Just give me a moment while I strap on my wooden leg." The teacher, through word and action, conveyed the message that if this was my idea of an identity, she wanted nothing to do with it.

My fear and discomfort crept beyond the borders of the classroom and accompanied me out onto the wide boulevards. Stopping for a coffee, asking directions, depositing money in my bank account: these things were out of the question, as they involved having to speak. Before beginning school, there'd been no shutting me up, but now I was convinced that everything I said was wrong. When the phone rang, I ignored it. If someone asked me a question, I pretended to be deaf. I knew my fear was getting the best of me when I started wondering why they don't sell cuts of meat in vending machines.

My only comfort was the knowledge that I was not alone. Huddled in the hallways and making the most of our pathetic French, my fellow students and I engaged in the sort of conversation commonly overheard in refugee camps.

"Sometime me cry alone at night."

"That be common for I, also, but be more strong, you. Much work and 25 someday you talk pretty. People start love you soon. Maybe tomorrow, okay."

Unlike the French class I had taken in New York, here there was no sense of competition. When the teacher poked a shy Korean in the eyelid with a freshly sharpened pencil, we took no comfort in the fact that, unlike Hyeyoon Cho, we all knew the irregular past tense of the verb *to defeat*. In all fairness, the teacher hadn't meant to stab the girl, but neither did she spend much time apologizing, saying only, "Well, you should have been *vkkdyo* more *kdeynfulh*."

Over time it became impossible to believe that any of us would ever improve. Fall arrived and it rained every day, meaning we would now be scolded for the water dripping from our coats and umbrellas. It was mid-October when the teacher singled me out, saying, "Every day spent with you is like having a cesarean section." And it struck me that, for the first time since arriving in France, I could understand every word that someone was saying.

Understanding doesn't mean that you can suddenly speak the language. Far from it. It's a small step, nothing more, yet its rewards are intoxicating and deceptive. The teacher continued her diatribe and I settled back, bathing in the subtle beauty of each new curse and insult.

"You exhaust me with your foolishness and reward my efforts with nothing but pain, do you understand me?"

The world opened up, and it was with great joy that I responded, "I know the thing that you speak exact now. Talk me more, you, plus, please, plus."

[2000]

Coming to an Awareness
of Language

Malcolm Little, born in Omaha, Nebraska, in 1925, was reborn
Malcolm X in his twenties while imprisoned for burglary. (He considered "Little" a slave name and chose the "X" to signify his lost African tribal name.) His conversion to Islam under the Nation of Islam
and his rigorous self-education led him to a life of political activism
marked by hatred, violence, and hope. For a time, as the foremost
spokesman of the Nation of Islam, Malcolm preached a separatist philosophy with racist rhetoric; on breaking with the Nation of Islam and
converting to orthodox Islam after a pilgrimage to Mecca, Malcolm
again changed his name (to El-Hajj Malik El-Shabazz) and philosophy,
moving closer to the integrationist goals of the mainstream civil rights
movement. Not quite a year later, he was assassinated.

   In "Coming to an Awareness of Language," from his 1965 *Autobiography*, Malcolm X relates his frustration at "not being able to express
what I wanted to convey in letters that I wrote," and describes the
"homemade education" that enabled him, to overcome that difficulty.
While an inmate at the Norfolk Prison Colony, Malcolm X challenges
himself to transcribe the English dictionary, thereby increasing his literacy, his world knowledge, and his sense of intellectual liberation
despite his being incarcerated. Reading and writing eventually become
Malcolm X's lifeline to an imagined future in which he could reach his
fullest potential.

I've never been one for inaction. Everything I've ever felt strongly about,
I've done something about. I guess that's why, unable to do anything else,
I soon began writing to people I had known in the hustling world, such
as Sammy the Pimp, John Hughes, the gambling house owner, the thief
Jumpsteady, and several dope peddlers. I wrote them all about Allah and
Islam and Mr. Elijah Muhammad. I had no idea where most of them
lived. I addressed their letters in care of the Harlem or Roxbury bars and
clubs where I'd known them.

I never got a single reply. The average hustler and criminal was too uneducated to write a letter. I have known many slick, sharp-looking hustlers, who would have you think they had an interest in Wall Street; privately, they would get someone else to read a letter if they received one. Besides, neither would I have replied to anyone writing me something as wild as "the white man is the devil."

What certainly went on the Harlem and Roxbury wires was that Detroit Red was going crazy in stir, or else he was trying some hype to shake up the warden's office.

During the years that I stayed in the Norfolk Prison Colony, never did any official directly say anything to me about those letters, although, of course, they all passed through the prison censorship. I'm sure, however, they monitored what I wrote to add to the files which every state and federal prison keeps on the conversion of Negro inmates by the teachings of Mr. Elijah Muhammad.

But at that time, I felt that the real reason was that the white man   5
knew that he was the devil.

Later on, I even wrote to the Mayor of Boston, to the Governor of Massachusetts, and to Harry S. Truman. They never answered; they probably never even saw my letters. I handscratched to them how the white man's society was responsible for the black man's condition in this wilderness of North America.

It was because of my letters that I happened to stumble upon starting to acquire some kind of a homemade education.

I became increasingly frustrated at not being able to express what I wanted to convey in letters that I wrote, especially those to Mr. Elijah Muhammad. In the street, I had been the most articulate hustler out there—I had commanded attention when I said something. But now, trying to write simple English, I not only wasn't articulate, I wasn't even functional. How would I sound writing in slang, the way I would *say* it, something such as, "Look, daddy, let me pull your coat about a cat. Elijah Muhammad—"

Many who today hear me somewhere in person, or on television, or those who read something I've said, will think I went to school far beyond the eighth grade. This impression is due entirely to my prison studies.

It had really begun back in the Charlestown Prison, when Bimbi first   10
made me feel envy of his stock of knowledge. Bimbi had always taken charge of any conversation he was in, and I had tried to emulate him. But every book I picked up had few sentences which didn't contain anywhere from one to nearly all of the words that might as well have been in Chinese. When I just skipped those words, of course, I really ended up with little idea of what the book said. So I had come to the Norfolk

Prison Colony still going through only book-reading motions. Pretty soon, I would have quit even these motions, unless I had received the motivation that I did.

I saw that the best thing I could do was get hold of a dictionary—to study, to learn some words. I was lucky enough to reason also that I should try to improve my penmanship. It was sad. I couldn't even write in a straight line. It was both ideas together that moved me to request a dictionary along with some tablets and pencils from the Norfolk Prison Colony school.

I spent two days just riffling uncertainly through the dictionary's pages. I'd never realized so many words existed! I didn't know *which* words I needed to learn. Finally, just to start some kind of action, I began copying.

In my slow, painstaking, ragged handwriting, I copied into my tablet everything printed on that first page, down to the punctuation marks.

I believe it took me a day. Then, aloud, I read back, to myself, everything I'd written on the tablet. Over and over, aloud, to myself, I read my own handwriting.

I woke up the next morning, thinking about those words—immensely 15 proud to realize that not only had I written so much at one time, but I'd written words that I never knew were in the world. Moreover, with a little effort, I also could remember what many of these words meant. I reviewed the words whose meanings I didn't remember. Funny thing, from the dictionary first page right now, that "aardvark" springs to my mind. The dictionary had a picture of it, a long-tailed, long-eared, burrowing African mammal, which lives off termites caught by sticking out its tongue as an anteater does for ants.

I was so fascinated that I went on—I copied the dictionary's next page. And the same experience came when I studied that. With every succeeding page, I also learned of people and places and events from history. Actually the dictionary is like a miniature encyclopedia. Finally the dictionary's A section had filled a whole tablet—and I went on into the B's. That was the way I started copying what eventually became the entire dictionary. It went a lot faster after so much practice helped me to pick up handwriting speed. Between what I wrote in my tablet, and writing letters, during the rest of my time in prison I would guess I wrote a million words.

I suppose it was inevitable that as my word-base broadened, I could for the first time pick up a book and read and now begin to understand what the book was saying. Anyone who has read a great deal can imagine the new world that opened. Let me tell you something: From then until I left that prison, in every free moment I had, if I was not reading in